Days of Honey

Days of Honey

The Tunisian Boyhood of Rafael Uzan

Irene Awret

SCHOCKEN BOOKS · NEW YORK

First published by Schocken Books 1984
10 9 8 7 6 5 4 3 2 1   84 85 86 87
Copyright © 1984 by Irene Awret

Library of Congress Cataloging in Publication Data
Awret, Irene, 1921–
  Days of honey.
  1. Uzan, Rafael.   2. Jews—Tunisia—Biography.
I. Title.
DS135.T73U933 1984   961'.1004924024 [B] 84–5338

Designed by Betty Palmer
Manufactured in the United States of America
ISBN 0–8052–3923–5

Contents

Preface

I first met Rafael in the aftermath of the Second World War, when Jews from all the countries where they had been persecuted were converging on the newborn state of Israel. Both our families, still young, were trying to settle in Safed, a small, sleepy town in the hills of Galilee, dreaming of its past of kabbalists and scholars. Handsome and sunburnt in his blue worker's shirt, Rafael would climb behind his donkey the steep stairs to our house to haul up concrete blocks and sell my husband antique coins that he had found in his yard. He had come from Africa and I from Europe. But although our backgrounds were widely divergent we had in common the same lingering euphoria to have survived the war and the urge to leave a mark, a fingerprint—to paint. We had the same desire to live as Jews in a country of our own. Another link was the French language in which we could converse before either of us were able to do so in Hebrew.

As told to me in my kitchen over daily cups of coffee, this is the story of Rafael Uzan, a native of a small town on the coast of Tunisia, a former shoemaker, pensioned gardener, and now successful primitive artist living in Safed.

The once-teeming communities of North Africa have been emptied of their Jewish inhabitants, abandoned. Famous synagogues have become shelters for goats and sheep. Few writers have attempted to redeem the rich patrimony of North African Jewry, or tried to recall the hardships of a people brusquely uprooted from surroundings they had been part of for two thousand years.

The East European shtetl is still with us forty years after its extinction thanks to the wealth of literature; not the smallest facet of its life, lovingly polished, is allowed to fade from memory. The colorful communities of the Maghreb—Morocco, Algeria, and Tunis—tend to be overlooked; the intricate pattern of their ancient customs and traditions has been left to disintegrate.

Listening to the nostalgic accounts of Rafael's Tunisian boyhood I soon found it impossible to detach myself from the eyepiece of his Arabian Nights kaleidoscope. How could I in good conscience let such a treasury of folklore, anecdotes, and adventure go unrecorded? Still I resisted writing, more accustomed to a painter's brush than to a pen. Writing in any language required some nerve on my part. Having as a teenager fled Hitler's Germany for the Belgium of the war years, I had little formal education other than painting. My life, by the force of circumstances, had been divided into varied spheres of languages and cultures: German, French, Hebrew, and Yiddish, with English trailing behind. But because even Rafael's charming pictures of his youth could not tell the whole story, I finally had to sit down and write.

My heartfelt thanks to Gruine Robinson, who led me safely through the lush but tangled thickets of the English language and became my good friend in the process. Her encouragement and patience were invaluable.

I tried throughout to keep as closely as I could to Rafael's truth as he saw it. If here and there a streak of my own more ironic disposition has slipped into his story, I apologize to the reader, as well as for a complete lack of regard for ideology.

IRENE AWRET

Falls Church, Virginia
May 1984

Days of Honey

1

Nabeul

Rabbi Hai synagogue has been closed up for over twenty years now. It closed the day that the last Jew left Bab Salah Street to settle in Israel. No more prayers mount through the paneless skylight in the middle of the vaulted ceiling. Instead, birds flutter in and out, nesting on the oil lamps still suspended in front of the empty Torah shrine. They were hung there in memory of kabbalists and sages. One small lamp at the end of the row is engraved with the name of my grandfather, Rafael Uzan, the same as mine. At his knee I learned, along with my first prayers, how to catch sparrows with the help of a string and my grandmother's couscous sieve. He showed me how to dry big, yellow butterflies and how to distinguish harmless snakes from vipers. To me, he was just my kindly shrunken grandfather, the oldest man in the world. But after his death, everybody, even the rabbis, said that he had been a saint.

"You carry his name, Rafael," people liked to remind me. "Don't forget, you are the grandson of a saint."

It was useless. God knows my father did not spare the belt, pushing me with a strong hand to follow in the saintly footsteps. But I was born under a star that led me, however safely, throught the dirt paths of life. My Tunisian and Israeli papers disagree on the year of my birth, which took place either fifty-seven or fifty-eight years ago in Nabeul, an ancient little town on the coast of Tunisia. There I grew up in a whitewashed house built of fieldstone and lime, in the one room my parents had rented to found a family. Having given birth to me on a Thursday, my mother always told me to stick to Fridays for important undertakings or decisions. Events bore out that she was right, for anything that I started on a Friday would prosper as if by magic. Even on ordinary weekdays I seem to have more luck than foresight, a fact that makes my wife Fortuna envious. Convinced that I have stolen her portion of luck to add to my own, she blames me when most of her little plans and schemes go awry. Fortuna is quite bitter about this alleged robbery.

"No wonder that with double luck there is always money jingling in your pocket," she lashes out. "But here, feel my poor purse— as flat as a flounder!"

Fortuna is very devout. She lights candles on the graves of all the great rabbis buried in Upper Galilee and even went as far as Bethlehem in Judea to measure the tomb of our mother Rachel with a blue thread. Every time she is worried about a grandson, one of our own children, or even about me, she will take the thread out of its tissue-paper wrapping to pray for help, and as she is almost always worried about one of us, the blue thread is much in use. There is nothing Fortuna is more afraid of than desecrating the sanctity of the Sabbath. On that day she will not come near anything with the faintest resemblance to fire. She would not dream of turning on electric lights. One temptation too great to resist, however, is the Egyptian love stories aired on Israeli television on Friday evenings, so she has me push the buttons on the TV set.

If, in spite of all these precautions, things still don't go her way, she becomes furious, blaming me for having stolen her luck. Nevertheless, I was fortunate in marrying Fortuna. At bottom she is very kindhearted, neat and clean, even still good-looking in a way. On top of all these qualities, she has been truly blessed as a cook and a baker. But there again, as I sniff the delicious smell of steaming couscous and stuffed tripe, I realize that this blessing can be weighed on my side of the scales as well. It is a mystery to me why I am luckier than she is. She tries so hard to please the Almighty, never straying from the narrow path prescribed to Jewish wives and mothers while I am careless; I walk the streets bareheaded, although I keep a cap ready in my pocket in case I run into my old father.

It's not as if I were an unbeliever, God forbid. But never having been a great stickler for rules, I pray in my own fashion, having at last managed to creep out of the maze of superstition I grew up in. Maybe I would still go to synagogue if today's rabbis were like the hooded figures of my youth who coveted neither honors nor money and averted their eyes whenever they passed a woman. Their memory I worship. From time to time one of them speaks to me in my dreams which is a sure sign that something wonderful is about to happen.

In a shoe box at home I keep their photographs. Their fading stares still cling to the yellowed paper—solemn, bearded faces all topped by the same kind of *tarboosh* worn at different angles. Stored away with the photographs are souvenirs of the rabbis as tokens of good luck: a shred from Rabbi Moshe's burial shroud, a filigree button from Rabbi Eliahu's Sabbath *bournous,* the precious copper spoon with which Rabbi Yitzhak Bishlino used to eat his simple meals. The smallest of the souvenirs are the most valuable, the amulets these holy men once carried in their pockets to ward off the evil eye; tiny charms of hands, silverfish, blue beads and pearly shells.

Some of the good rabbis must be pleading my case in heaven, for there is no doubt in my mind that I am luckier than most people. Though I had learned the trade of shoemaker in Nabeul, here in Safed I became a gardener. I myself was amazed to see how every seed or plant I put into the soil would grow and flower. Along with my green thumb I also discovered that I had fortunate fingertips. Wherever my spade turned the ground I would find something: antique coins, a golden earring, beads that had clasped some neck a thousand years ago; on meager days, a broken glass-bracelet from the times of the Mamelukes or a shard from a carved clay-pipe.

I am just as lucky when it comes to business, a fact that has earned me much jealousy besides getting me into trouble with the income-tax people. There are close to a hundred galleries in Safed and as many painters, yet it is to me that buyers cling as flies to flypaper, running after me in the street: "What are you hiding inside that newspaper, Rafael—some new painting?" For the contents of my pockets or the oddest objects to be found in my little flat, people beg me to name a price. Old buttons, seals, and amulets, even the pair of finches I keep in a cage at home. The less anxious I am to sell, the more they are set on buying.

Fortuna has overheard these people calling me a primitive painter. "Primitive? Crazy!" she hisses. "Who has ever seen green donkeys and red camels? Spending all your money on paints and brushes instead of buying a bathtub. . . ."

I answer her tit for tat. "With you everybody who buys my paintings must be crazy. To you the jury that awarded me first prize must be completely out of their minds. And the Mayor's wife from Tel Aviv? She must be primitive *and* crazy to let herself be photographed handing me the check. . . ." That hits home.

"Of course," she now says in a low, sly voice. "With stolen luck you can trick anybody, mix up heads as you mixed up mine—otherwise why would I have married you?" She does not really mean what she says and I show off like that mainly to make her furious. At heart, I am not all that sure what people find in my paintings.

When we first came to Israel and settled in Safed we quarreled very seldom. Times were difficult then with not much luck to quarrel about. Three months after our wedding, I took my bride and two trunks packed with our new clothes, prayer books, salt, olive oil, coffee and plenty of dried peppers to return to the land of my fathers. But that was thirty years ago.

Never again have I set eyes on Nabeul, but deep in my memory my town lies glowing in the sun as on the day I left it. I can yet see white and blue houses in the blinding moonlight, hear the trample of goats, sheep and cows running down our sunbaked street. Their bells still fill my ears with their metallic clank. I see a *fallah* passing by, proudly seated on his donkey, his barefoot wife following with a heavy load of firewood on her head. Farther down, alongside narrow plots of corn and vegetables, some camels are grazing. Lush green fields stretch out toward the golden circle of the dunes, in their turn caught up by the moist sapphire blue of the Mediterranean.

I must have been at least ten years old when I became first aware that there exists something called mountains. My world was completely flat, made up of Nabeul, the sand, and the sea. Without even climbing onto my lookout on the roof I could gather the height of the waves by wafts of salty air coming in from the direction of the shore. I can still sniff the rich aroma of freshly baked barley bread escaping from the ovens, the acrid, tangy mixture of charcoal smoke, pepper, spice, and dung that pervaded Bab Salah Street. My nose will remember it forever.

In summer I would awake before dawn, roused from sleep by a great din, our Arab neighbors chasing swarms of sparrows out of the millet fields. All of a sudden the silence between night and day was broken by loud shooing, clamoring camel bells and the "thump-thump" of sticks striking empty tin cans as clouds of birds darkened the paling sky. It was the hour when young mothers fed their children and took them down to the beach. On a secluded strip of dunes they got out of their ample clothing, clutched their babies tightly to their bodies and ran into the waves after the toddlers who were chasing tiny fish.

Summers went on endlessly, with mornings at the beach and afternoons at play, one day melting tranquilly into the next like frothy little waves toppling on each other, dissolving in the sand. Winters were short and so mild that I had never seen snow before settling in Upper Galilee. Rains, winds, an occasional hailstorm would never stay with us for long, yet everyone prepared for them as if for a hard time. Already early in October, when west winds swept the first rain clouds into a sky that had been stark blue for as much as seven months, my father used to come home from his weekly peddling trips with sacks of sorghum, durra, and dried corn for which he had bartered in exchange for lace or satin. Loaded on his donkey were dried fish, salted meat and tin cans gurgling with thick greenish-brown olive oil in addition to its usual bales of cotton, silk and muslin. My parents' bed, an odd assemblage of planks, covered a hole which was deep enough to stow away the earthenware pots, linen bags and canvas sacks with our provisions.

When the winds began to whistle and the rainstorms left puddles on the floor under the paneless lattice window, I had a wonderful time. Our room would fill with visitors, aunts and neighbors passing whole days in our company while I would play games with my little cousins. Our mothers cooked, baked and gossiped, telling each other the hidden meaning of their dreams.

"Mother," I remembered, "I also had a dream last night."

"What was it, what did you dream, n'doralnik, my darling son?" inquired my mother, who always addressed me in such terms of endearment.

"A big, big man was sitting on my belly; he was so heavy that I couldn't move my arms to push him off. I could not even shout for you."

"Oh, oh, what a pity; why didn't you grab his hat!" all the women cried as one, their voices squeaky with excitement. "That heavy man, he must have been a *Bootalish*. Had you only looked up you would have seen his tall hat, covered with diamonds and precious stones for you to snatch!" My mother begged me very seriously to be more watchful next time Bootalish would appear in my dreams, but though I tried hard to remind myself of my promise to her I could not lift my eyes and even less a hand in dreams where someone heavy was sitting on my chest.

The rains would stop as suddenly as they had come. The moment the sun was out again it would dry our muddy street in a matter of minutes. Then I would shoot marbles with Mahmood, Kasham and Abdel Kader, my little Moslem friends. I'd sometimes swap my "marbles" (apricot pits saved from last spring) for delicately tinted butterflies and tiny colored fish caught by my playmates. On warmer days, I was allowed to run in and out of the houses of our Arab neighbors on the condition that I refuse nonkosher food and be back home at sunset. The latter rule I followed very strictly. My mother did not have to call me more than once when dusk was falling. No game could keep me outside after dark.

Fearsome stories were going around about Roola, the black she-devil. Some of my young cousins had told me how they had escaped her clutches by the skin of their teeth. One had had the presence of mind to jingle coins in his hand. Another, big Eli, had made her vanish by lighting a match into her hideous face. (Shishi, the dwarf next door, had once shown me the golden ring he had snatched from Roola when she tried to entice him.) They said she had yellow

wolves' eyes peering out from behind black shags of hair. Her sagging breasts were only half hidden by her dirty rags. After dark she
would come out, hiding her ugliness in the gray cactus hedges fenc-
ing the sheds of our Arab neighbors.

"I am not afraid . . . Roola, where are you? Roooola. . . !" I
shouted into the prickly pear hedge as my admiring little friends
stood openmouthed at such pluck.

In broad daylight I had been daring. At night things looked different. Lying very quietly on my sheepskin, my eyes would carefully
avoid a certain corner—the dark one beside the door. What if she had
heard me, lurking over there in the tangle of thorns and leaves in our
neighbor Nisria's yard, waiting to sink her fangs into me. . . .

Stretched out flat on my back I'd rather try to make up images
from the long shadows the oil lamp was projecting on our bumpy
walls. Those walls were the picture books of my childhood. Its pages
were filled with an unending, ever-changing line of animals, funny
profiles and frightening monsters. When I grew up a little and started
studying the Bible, my jumping horses, humpbacked camels, rabbits
and hedgehogs were taken over by Lot's wife, Jonah's whale,
crowned kings and a menacing Moses brandishing the tablets of the
Law.

My parents would sit stiffly upright on the stuffed mattress at the
far side of the room, cross-legged, facing each other from opposite
sides of the big bed. One arm folded around her knees, her delicate
face cupped sideways in the other hand, my mother alway seemed
deep in thought at night.

"What is the matter, Mother?" I would ask a little worriedly.

"Fish soup or bean stew, carrot salad or beets with pickled
lemon. . . . I can't make up my mind over tomorrow's dinner," she
would sigh and cup her chin in her other hand.

Winter Nights' Tales

On long winter evenings my father used to ask Yedida, the storyteller, to come over at bedtime. Yedida was one of those women with
an unusual trade. There were quite a number of such women in our
community. Blind and widowed, she occupied a small room in the
courtyard of our synagogue across the street, eking out a living with
her stories. Already from a distance I could hear her grope her way to

our house and as the tapping of her cane drew close, I would rush to spread out my sheepskin, lying down in happy expectation.

"*Shalom Aleichem*," her deep voice would greet us from the threshold. Yedida's heavy bulk would squat down on the floor and her voice boom at once into a story: "We all know what happened to us under the hard rule of the Turks," she began, staring at me with unseeing eyes.

During the reign of Hamuda Pasha—may God blot out his name and memory—a long, long time ago, our people had to live inside the ghetto, hem their sleeves and trousers with black ribbon, wear black *babooshes* to mark them as inferiors. But that was not all. Hamuda Pasha decided that he would show the Jews who was lord in Tunisia and commanded them to bend down and lend their backs to the boots of their Moslem masters whenever an Arab wished to mount his donkey or his horse. His decree did not only hurt the backs of our people but also hurt their pride. Nevertheless, it did not hurt their pockets.

So the Pasha thought of yet another humiliation. He let it be known that the great number of poor among his Moslem subjects were thenceforth permitted to pay the Jews with "orange money." Furnished with round slices of orange peels they could enter any Jewish shop, buy anything they needed, put orange peel coins on the counter and demand the change. What Jew in his right mind would have wanted to leave tranquil Algiers and settle in Nabeul under these circumstances? Nevertheless, there was one.

"I will wrangle back from the rich what I lose to the poor who pay with orange money," he said, and opened a shop in the market. Against all odds he prospered and in time he became wealthy and respected—so much so that the day arrived when he dared to refuse the use of his back to a Moslem who wanted to mount his horse. Furious, the Moslem pulled a dead cat out of the gutter, grabbed it by the tail and hit the Jew over the neck with the stinking carcass. The Jew, in turn, struck the Arab in the face. It became a fight. With the intervention of some bystanders the Jew was overpowered, bound and brought before the Pasha. Witnesses testified that he had refused to let the Moslem step onto his back and had struck him in the face on top of it all. The Jew was condemned to hang.

"State your last wish and I will see to it that it is granted," Hamuda Pasha said to the Jew who was about to be led away for execution.

"My wish is simple," said the Jew. "Show me the parchment with the Pasha's decree on backbending."

It was unrolled before him, he began to read and as he came to the part spelling out what kind of punishment was to be administered to disobedient Jews he exclaimed, "Here, here it is written in black and white: 'One blow with folded hands on the Jew's neck. . . .' It says nothing about dead cats here!"

Even the hardest Pasha has to stand by his own law. The Jew went free and later the cruel decree was done away with altogether.

On those evenings when my mother found it hard to fall asleep and if Yedida was not available, it was my father who read to us from worn-out storybooks. They were printed in the script of our holy tongue, but the words were Judeo-Arabic, a language only old men still can read today. My father's stories were all fairy tales filled with kings in magic glass castles, innocently slandered queens, princes who were changed into howling dogs and bewitched princesses who hopped about as feathery pigeons.

"There was once a widower king who had an only son . . ." my father began reading as my mother Meesha was making ready for bed. Night after night she did so in the same fashion. First she would untie the coquettish butterfly knot over the middle of her forehead, take off the striped kerchief hiding her thick, brown hair, then put it on again, this time modestly fastened in the back. Seated cross-legged on her side of the bed she would swing the wooden cradle hung up nearby. How drowsy I became with her low singsong and the creaking of the chain!

My father's voice brought me back from the edge of sleep.

His queen had died giving birth to the prince, who was the apple of his father's eye. So afraid was the king for his son that he had him brought up in a chamber of glass that only the wet nurse and himself were allowed to enter. Even after he had grown up the nurse would still mash his vegetables and spoon-feed him, watching over the prince day and night.

Having never been in touch with the outside world the young man lived quite happily in his glass chamber, but when he reached the age of eighteen, the old nurse died and another woman took her place. This one was careless enough to serve him a hard-boiled egg unpeeled and the prince, in a rage, flung it at the transparent wall. The glass broke and the egg landed in the honey fountain in the middle of his father's courtyard, smashing an old woman's honey jar. The poor of the country were allowed to scoop up honey from the king's fountain after sundown and the old woman had just scraped together the last of it when the egg hit her jar.

"Clumsy fool!" she shouted at the prince behind the broken glass wall. "Who do you think you are? Sandra, princess of the Romans?"

"And who is Sandra, princess of the Romans?" asked the astonished young man who had never heard of princesses.

Throughout my father's reading my mother had not changed her upright position on the mattress, but now her head sank slowly forward, nodding lower and lower until she finally lay down. My own eyes were closing and I remember the rest of the story as if bottled up in thick mist. . . . How the poor prince became sick with longing for beautiful Sandra who was kept prisoner by the cruel demon Obeita in a cave behind the Land of the Winds, of Fire and of Water. . . . How the king wept when his only son took leave to go and search for the princess. . . . Having overcome terrible dangers, the prince arrived at last in the demon's realm and just as Obeita nibbled off one after another of the royal horse's legs, I would fall asleep.

I barely noticed how the lamp was blown out or how the red curtain that separated me from my parents' bed was drawn shut.

My Mother Meesha

Never have I felt richer or more secure than on those winter nights, lying on my sheepskin on the floor of my parents' room, though I cannot recall many items in their entire household that would fetch more than a few francs today. The exceptions were my mother's three golden jewels: a chain of old French coins, a heavy bracelet, and a pair of dangling earrings that she wore to her dying day.

We were only one of five families living around the same courtyard in an old one-story house. It was built from fieldstones plastered over with a thick mixture of lime and mud; the floor was beaten earth covered with blue wash. I cannot remember entering the room without first kissing the glass *mezuzah* embedded in the doorpost. Only after I had rinsed my hands with water from the earthen pitcher on the threshold was I allowed to sit down for my meals.

My mother would serve food in a big bowl she put down in the middle of the rush mat. Squatting around it in a circle we held our wooden spoons in readiness, waiting impatiently for the moment my father would be finished with the blessing. Fresh homebaked barley bread, rice, beans and cooked vegetables were our staple, rounded off with salads and fish. On the Sabbath we always had delicious white bread with *hameen,* a calf's foot or an oxtail stewed with chickpeas and red peppers. It would have been dangerous to keep cooked food for more than a day in our hot climate, and so we had to clean out my mother's big bowl to the bottom, a task for which I did not need much urging. On the rare occasions when my appetite was flagging, a jug with leftovers would be hung into the cool water of the cistern or else I was sent with a little pot to poorer neighbors. To throw out any food was unheard of and would have been considered a great sin.

By dawn my mother would already have lit the charcoal tripod in the courtyard, a chore I tried to make a little easier for her by asking for a chunk of glowing embers from a neighbor and fanning the flames with a palm leaf. After the smoke had subsided she would carry the tripod to the "kitchen," the cavernous terrace she shared with five other women. Only then could she put on the kettle to prepare the morning coffee. Since for every hot meal or cup of tea she had to go through the same steps again and again, it was no wonder that the best part of my mother's days were spent in that old cooking hole. Relations in the kitchen were friendly and helpful. I never saw my mother quarrel with her neighbors. True, my mother was so good-natured that she never quarreled with anyone. She would not even talk back to my father.

Being obstinate and short-tempered he was not an easy man to live with at the best of times. Today, well into his eighties, his most outstanding traits—stubbornness and piety—have hardened him into a rock of loneliness. Though he loved my mother dearly and still laments her early death, he would often treat her harshly. She, on the other hand, would take a hard word in her stride and did not seem to mind much my father's tightfistedness with household money. Always gay and ready for a joke, she was an expert in the use of gold and silver yarn, a craft with which she made some extra money for little luxuries and presents. Merchants trusted her with the expensive, carefully weighed thread to tat lace and do embroidery on wedding outfits. For a small fee she would stitch intricate flower patterns of her own invention on silken slippers; also, for good measure, she would generously throw in a peacock here, a swan there.

Crouching on the rush mat by her side I loved to watch blossoms and leaves grow into shimmering life under her fingers, but most of all I liked to see my mother making lace. Seated cross-legged behind her lace board she would throw the whorl, pat my head and accompany the click-click of the little sticks with the latest Nabeul hit song:

Rimona pomegranate-girl enters the grocery.
"Sell me fruit, pomegranates."
Rimona pomegranate, Rimona pomegranate, with six and seven,
Six and seven in a bunch.
"Now I want milk," she skips and trips,
"Pay money," says the sniffy dog,
the grocer they call hunting dog,
"And drink it in good health!
"Want to taste dates?" hunting dog smiles,
"tuck up your skirt, let's see your knees—
and eat them in good health. . . ."
Rimona pomegranate, dance with me pomegranate, with six and seven
six and seven in a bunch. . . .

The time my mother could spare for lace making and needlework was limited. She had to take care of me, the eldest, and the brothers and sisters who had followed me, more than half of them dying in infancy. Though my father was away peddling most of the time, she was busy from morning till evening, cooking, baking, sewing our little tunics, vainly trying to keep us clean. On Thursday, when my father came home in time for Sabbath preparations she would become even busier, washing his clothes, baking white bread, steaming couscous and stewing hameen.

Our needs were simple. There were two nooks in the walls of our room. One served as a cupboard where my mother kept the precious set of glazed earthenware dishes we used only once a year during Passover week. The other served as a wardrobe for storing some handwoven blankets and our winter clothes, one pair of woolen socks and one sweater for each member of the family. Add new sandals for our great spring festival, a pair of shoes at the time of the High Holidays in the fall, and we were set.

The outfit of my Arab friends was still simpler. For the first nine or ten years of their lives they were running around barefoot and trouserless, dressed only in long shirts. Our parents were mostly craftsmen, shopkeepers and hawkers, while they were farmers' sons, proud to help shepherd their fathers' herds or weed the fields and orchards.

Before every one of our frequent holidays, our Moslem neighbors would bring us presents of their produce, huge ears of corn, lemons, carobs, sometimes pots with milk and honey. There were days when I was sick and my friends would miss me at play outside. Their mothers would soon drop in to inquire about my health: "How is our Fallu today? Here, a little gift from Mahmood, Kasham and Abdel Kader to make you well again." A delicious touch of cool glass on my feverish fingers, then Mahmood's mother would open the small bottle of orange blossom essence and rub drops of sweet-smelling oil into my temples. Arab women know how to grow fruit and tend their vegetable plots; Jewish women were the better cooks. Returning our neighbors' gifts in kind, my mother would reserve some of her holiday specialties for them, such as honey pastry, but nothing was more appreciated than our Passover *matzohs*.

Fat Lajla, our next-door neighbor, was the only Jewish woman who never sent food to anyone. She ate everything herself. Here is how I knew. Playing in the yard with her scraggy children I had heard funny, sucking noises coming from behind her door, the smack and crunch of a feeding animal. What creature could Lajla be hiding in her room? Every time I questioned one of the children they would either talk about something else or run away. One hot afternoon with nobody around I had an idea; hoping that it would make me tall enough to get a peep at Lajla's mysterious pet, I dragged an empty oil can under her window and climbed on top. Hiding behind the wooden lattice, I could survey the room with ease. I held my breath, but there was no mistake, the animal was fat Lajla herself; loudly groaning she was crawling on all fours toward an enormous pot of noodle soup standing in one corner. Having helped herself to a generous portion, she crossed back to the other side, pushing the overflowing bowl in front of her. Standing spellbound on my upturned oil can I watched how our neighbor hoisted her mighty, panting torso to prop it up against the wall.

Too fat to eat cross-legged like the rest of us, Lajla shut herself up to take her meal in solitude, but her lot did not seem to trouble her enjoyment. Seated spread-eagle fashion, she had squeezed the soup bowl in between the overblown flower pattern gracing two bursting trouser-legs, splashing, gulping and gurgling to her heart's content. After every plunge into the noodles she would lick palms and fingers, then crawl once more back to the cooking pot.

I was deeply impressed. The same evening at dinnertime my mother was appalled to find me on all fours, huffing and puffing over the big bowl she had just set down in the middle of the rush mat. Dipping my fingers in the millet pap I licked them with loud delight. For once my mother was angry.

"It's a great sin to play doggy with the Almighty's blessings," she chided, pulling me out of the millet bowl.

"I am no dog. . . . I am fat Lajla," I tried to defend myself, only to get out of the frying pot into the fire. My mother became even angrier.

"Who are you to make fun of your neighbor . . . as good a Jew as you and me? Is it her fault if the Almighty made her fat? He certainly knows what He is doing, and I don't ever want to see you mock Lajla again. . . ."

My mother very seldom lost her temper, in contrast to my father. But though he would boil over at the slightest provocation, I have never heard him swear. I cannot have reached far above his knee when he already took great pains to warn me against cursing.

"Why the rage, Fallu, what has happened?"

"Hooo . . . hooo . . ." I cried, "Cousin Eli bit my thumb."

"So far as I can see it is still in its place . . . isn't even bleeding," said my father sternly. "Shame on you, I heard every word you said. For one bite you call a triple curse upon your cousin's head? To lose all his teeth you wish him? To have his right hand fall off? To burn like a roast? Don't you know what awful risk you're taking, Fallu? The Gates of Heaven swing open a hundred times each day. . . . Angels have to get in and out, you can understand that, can't you? Now imagine only one of those ugly curses popping so easily out of your mouth getting through that gate and flying straight into the ear of God? How would you feel if it comes true, God forbid?" With repeated warnings such as these I learned at an early age to suppress anger and to make requests that I wished to reach His ear more worthwhile.

My good-natured mother managed easily to do without cursing. However, I vividly remember one occasion when fouler language poured from her dainty lips than I could have believed she knew. Here is what had happened. A Bedouin woman had helped her with the weekly wash, perhaps misjudging the contents of my mother's purse. Having raised countless buckets of water from the cistern, rubbing and squeezing our dirty clothes for hours on end, she had accepted her miserable wages in silence. In the afternoon she came back to our house, and before we could grasp what she was up to she rushed into our room, scattering the contents of a small box over my parents' bed. As much as we strained our eyes, we could not find a thing on the mattress, not even a trace of some magic powder or a written curse. Only when we all began to scratch did we understand the mystery. We were infested with lice. For a whole week we did nothing but try to get rid of the washerwoman's blessing. As DDT was still unknown our heads were rubbed with kerosene, our clothes washed anew, the mattresses beaten, sunned and scrubbed, our sheepskins combed and brushed—and still we kept on scratching.

Kerosene trickles from one end to the other of my childhood, soaking the endless battlefield on which my mother fought the good fight against lice. Sometimes it was a cold war struggle: dire warnings not to come close to certain people. Then, all of a sudden, it would flare up into open battle where heads were shaved and kerosene went into action. With other vermin, mice for instance, I was on the best of terms. So I was with our donkey, the various cats in the yard, the songbirds nesting under our roof, not to forget the house snake. They all fed off each other, yet their numbers never seemed to change. The birds were useful against bugs and caterpillars, cats and snakes took care of rats and mice, and although the latter were simply a nuisance, I was very fond of the funny little creatures. After many fruitless efforts I managed to catch one and dragged my pet everywhere behind me on a string attached to its tail. Small wonder that the mouse did not last very long with such treatment. Finding it dead in the morning, I cried with sorrow.

Warding Off Evil

My Atonement

My next pet was a rooster.

"It's for you, Fallu, for your *kappara*," said my father who had bought the bird in time to fatten it up for the festive meal that breaks the fast of Yom Kippur. Little did I know what kappara meant, but I took good care of my rooster. I fed it tidbits saved from my own meals, and nice, plump worms dug out of our courtyard. Before long the rooster was following me around like a dog. Its comb grew bigger and redder every week; its call changed from a short, hoarse squeak into a drum-splitting, drawn-out crow. By Rosh Hashanah the rooster reached up to my shoulders as it tiptoed after me with flapping wings, its flag of green, gold and scarlet tail feathers rippling behind both of us. Its time had come. One day before Yom Kippur my grandfather forced my rooster and several more chickens into his big basket, hung it over his arm and took me for a walk to Rabbi Haim Shushan, the slaughterer.

"What is the man doing, Grandfather?" I asked worriedly as the rabbi grabbed my wildly flapping rooster by the legs.

"This is for my atonement—an exchange—for my sake this rooster is going to its death. . . ." Seven times the rabbi half-muttered, half-chanted the same incomprehensible Hebrew words, seven times he swung the bird over my head before my grandfather's callused old hands closed my eyes. Awful shrieks pierced the dark, and when the hands let go again I saw Rabbi Shushan facing me, a bloody knife in his right hand. At his feet in a flutter of colored feathers my rooster was trying to lift itself with funny little flaps and jerks, then fell back on its side and lay very, very still. Vaguely understanding what had happened I cried so hard that the whole family began to worry, especially as I would not stop rubbing my red, swollen eyes. I was going to come down with one of those eye sicknesses that leave children blind in one eye or both, God forbid, said my mother, and she sang little rhymes to cheer me up:

"Say Dibdib, say Hidwid . . . where did you sleep last night?

"Close to my Arab woman . . .

"Off with you, little mouse, off with you, little mouse, run to the butcher's shop!"

She hugged me, tickled me to imitate the running mice, but nothing helped. My father made funny faces, my grandfather cradled me in his arms and fed me sugar lumps.

"Can't you understand, Fallu? It's for your own good . . . . That rooster has taken all your sins away. . . ."

"I want them back, I want them back!" I shouted. "I want my rooster alive and not dead!" Chicken being either for the rich or for the sick, it was a rare treat in our house, yet for years I would not touch its meat; forgiving Rabbi Shushan took me even longer.

The Evil Eye

With a beautifully brown-and-black-marked viper I had a more distant relationship. Holding its three-cornered head proudly erect it would nonchalantly wind its way through our room. "Sheikh bait," we would greet it courteously as it passed by, flipping its thin, forked tongue to catch a fly without honoring us with a glance. Ignoring our advances, it was nevertheless aware of its duties as guardian of the house, never once attacking one of its inhabitants or guests. It would not even steal from the chicken coop, patiently waiting for the egg we let it have from time to time.

Although no one will cast doubt on the protective power of house snakes, more than snake power was needed for the well-being of a family that never saw a doctor. The symbol of a hand with five raised fingers stretches out from the past, a time-proven guard against the evil eye, passed down to us from our ancestors. So hands it was, scattered all over our home: hands of every shape and material, hands of copper and of glass, hands embroidered on silk or drawn on paper. Already on the threshold visitors were welcomed by five eggshells dangling from a chunk of charcoal, a contraption meant to strengthen the powers of the mezuzah embedded in the doorpost. Palms dipped in blue lime were pressed on the walls of our room. Outside, the imprint of a single reddish-brown hand over the gate could be seen from afar. Every year before Passover, after all the walls had been duly whitewashed, my father would plunge his hand into the blood of a freshly slaughtered sheep and slap it on the snowy lime. Had not the Angel of Death spared every Jewish home marked by just such a seal of blood a long, long time ago when we were slaves unto the Pharaoh in Egypt?

It is common knowledge how vulnerable baby boys are to the emanations of the evil eye and no end of precautions had to be taken to protect them. Girls, of course, could be left safely to their own devices. Who in his right mind would begrudge a mother her daughter, as pretty as she may be? But boys under the age of two had to be protected with the most potent spells available. A day or two before the *brit milah* (circumcision), the father would go shopping for a tiny silver hand or even a charm wrought of gold if he could afford it. Was he in such straits that he could not even buy a glass fish, then he had the whole seashore to search for a small, round shell of immaculate white, which was quite efficient when well chosen. Tied in with a couple of blue beads, the talisman would be sewn on a tiny cloth bag which was then pinned to the baby's shirt. Bulging with handwritten charms, the bag also contained round, black grains of the brightest polish, hard and shiny enough to deflect any evil eye.

Although every little boy in Nabeul would wear his talisman day and night, more than half of our children would never see their second birthday.

My own mother gave birth to seven boys and girls of whom only three survived. My brother Michael was among those who left us. A beautiful, healthy child loved by everybody, I can still see his friendly eyes and his plump little arms and legs before me. My grandfather adored him. To throw the evil eye off his tracks he would smear the round baby face with coffee grounds, would not let him wear the pretty blouses with my mother's needlework so as not to arouse the envy of our neighbors. The old man must have had forebodings of what was to happen. My little brother had just taken his first steps and learned to say my name when he came down with a dry cough and a high fever. All of the rubbings with salt, the candles, prayers and incantations by the rabbi did not help. Michael died, leaving my parents very sad and my poor grandfather heartbroken. It was then that he came upon the idea of the whistle. Wanting me near him in his distress, he hung one from my neck on a string, and every few minutes I had to signal him with three blows that all was well with me.

Any child's death brought great grief, but since it occurred so frequently it seemed inevitable and it was accepted as the will of God. The moment a boy showed the first signs of an illness his mother would run to buy more charms to add to his already overstuffed little bag. If the symptoms did not subside, Haia, the exorcist, was called in. Murmuring incantations suited to the sickness, she would drive out evil spirits by the application of coarse kitchen salt into the afflicted parts of the child's body. Seven times she would vigorously rub salt into her patient's skin, spit seven times, utter three sonorous "poo, poo, poos" over her shoulder, then throw out the tainted salt into the street.

Of course, as I already said before, only for boys would one go to such lengths and take all that trouble. When I came down with the measles my mother used another cure, though, simple but time-honored. "Red" was the name of her remedy, red as the red rash itself. I remember lying prone on my sheepskin, a red woolen bonnet drawn over my ears. I was dressed in a red blouse and was covered with a red blanket as I faced the red curtain hiding my parents' bed. After a few days of the red treatment the rash subsided, the fever passed, the cough loosened up. I could return to my games with the children of the neighborhood.

I was my mother's firstborn, strong and healthy. How she loved to recall the days of my babyhood.

"Fallu was the prettiest boy in all of Nabeul," she would tell my wife Fortuna when we were newlyweds. "With a head of curls . . . a black lamb, I tell you. . . . Every time he caught lice and we had to shear them off I cried. His skin . . . fresh brown cake crisp from the oven, and his eyes . . . chocolate with almonds. . . ." No wonder my parents would take no chance with their treasure. In a brown paper bag at the back of Fortuna's wardrobe I still keep the tokens of their love, all the tiny charms and amulets they had given me for my protection. There are the scented wooden beads, the old silver coins inscribed with portions of the Koran, strangely formed crystals with magic properties and pink and brown pebbles worn smooth by a thousand years of rushing waters. An iridescent white shell, not bigger than the tip of my little finger, is the most potent spell of them all. For countless centuries it had been lying on the bottom of the sea until it found its way into the scant belongings of my great-grandfather Mordehai. He somehow managed to provide for his wife and children on a very slack trade in grain and was convinced the little shell had helped him muddle through. On his deathbed he gave it to my grandfather Rafael who was just building up his flower and myrtle stand in the market. He in turn left it to my father Hamus who would never go on a peddling tour without first making sure the talisman was at the bottom of his pouch.

Since my father's retirement the little shell has not left my pocket except once, when I used its powers to help my son who was out of a job. As he will have nothing to do with "such nonsense" I found a way around his stubbornness, secretly sewing the shell into his lapel. To this day he is convinced that he got his job thanks to his handsome looks and smooth talk but I know better. I know my shell is worth a fortune, much safer than a bank account in these inflationary times.

"Give it to me . . ." Fortuna keeps nagging. "For thirty years you have been running around with my luck. Lend me the shell for a few days, it's the least you can do. . . ." Why should I? Hard currency melts in her hand like ice cream, our poor paper shekels in her purse go up—poof—into unnecessary presents. Fortuna does not accept no for an answer.

"Oh, where have they gone?" she laments. "Where are the days when I was still in my father's house, sitting under my own star and on top of my yellow camels?" What camels can she mean? She likes to feel sorry for herself, and I am used to seeing her eyes get watery every time she remembers her lost star, but the camels are new to me.

"Fortuna, for God's sake . . . what camels? On what camels were you sitting in Nabeul? Did I marry a good Jewish daughter or a Bedouin? As far as I know the only thing you rode in your father's house was a sewing machine. . . ." That does it—the sewing machine brings it all back to me. I recall the big camels Fortuna had been sitting on—the caravan pictured on those large Tunisian one-thousand-franc notes hidden under the rush mat. From early morning until late at night she and her five sisters had sat on that mat sewing trousers for Arab women, hatching their camels as would so many hens sitting on their eggs. The notes had been the sisters' dowry, one thousand francs for each of them. Why on earth would Fortuna remember them now, weeping for her camels as for some long-lost relatives? Throughout years of hardship she never once mentioned her camels, why does she have to bring them back now, she being a grandmother of almost five and, thank God, lacking nothing?

To dry her tears I let her have some rubbed-off antique coins, a small picture on parchment. Those she can easily sell for pocket money. Not always will a little present calm her down. She will go on pestering me until I become too upset to take up my brush and paint. Then I will go into the bedroom, open the wardrobe and take out the tiny, fifty-eight-year-old bag with the black grains, the blue beads and the silver hand. A few weeks before her death my mother gave it to me, and always when I feel sad or unwell I wear the bag close to my heart. How I miss my mother's love. Worn out, she left us early, a short time after she had embraced her first grandson in Israel.

Healing the Sick

Mama Hafzeah—Healer of the Sick

One of the most popular figures in the Nabeul of my childhood was Mama Hafzeah. Not a week would pass without my mother sending me on an errand to her tiny shop in the heart of the Arab quarter. Entering to ask for a few sous' worth of incense or a concoction against headache, I had to hold my breath—the smell of herbs was overwhelming. In the sudden darkness I could not see a thing but little by little my nose adjusted, my eyes made out Hafzeah's hump-back not far above the counter.

"*Aslama*," muttered the bent shape. With eyes half-closed in sunken sockets, her wrinkled nose forever sniffing herbs, the old Jewess, who had never learned to read or write, would label her merchandise by its smell. Goods were lined up all around her on dusty shelves: tin cans, wooden boxes, jars and bottles filled with a greater variety of dried leaves, shrunken fruit and roots than ordinary people would ever suspect existed. Most of these remedies she had gathered herself in fields and orchards; rare plants not to be found in Tunisia, however, came from as far away as Algiers and Morocco, some even from the Moslems' holy Mecca and a place called Zanzibar. There is not a pharmacy today with such a wide choice of remedies as was packed into Hafzeah's tiny shop, and an illness the old healer could not get under her thumb has yet to be invented.

"Mama Hafzeah, Father wants something for his foot; it's very sore and all swollen."

"Does it hurt all the time or only when he stands on it? Is the swelling red, purple or yellowish?" While I was trying to find the

answers Hafzeah already had mixed salve and, having gathered from
my answers that a house visit was indispensable, closed shop to
accompany me to Bab Salah Street. Diagnosing the thorn of a prickly
pear lodged deep inside my father's suppurating sole, she applied
salve to bring both pus and thorn to the surface and advised complete
rest. The next day she rubbed in more unguent; on the third she
pulled out the thorn and finished her job with a neat white bandage.
The fee for three visits, two preparations and a minor operation came
to whatever a more or less grateful patient pushed into her hand.
Usually this would not exceed a few sous which Hafzeah, who considered healing a vocation, let glide unseen into her pocket.

I was perhaps nine years old when I broke my forearm. She set it
so well with a splint and a plaster cast that today I could not tell for
the life of me whether the injured arm had been my left or my right.
Propped up on a cane, a bag with herbs slung over her crooked
shoulder, the old woman would walk the streets of Nabeul in her
brisk limp, bringing her gift of healing to the sick.

"Working in the greatest heat, Mama Hafzeah?" Passersby
would approach her amicably, then murmur, "Beware of the old
witch, she will sell you Roola's milk and devil's potions," as soon as
her humpback was turned. Yet the same people would never set foot
in a pharmacy. Were not Hafzeah's herbs more powerful and also
much cheaper? There was some truth to the rumors though, for next
to bottles with cough medicine, jars with various teas against upset
stomach, bladder cold and kidney stones (God forbid!), sharing the
gloomy corners of the shelves stood pots with more subtle potions.
Blue glass goblets with balm to cure lack of sex appeal in unmarried
maidens stood side by side with flasks of elixir to strengthen potency
in men.

When Bedouin and fallahs from the surrounding countryside
streamed into Nabeul for the weekly market, Hafzeah saw a flurry of
activity. A line twenty or thirty deep could be seen opposite the
prison on a Friday morning, waiting to gain entrance to her shop.

"Take him home for now," Hafzeah said to the son of an old Jew
bent over with back pain. "I will come before the start of the Sabbath
to give him a good massage, maybe cup him too. . . . Who's next in
line?" A Bedouin advances. With much dignity he coughs his soul
into the white woolens wrapping his tall figure from head to naked
feet; only black eyes consumed with fever peep through an opening.
Hafzeah listens to the cough, mixing with one hand roots and leaves
for his tea as the other chases flies off the crusted, inflamed eyes of an
infant the Bedouin's wife carries tied to her back. The Bedouin
mother is handsome. In contrast to the fallah women in the line, her
face is unveiled under a black kerchief, dark and pretty despite the

bluish tattoos on her chin and cheeks. Her robe, of the same plain black cotton as the kerchief, is weighed down by rows of necklaces, and massive earrings have torn big holes into her sagging lobes. All these ornaments are made of copper, but her front teeth flash a smile of pure gold at Hafzeah.

"Here, boil *hush-hash* with camomile and with the liquid wash the child's eyes at least ten times a day . . . ten times." The old woman raises her ten bony fingers. "In the other bag is the tea for your husband—five sous altogether. Who's next?"

A heavily built farmer's wife on broad, bare feet clanks her silver anklets one against the other.

"Mama Hafzeah," she says worriedly behind her veil, "little Ahmed's tummy is tight as a drum. . . ."

"It must be from too many prickly pears," decides Hafzeah, handing her a potion of castor oil. More purgatives, more teas, until the approaching Sabbath makes her at last close shop.

Were you burning with desire and your love left unrequited? The old woman would deliver you the goods, yellow cumin seeds together with advice on how to use them. Follow her instructions to the letter, cast your spell right—and the object of your affections would fall madly in love with you. Now light a fire in the seclusion of your home and let the flames kindle your yearning. Cast the seeds upon the red-hot coals and as their aroma gently titillates your nose, whisper into the fragrant smoke:

"*Yah camoon—jebo majnoon! Yah tabel—jebo habel!*" Oh, cumin seeds bring foolishness! Oh, tabel seeds bring madness! Call the name of the adored over and over, press a shred from his clothes to your bosom, stroke a lock of the beloved's hair and the spell becomes infallible.

From the perfume poured over the bride's head down to her henna-painted soles, wedding preparations without the services of Hafzeah were unthinkable. It was amazing to see how the old witch's cosmetics could transform the plainest girl into an enchanting temptress. First there was kohl, a blue-black powder to darken the lids and lend the eye the brilliancy of deep desire. Hafzeah produced it from the ashes of the charred heads of chameleons, while the roots of a thorn bush pounded into a lush, pink salve, were used to make enticing lips. Smooth ebony arcs painted on with the help of an unguent obtained from acorns replaced the natural brows pulled out with their roots. Luminously red henna applied to the bride's soles, her toenails, palms, and fingertips was not only a harbinger of good fortune and fertility—it also added an alluring glow of bashfulness. Douse the girl with a generous dose of orange and lemon flower scent, dress her in a white gown trimmed with gold and silver lace—

now fire the imagination with a veil and any groom will face his lot
with confidence.

Dance Away the Demons

Not everything, however, was in Hafzeah's domain. Cases for blood-
letting she would refer to the Arab dentist-barber, but if a Jew was
stricken with melancholy or any other sickness of the soul she would
recommend the *hadra*. This age-old word in Aramaic grates on the ear
as the music it so well describes—the music of the demons. In Nabeul
the word hadra stood for a three-man band playing tunes of such
devilish charm that no evil spirit could resist them; the most obdu-
rate, pigheaded of demons would be lured out of their victims by the
hadra's unearthly melodies and frantic rhythms. As they joined the
din and dance inside the sick room, the patient got a respite from
suffering which usually lasted for months and sometimes even years.

Spirits, demons, jinn and ghosts keep late hours. Because they
love to putter around in the small hours of the night, a hadra would
start between nine and ten in the evening to let it reach its peak at
midnight. Hours before the event, the neighborhood would wait for
darkness to fall. Every few minutes someone would step out to look
up at the sky. When it had turned so black that stars sparkled like
diamonds, the guests began to drop in. First come, first served. They
squatted down on the best seats the sickroom floor had to offer,
stolidly munching broad beans and chick-peas passed around as refreshments. Women suckling babies were cracking sunflower seeds,
admonishing their offspring not to rub the sleep out of their eyes, not
to yawn either as gaping mouths might attract the evil eye. Everybody's attention was fixed on the doorway from where the musicians
would make their appearance rather than on the prostrate patient
who, with profuse sighs and much groaning, did his best to contribute to the success of the evening.

The people of Bab Salah Street knew no cinema, no theater; radio
and television were still a long way off. In their place they had something much better: neighborliness. Had misfortune struck one of our
families, all the others would take part in the sorrow, trying to help
and comfort as best they could. If, on the other hand, a happy event
called for joy and celebration, the whole street was invited to attend.
Oddly enough, a hadra was counted among the latter, an occasion for
pure merrymaking. Long before the start of the ceremony, the sick-

room would be so crammed with spectators that a needle could not fall to the floor, and latecomers had to watch proceedings from the courtyard.

When finally flute, drum and tambourine made their entrance, people squeezed out a little stage where the three crouched down with their instruments. Full and throaty the flute took the lead, then let out a sudden, high-pitched wail, the signal for a woman, preferably a relative of the sick, to take up position in front of the musicians. Standing upright and with much dignity she removes the kerchief hiding her hair, winding it tightly round her waist and, opening her tresses, starts swaying to a sad, captivating melody. The audience is eager for more noise and movement. *"Fisha, fisha, Yah sidi! . . ."* they urge on the drummer. His fingers quicken, his palms smack the taut hides: Ta tera-tam, de ta-teratam, tam-tam-tatera-tam . . .

Carried away by the sound of the *dar'booka*, the dancer's bare feet tap and glide, her copper anklets glimmer in the dull light of the brazier. Acrid and sweetish, the scent of frankincense mounts from the coals. Her hands protected by wet rags, the woman lifts the tripod by the legs, swinging it round and round until the whole room lies veiled behind a yellow smoke screen. Children cough and shout, wide awake now, "Fisha, fisha . . . let them jiggle . . . make them waggle . . ." they spur on the dancer shaking her breasts to the trills of the tambourine. To abandon herself more freely to the frantic rhythms, she puts the smoking tripod down. Breasts rock, head and haunches roll wildly, long black strands sweep her face as she throws her long hair from side to side in mounting frenzy. "Uhululululululu- lulu . . ." To heighten the excitement, all the women present vibrate their tongues in a shrill, drawn-out howl of joy, the *sahruta*, while from the flute rise wails that tear one's ears and soul apart. The music has reached a hellish pitch—the scented smoke is thick enough for any dancing demons to hide in. "Do you feel any better? Have the black thoughts gone?" Remembering why they have come here in the first place, some of the guests yell polite questions in the direction of the sickbed. As the music suddenly stops, the dancer stands dazed. The dar'booka could take no more—the hide has burst. Still in a trance, trembling and exhausted, the dancer sinks into the arms of waiting women who revive her with sugar water. The guests step outside to fill their lungs with fresh air. The patient is beginning to feel better. Sighing only occasionally, he orders his wife to treat the musicians to coffee.

Then the next round starts. Another woman prepares to dance. More incense is thrown on the coals and the drummer takes hold of a brand-new dar'booka. Unlike Nabeul's bigger Jewish wedding band which boasted of a fiddle and a flute, the hadra musicians played nothing but demon music. Much in demand, they took their task very seriously. Tireless, the three would drum, blow and shake the tambourine until they had made sure that the last of the brooding demons of melancholy had been expelled and the patient had regained his spirits. In the morning he would almost always be able to get up and go to work. If after some time symptoms of illness reappeared, the hadra would simply be repeated to the great elation of the whole neighborhood.

Tootoo the Seer

If an important decision had to be made anywhere in Bab Salah Street, if a marriage was in the offing, a trip or a business deal up for consideration, then Tootoo the seer was sent for. With her unfailing sixth sense she made a living the easy way—all she needed for her trade was a glassful of water. Seated on the ground opposite her client, she would fixedly stare into the glass before her, ask some questions and stare some more. Tired at last of gazing down her long, narrow nose she would lift her sharp eyes and ferret out those of her visitor. Halting questions would probe into the furthest corners of his memory, explore forgotten chambers of the mind where events of the past are stashed away along with secrets never confided to a living soul. If the visitor's head was so muddled the images in Tootoo's water glass remained a mystery even after addition of a magic powder, she would ask her client to come back on the first or second night of the new moon, propitious to fortune-telling.

Huddled under the grapevine in Tootoo's otherwise bare courtyard, in the twilight of a crescent as thin and sharp as the soothsayer's nose, two shadows mingled whispers with the autumn breeze. Tootoo's scraggy one was hovering over her glass as usual; to whom did the other shadow, the dismal heap of woe crouching in front of her belong? It was Laloo the candlemaker, a pillar of our congregation, pouring out his bag of troubles into the rustling leaves.

"Finished, Tootoo, I am finished. . . . I can feel the Angel of Death sitting between my eyes—a curse has gripped me by the neck. It all started a week ago. Monday my star began to totter. I stumbled on the steps of my own shop. Still limping Tuesday morning, I dragged myself out of bed to drink my coffee. I was drinking worms! I limped over to look at the cistern—there were millions of them squirming in the water, red as the river of Egypt. I tell you, Tootoo, a plague on Pharaoh (may his name be erased!). Now what happened on Wednesday? I can't even think . . . my poor head's become a dar'booka, drumming with trouble. . . . Oh, yes, Wednesday my wife—gone nine months with child—wanted to cook beans. But she nearly fainted when she saw the big sack I bought two weeks ago. Black beetles popping out all over, peeping at her from every bean. And that's not all. The almonds I put away for Passover were bored through and through. Worms as fat and pink as pigs (may God erase their name and memory) curled up inside. Thursday is a good day for selling Sabbath candles—if there are candles to sell that is. But what is left after the rats have gnawed their way into the candle shop? Now comes the worst day, Friday, Tootoo . . . or was Sabbath even worse? Friday at the market my donkey was stolen. God has given me only daughters . . . that donkey I brought up myself . . . loved it as my own son. . . ." Laloo sighed, then took a deep breath: "What happened yesterday, Sabbath, everybody knows. The whole town is laughing—twin girls she bore. . . ."

"Are you through, Laloo?" asked Tootoo coolly and rose to pour water into her washtub. "You made a mistake. You should have come earlier to see me. It's a clear case of the evil eye," she said firmly, looking upon the broken sickle of the new moon floating in her tub. "We must stop it at once or worse is coming. Tell me, Laloo, who was around when you stumbled on your doorstep?"

"Nobody . . . nobody but Hanan, the ragpicker. He wanted to buy candles on credit. He never pays, so I sent him away."

"That was unwise," said Tootoo sternly. "Haven't you ever looked at his eyebrows? Grown together over the nose . . . the mark of the evil eye." The seer gave Laloo three almonds soaked in green moonlight, and while he was still chewing them she wrote out something with her finger on a plate, then quickly rinsed off the invisible charm with water. "Now you go straight to your shop," she recommended, "walk up and down the steps where you have stumbled and cry over them—remember what Hanan, the ragpicker, did to you. My name is not Tootoo if his curse will not come down upon his own head!"

I don't recall whether Laloo's donkey came back or what happened to the ragpicker who was miserable enough with or without a curse upon his head. I do remember though that later on Laloo's wife gave birth to a son.

The Miracle Worker

Tootoo was not the only one helping poor Jews solve their problems. An old man crouching on some sacking in the farthest corner of the market could also be turned to in times of trouble. For three sous he would write down a short charm, for six a lengthy invocation, for seven he would squeeze the names of all the Archangels into one small piece of paper to be worn over your heart or concealed inside your pocket. Old maids in search of a husband, sterile women craving pregnancy and mothers with a house full of nothing but daughters were his steadiest clients. To men afflicted with quarrelsome wives he sold herbs which worked wonders when secretly added to their spouses' tea. Served at the right moment with sugar and mint leaves, such a potent nightcap would, at least for a while, transform a snarling tigress into a cooing dove.

Keeping me at her side, my mother liked to linger in the miracle worker's shady corner. I was puzzled. "What is the old man doing?" I would ask, seeing him inscribe a charm in diminutive Hebrew letters.

"It's a prayer for us, Fallu. God willing it may help bring a little brother for you," my mother would say with a sigh, pay the scribe and tuck the bit of hope into her bosom.

From there we would always continue through the arcades where the craftsmen had their shops, then cross into the dank, smelly passage of the Arab butchers. Here dark vaults gleamed with slimy-looking meat; heavy sides of camel were hooked up side by side with grotesquely formed tripe and intestines dangling from the ceiling. In front of me severed black cows' feet, piled up high, were watched over by the heads of their former owners, their hairy hide clotted with blood and full of flies. From behind I could feel the reproachful stare of naked eyeballs of skinned sheep hung up by their hind legs—a priceless delicacy for Moslem gourmets. Slightly shuddering, yet strangely captivated, I would let myself be pulled along, taking a deep breath when we finally stepped into the light of the big, open marketplace.

V
Market Day

Every Friday, farmers from the surrounding countryside converged on our town, some to sell livestock and produce, others to renew their stores or simply to enjoy the bustle of lively crowds. Entire families would arrive early in the morning, on foot, on donkey back, on camels, horses and in carts, to disperse again in the afternoon weighed down with bargains.

Although Nabeul was famous for its fish and for its pretty blue-and-white-glazed pottery, its true pride was peppers. Who did not envy our town for its pungent red pepper pods, the crowning grace of every dish stewed in the earthen cooking pots of Tunisia? They were the spice of the earth, so hot that tears would come to one's eyes at the first bite. Wherever a traveler from Nabeul revealed his origins he was greeted with an embrace as fiery as our condiment and an old joke reserved for the hot-tempered citizens of our town: *"Takel shakshooka, tadreb dar'booka!"* (Eat pepper omelet, then play the drum!)

Pepper pulp was the lifeblood pulsating through the veins of Nabeul, and in our market one literally saw red before one's eyes. Countless strings of pepper were hung to dry from the roofs surrounding the wide market square, like vermilion curtains streaming over whitewashed walls. Peppers in heaps or stuffed into sacks, fresh or dried, in pulp or in powder, everywhere their sting hung in the air, tickling and tingling in my nose until I, like everybody else around me, joined in the resounding sneezers' choir.

Swaying under broad pepper baskets suspended from its humps, a camel advanced on a narrow path squeezed out by throngs of shoppers. In its tracks screeched a camel cart on giant wheels. Piled high with fiery pods, the cart swung from side to side like a Cape Bon fishing boat with bright red sails. One shade darker were the tarbooshes worn by Arabs and Jews alike, moving back and forth in scarlet waves broken only by a jug or basket atop some woman's head. Farmers' wives were used to carrying the heaviest loads in this fashion, needing both arms unencumbered to tote babies and keep toddlers safe in the big folds of their skirts. Stolidly they steered their course against the stream, pushing obstacles out of their way with hips and bellies, showing greater strength than one would expect in such modestly veiled figures.

Hoarse from long hours of praising the merits of their merchandise, the shouts of hawkers were echoing from all sides in raucous bursts. Coming on top of the loud bargaining of the shoppers, the braying donkeys, bleating sheep, and the universal sneezing, the din was deafening. Pounding on my ears as breakers on the cliffs down at the seashore, the happy giddiness I always felt amidst the roaring of the surf was sharpened by the brilliant colors all around me. With the blue sky above, white houses, and red peppers, our market was one huge tricolor scene spattered with squash, cucumbers, cabbages and lettuce. The silky purple of eggplants and fleshy pink of open melons were outdone by the garish hues of oranges and lemons. Tomatoes were thrown into the shade by the mass of red peppers. The final, festive touch, however, belonged to the fish. Fresh, silvery fish were laid out in rows, glittering heaps of rainbow in brown puddles; their strong smell made me itch to run down to the shore.

My mother paid for two gray mullets and we made our way toward the fallahs offering earthenware pots with goat cheese and honey. In the open market there were no stalls. Vendors sat cross-legged on the ground with their merchandise spread out in front of them. Side by side with Arabs offering rush mats and palm-leaf baskets for sale, bearded Jews were squatting, hawking clothes and footwear of their own manufacture. Here pointed leather slippers, hand-woven woolens for bournouses, and striped cotton for long gowns called *kashabias*. There plain white fabric for the enormously baggy trousers of the men and colorful flower patterns for the long pants of the women. Some young girls were lovingly stroking the bales of bright satin meant for dowries, dark eyes over black veils were trying to match ribbons, lace and gold buttons laid out close at hand. Farther down the row stood two donkeys amid mounds of glowing water jugs and stacks of bowls and plates, waiting resignedly for someone to release them from a load of pottery packed in straw.

It did not matter where my mother stopped to buy onions and tomatoes for her pepper soup or bargain over cabbage and carrots for her couscous, I knew in which direction to pull her. For a whole week I had been dreaming of getting behind that wall of latticed, wooden cages from where now came the sound of flutes and drums and the shrill cry of a monkey. Straining on my mother's hand to move beyond those cages, I was much too impatient to pay attention to their occupants, nervously fluttering songbirds or listless hens and pigeons, their beady little eyes frozen with fear.

At last we turned the corner and the snake charmer came into view. Knees drawn up to his shoulders, ballooning cheeks pushed forward in between, he crouched on his carpet playing the flute in an effort to coax his cobra out of its laziness. I loved to tease his green-and-orange-colored parrot, driving it so mad with my hissing, whistling and stamping that the ruffled bird would hop onto his master's turban, a secure spot from where to call me names. Satisfied at last, I could draw my mother over to the next attraction—the monkey men from Algiers.

Silent people gray with the dust of distant regions, they used to camp under an equally gray tree, carrying monkeys on long chains perched on their shoulders. Every time one of the animals uttered its sudden, piercing cry it was a signal for the other monkeys to jump onto the nearest branch and take some exercise, somersaulting or balancing themselves by their tails. One of the men would order a female out of the tree to dress it in a striped skirt; another collected a fee from the public and the performance could begin. The animal was trying to imitate an old woman. Heavily leaning on a short cane, it shuffled and dragged its feet, advancing as if with great difficulty. Finally, it went down on all fours exhausted, trailing its belly through the dust.

Now her old husband stepped forward, a male wearing fashionably baggy trousers and a tiny tarboosh greeted the spectators with the low, dignified bow of a devout Moslem. The animal then spread out a prayer mat and knelt down on it. It rested for a while, chin in hand, absorbed in meditation, then lowered its head until its forehead touched the ground to go through the motions of Moslem prayer. The more we clapped and laughed, the harder the monkeys would try to please us, but after a few more numbers we were through the repertory and I was out of peanuts.

The Booshadia

"Let's go to see the *Booshadia* now," I begged my mother, dragging her toward the dense circle of people forming in the shade of the arcades. Heedless of their grumbling owners I pushed my way across trousers and skirts, until I finally caught sight of the market goblin, the highlight of my Fridays.

The Booshadia was a poor but ingenious black man who had knocked together a monstrous costume from bits and pieces anybody would throw out with the trash—even the people of Nabeul. The fantastic creature must have lost its way, must have landed in our midst by mistake. Perhaps it was a jinni from the weird world down under. Curiosity getting the better of caution, I risked a second glance and recognized the Booshadia for what he was: simply a big, dressed-up black man.

Lustrous rooster's feathers tied in with green-blue and golden plumes from a peacock, rows upon rows of empty snuffboxes, colorful rags and bells stolen from the very necks of sheep and goats were the main ingredients of his outfit. Bushy tails, hairy tails, once the pride of a great many animals, were dangling from his back or sprouting out from unexpected parts. His feet in their enormous slippers resembled fishing boats with black masts instead of legs. One might well say that the only human touch about this strange being was the tarboosh on the Booshadia's woolly head. Eyes wildly rolling, in turn sticking out a fleshy tongue or baring his teeth in a terrific grin, he belabored his drum like a true savage. One moment he was leaping up into the air with crazy laughter, the next moment he was wallowing in the dust with squeals and grunts, bells ringing, boxes rattling, giving everybody a marvelous time. Taking a break from his strenuous activities, he would use the intermission to make the rounds with a broad smile and a wide-open bag. Who would not readily give something to our Booshadia, a coin or two, a fruit or a chunk of bread for his many children?

Thinking back it seems to me that I never missed even one of his Friday performances. Today I would gladly give up all the newfangled, fancy entertainment and throw in color television with the rest could I only once more watch that poor, crazy Booshadia do his stunts.

Grandfather Rafael

In the cool shade of a half-crumbled wall, screened from the noise and bustle, my grandfather Rafael was selling myrtle branches and bouquets of flowers. A very old, bent Jew, his snow-white beard enveloped in the scent of roses, myrtle and carnations, he seemed forever to be snipping away at stems and twigs when he was not reciting prayers.

Rich or poor, it was an obligation for every Jew to receive the Sabbath with fragrant flowers as befits a bride or queen. If one could not afford an expensive bouquet with which to greet the Sabbath, one had to make do with the more modestly priced myrtle which also gives off a nice, fresh smell. Since nine out of ten of our Jews were poor, my grandfather's myrtle trade was as hardy as his flower trade was slack. Only a handful of wealthy merchants, jewelers and owners of pawnshops or olive presses could afford such Sabbath luxuries. Moslem clients, however, preferred tiny bunches of white jasmine with a red rose or carnation tucked into the middle.

If a businessman came into a sudden windfall or if a young man passed a veiled beauty on a summer afternoon, he would buy himself a fragrant nosegay to let everybody see his happiness. Even a simple, stout family man, in high spirits for no reason at all, would often stick flowers behind one ear, wear his tasseled tarboosh at a rakish angle and strut off twirling his mustache and swinging his walking stick.

In short, what I want to say is that my grandfather Rafael, after whom I was named, took care of loftier needs than ordinary hawkers.

Every Wednesday morning before sunrise he would mount his donkey and trot off to a ravine outside of Nabeul where myrtle bushes grew. He would return in the afternoon with a big load of branches. Sitting down at once to clean them with his long, black scissors, it took him all of Wednesday night and Thursday to cut, prune and bundle the myrtle. They looked terribly old, the donkey and his master trotting to market together on Friday morning. My grandfather heavily leaning on his cane was so stooped that his white beard reached his knees. To me he was the oldest, nicest grandfather on earth.

When he came to visit us, with my little grandmother shuffling behind him at a respectful distance, the scent of myrtle clinging to his clothes would bring sweetness to our home. My father would bow very low to kiss his father's worn hand; my mother would run off to the kitchen to fetch cool lemonade and soft food that needed little chewing. Meanwhile I was standing on the tips of my toes, unable to tear my eyes from the wrinkled face. I was eagerly waiting for one of my grandfather's fond smiles so that I could catch a glimpse of his teeth. With the years he had grown a fascinating third set of them, resembling needles or fish bones rather than trappings for biting and chewing. Having made sure the funny little things were still safely in his mouth, my eyes would then drop to the snake head carved out of the knob of his walking stick and from there it was not far to the pocket in his bournous. My grandfather's hand was already inside, coming up with a checkered handkerchief. Slowly, very slowly he would untie the knot, letting me help pull until I finally arrived at the core, a small cluster of raisins and almonds.

One day my grandfather opened the door to our room and, without even taking notice of my presence, sank down on the bed.

"Meesha, Meesha," he called my mother, "you won't believe this, but I saw it with my own eyes. A man not bigger than my fist is sitting in a box—the whole town is at Rahamim's café to get a look at him. He sings so loud even I could hear him, and you know my ears are not what they used to be. A nightingale sent from heaven I tell you!" Completely out of breath, the excited old man had to gather his strength before going on. "God knows I've never been much inside coffeehouses, Meesha, but that singer I had to see. People let me through and there was that box on the table with a trumpet sticking out. Rahamin was just feeding him after a song. . . ." My mother was hastily hiding all but her eyes and hands behind her big white wrapper and, leaving me in the care of my grandfather, ran to see the wonder for herself.

"It's really true!" she shouted as she came back with glowing face. "That little man has the biggest voice I have ever heard." The first record player had found its way into Nabeul, gradually to be followed by still more astonishing inventions like cars, radio and electricity.

Whether my grandfather was accompanied by my grandmother or not did not make much difference; she was so quiet that one hardly noticed she was there. Speaking seldom and then only in whispers, she was, if possible, even more pious than my grandfather. Only by her gray eyebrows could one tell the color of her hair; not a single lock was allowed to peak out from under her striped kerchief. Her plain white pants reached down over her ankles; her whole shrunken, fragile person would have gotten lost in the maze of her shawls had not one of them, tightly wound around her middle, held everything together. Having swallowed the last of my grandfather's raisins, I would wait for a wink from her eyes to slide over to her side. Poking with thumb and gnarled forefinger into the depths of her wrappings she would fish out half a dozen cooked chick-peas or broad beans and pass them into my hand delicately, as if they were so many precious stones.

My Uncle Goliath

In her youth my grandmother had given birth to a great number of children. She had had a hard time to bring up the six surviving ones, of whom my uncle Goliath was the eldest. It was the custom with the Jews of Nabeul to give every newborn boy a nickname because parents believed and hoped that if the Angel of Death remained ignorant of their son's true name he would be powerless to harm the child. It is a sad fact that the Angel of Death was seldom misled by this subterfuge. In the case of my uncle Goliath, however, the benefits of his nickname surpassed all expectations. Surviving babyhood without a hitch, he wore it later on so well that he was called Goliath to his dying day. He was an awe-inspiring figure, probably less tall but on the other hand as thickset as the giant of the Bible. How his frame could have sprung from my tiny grandmother remains a mystery. I remember him walking into the steam bath on a Thursday evening, his gait a little clumsy because of all that muscle on his thighs and calves, his wet body glistening with an abundance of red fuzz. He was the envy of every Jew in town. No one dared talk back to him. Even my father, robust and short-tempered enough in his own right, would keep quiet when his older brother charged into our room in one of his frequent rages.

"Shame on you, Hamus!" he thundered at my father. "Your parents' cesspool is stinking to the heavens. Who do you think will clean it, me perhaps? As for you, Meesha," he now turned to my mother, "where were you when my wife was lying in with her tenth child? Watching Fallu run around with all the good-for-nothings of the neighborhood?" How frustrating it must have been for my uncle that apart from one tottering set of drawers we did not possess any piece of furniture to bang a fist on. In his own home he let it crash down with such gusto that the four legs of his table would jump up as one, his red face would turn to violet, sparks would fly from his copper-colored handlebar mustache and his bulbous brown eyes would nearly pop out of their sockets. So scared was I of my uncle's protruding eyes and the fiery mustache poking accusations at everybody that I would take any detour not to come across him in the street. Only my innate, voracious appetite would sometimes get the better of my fright, driving me over to his house at hours I was more or less sure to find him absent. Always a freshly opened ten-pound can of roe or tuna fish was sitting on the aforementioned table, my aunt forever doling out big chunks of fish and bread to her ten children. My uncle Goliath being a prosperous man, nephews who happened to be present were also treated. His job paid well. As watchman for a combined loan company and pawnshop business he had to

get rid of disgruntled debtors unable to reclaim their pawned belongings, an occupation cut out to his measure. There was one flaw in the
cast-iron nature of my uncle: he would crack at the sight of human
blood.

Having grown very wealthy with their loan and pawnshop business, the family of his employers had sent one of their sons to a famous
school in Paris from where he had returned as a qualified physician.
Occasionally called in to assist a wealthy resident sick in an outlying
village, he liked my uncle to accompany him as bodyguard. One day as
the doctor had hurried to the bedside of a rich Arab landowner, he
found the patient with one foot already in his grave and sure to get
there with the other too if not given a blood transfusion on the spot.
Goliath let the doctor coax him into giving a few drops of blood from
his finger, but on seeing preparations for an actual transfusion, my
uncle realized what was about to happen. Some of the effendi's
mother-of-pearl-encrusted furniture was smashed to smithereens before three strapping fallahs together with the doctor were able to rope
Uncle Goliath to the one remaining armchair. I only heard of the incident through the mouth of strangers. The thought of having his blood
flowing in the veins of an infidel, later on possibly also in those of the
cured effendi's offspring, was so intolerable to my uncle that nobody in
the family ever mentioned the fateful event.

Having given my uncle ten robust children, my aunt, a sickly
image of silent suffering, was withering away behind her cooking
pots. She went on ailing through the years and, now in her nineties,
is still living in a small town in Israel while my uncle, strong as an ox,
was cut down very early by a stroke. Though a terrible bully—may he
rest in peace—the death of this pillar of our clan was sorely felt by all
of us. Ordering us around, giving plenty of unwanted advice, he had
nevertheless felt responsible for the entire family, helping out with
food and money where they were most needed. At the time it had
seemed extravagant, but having taken it into his head that knowledge
was important, Uncle Goliath had sent all his children to school, even
the daughters, and woe to anyone who brought home low grades!
Whether they were born bright or studied out of fear, what matters is
that down to the last of them they became very educated people. In
fact, they hold such important jobs here in Israel that I don't get to see
them anymore. Take for instance my cousin Shlomo, assistant man-
ager in a bank. How could I reasonably expect him to find time for his
family in Safed?

Too much progress at one jump can turn a girl's head, which is
what happened to my cousin Yaffa. I don't know if a year had passed
after her father's death when she went to buy herself a short skirt.
However, looking at her image in the mirror she got cold feet and

asked me, maybe then sixteen, to chaperon her on a visit to the market. The farmers and hawkers had a heyday. Clapping and singing, making tin cans and cow bells ring to the rhythm of her steps, they sprained their necks or sprawled out on the ground to catch a better view as she was passing through their ranks in front of me with her nose in the air.

Rain Making

The Talmud-Torah School

So much for modern education. My own schooling was more traditional and it started when I was about five years old. Taking me by the hand one morning, my father walked me to a square stone house with a dark gate badly in need of repair. This building was the Talmud-Torah school, a venerable institution kept up by the Jews of Nabeul to put the fear of God into the sons of poorer families, assure them of one hot meal a day and hand them down clothes. One never knew, some of them might even become sages of the Book.

Inside the forbidding-looking gate my father left me in the hands of a sharp-eyed, bearded man and went back about his business, his breast swelling with hopes for the future of his firstborn son. The man was Rabbi Haim Parienti, my teacher for many years to come. Making me recite prayers and blessings I had picked up at mealtimes or on my frequent visits to the synagogue, words of whose meaning I had no idea, he brought me into his class, favorably impressed.

For six hours every morning I was taught reading and writing in preparation for the study of the Holy Book. Skullcaps on our heads and Hebrew primers before our noses, we were eighteen little boys in similar plight, forced to sit still on a stone bench around a long table. At its end stood the rabbi's desk and behind that the armchair from whose lofty heights he presided. Rabbi Parienti's white beard and a myrtle twig lying beside his inkstand reminded me pleasantly of my grandfather, but it did not take many lessons to teach me the difference between myrtle branch and myrtle cane. While the rabbi sat unperturbed, his eye fixed on some point of interest beyond the window, the twig would shoot down on my hand the moment I tried to stand up or started chatting with a neighbor. Hard as the new discipline was to take for a five-year-old unaccustomed to beatings, it brought results. One sidelong glance at the myrtle cane and the square Hebrew characters swimming menacingly behind a veil of tears would yield their hidden meaning.

Those children God had not graced with intelligence never got to feel the cane. Silently and with blank faces they sat at the far end of the bench, thanking me with a shy smile every time I had been ordered to wipe their noses or help them rearrange their dress. Anyone daring to treat these simple souls roughly or trying to make fun of them would be mercilessly punished by our teacher.

The study of the Torah is so sacred that language unworthy of the Holy Scriptures was forbidden during lessons; anybody needing permission to satisfy some earthy need had to use signs instead. Why those needs would creep up in class more frequently than elsewhere I don't know. Tirelessly, I kept making signs: one raised finger for a drink of water, two to piss and three to . . . Should the faint smell of a fart reach the rabbi's nostrils the heresy of it made him speechless with fury. Hurriedly an older pupil would be brought in to sniff out the culprit and we would have to stand in a row, waiting to learn whose behind would be selected to bear the brunt of the rabbi's rage.

Aware of my grandfather's trade, Rabbi Parienti naturally wanted to exploit his connection for a free supply of myrtle cane.

"Fallu," he took me aside after class, "give your grandfather my regards, may the Almighty grant him long life, and ask him for a few nice, strong branches as a favor to his grandson's teacher." I was not all that dumb. Go willingly to my own slaughter like a sheep—never! At first I would pretend that the rabbi's request had slipped my mind, then that all the myrtle had sold out, next it was the donkey that had gone lame. Having at last run out of ordinary fibs and feeling cornered, I invented a wretched story about my beloved grandfather being sick. Now the rabbi understood that he had gone too far.

"Come here, Fallu," he said, "I offer you a deal. You bring me fresh canes every other week and I make you guardian of the class." By right, this assignment, exemption from thrashings, belonged to the best student; although suited to the job like a goat to be gardener, I grabbed it with both hands.

The rabbi kept his word. Rarely requested to proffer my palm to the hissing cane from then on, I could let my thoughts wander more freely during lessons. Many of my classmates would come to school on an empty stomach, dressed in tatters and torn sandals, shirts either so short they kept escaping from their trousers or else so long they reached their knees. Why was it that, better dressed and better fed than most of them, all my daydreams gravitated toward food?

"Seven scrawny cows swallowing seven fat ones—they are seven years of drought and famine, the Lord's curse upon the land of Egypt." While Rabbi Parienti was going through the weekly portion, explaining Joseph's funny dreams, I had visions of stuffed tripe and calves' feet. I could not have been all that hungry, for in between early-morning services at synagogue and school my mother always served me a good breakfast. At the time of my father's childhood, hunger for bread rather than the thirst for knowledge had driven him to school. I, however, never knew such near starvation—not until Hitler's wars.

Trying hard to stay awake so as not to attract the rabbi's attention, I would drowsily sit through classes, waiting for the lunch bell to ring. Our teacher, always on the watch for bobbing heads, had a knack of ever so gently poking his cane under a sleeper's skullcap. Lifting it with a sudden jerk, he startled snoozers out of their wits. Finally the lunch bell would ring. Kissing the Bible before we rose, Rabbi Parienti's myrtle cane would lead us in a joyful song: "Yehi Rabbina ali karifina!" (Long live our rabbi who teaches us to read). Then began the mad race for the bucket, a pail with water standing near the entrance to the dining room. The first ones to wash their hands were the first to enter, getting a good chance of finding a bowl with an extra piece of bread. Hurrying through the blessing I would gulp down my beans, rice or lentils as if I were the hungriest and poorest of the poor. Then I would finish the meal with another much slower prayer. Freed for a short while of my obsession with food I would go out to play with my comrades in the courtyard. Sometimes the largess of a donor would fill up the usually meager stocks of the school kitchen. Slowed down by a full belly, I would then fall asleep on the stone pavement. My friend Dooha would pinch a fly between his thumb and index finger and hold the struggling insect at my ear, brutally waking me to two more hours in the classroom.

Nobody needs to point out to me the importance of Torah studies. To this day I know portions of it by heart, but as a child, sitting through those interminable afternoon lessons, I would often desperately seek for an escape. Winking at my friend Palmidi, I would raise two fingers; he would raise three and out we went. Inside the walled courtyard of Talmud-Torah school I rose to some of my loftiest moments. Pulling out a small chunk of bread saved from my lunch, I would nearly choke with love and noble feelings as I shared the morsel with my bosom friend.

"Palmidi, let's pretend we are David and Jonathan and that it's our last meal before the big battle. You can be David because you

have red hair," I whispered as the rabbi's voice cut the wings off my
lovely fancy.

"Jackasses!" he rasped and grabbing Palmidi and me each by one
ear pulled us back into the midst of our giggling classmates.

Welcome Interruptions

It was lucky that a number of special duties to be fulfilled by the
pupils of Talmud-Torah school were always interfering with the regu-
lar flow of our lessons. The sick had to be visited, the bereaved to be
comforted, and then there were, of course, also more pleasant inter-
ruptions, such as the news that a high-ranking member of our community was ailing. All smiles and excitement, we would assemble in
the dining room where the smell of stale beans was for once drowned
in an aroma of honey cake. It had been sent by the stricken one's
family to encourage us innocent souls to pray from the bottom of our
hearts for his recovery. In fact all we did was say "amen" at the end of
the rabbi's prayer but never has cake tasted as delicious as those
easily earned slices.

If this was perhaps not the best way to learn charity another
custom, more straightforward, taught us humility. Every time the
flour ran low in the school's pantry, which happened quite often, we
were sent out to collect bread in streets and courtyards shouting:
"Bread for the Talmud-Torah, bread for the Talmud-Torah." We
would wander through the Jewish neighborhoods in groups of two,
toting a wide open basket between us. Chunks and loaves would
thump in; even the poorest Jew wanting to share in our traditional
upbringing would contribute a small piece with his blessing. There
were other occasions when we took to the streets—two pupils to a
basket. If a baby boy showed signs of retardation and did not walk by
eighteen months or did not babble his first words because of deaf-
ness, he would be carried through the neighborhood so that as many
Jews as possible might pray for his well-being. Usually I was one of
the two robust fellows chosen as basket bearers. "May God Almighty
help this child to walk (or hear)!" we would shout at the top of our
lungs as women holding pots of broth or porridge would stream out
of every doorway. Gently cooing and murmuring blessings, they
would feed the toddler by the spoonful, while others put sweets and
fruit into the basket by his side. After about an hour of this we would
take the bewildered boy back home to his mother who would take

fresh hope on seeing her son all smeared and sticky, smothered in delicacies and good wishes.

Singing psalms at the weddings of the rich was another duty of the Talmud-Torah boys which I certainly preferred to the chanting of the same at funerals. Singing while following the bier to its final resting place was not so bad. What I hated were the silly caps, kind of gondolas, that we were forced to wear on those sad occasions.

On one radiant, warm winter morning, Nathan, Chief Rabbi of Nabeul, ordered us to assemble at the cemetery in our mourning outfits, the aforementioned caps and our blue prayer shawls trimmed with a single white stripe. "Who has died? What has happened?" we asked each other, running to the cemetery as fast as the flapping prayer shawls allowed. But a death was not the reason for this extraordinary meeting.

Rabbi Nathan's Last Call

A terrible drought had struck our region that same winter. Though we were already far into December not a drop of rain had fallen. Parched by thirst the earth had cracked up into a giant puzzle and in our Arab neighbors' fields the shoots of corn were brown and wilted. Cisterns were running dry; a thick, salty liquid brought up from the deepest wells was used to water cows and camels whose ribs protruded like sticks from their sides. With hundreds of sheep and goats having to be slaughtered, meat, lean and dry as the weather, was getting cheaper every day. The price of other foods rocketed to the sky.

A few days earlier the *Qadi* had summoned all Moslems to the mosque, asking them to pray for rain, but still the sun would travel up and down relentlessly, unhampered by the smallest cloud. Desperate, the Qadi was ready to accept help even from the devil. Trying Rabbi Nathan instead, he requested that venerable sage to beseech our God to please open the floodgates of heaven. Chief Rabbi Nathan was in a predicament. A request from the Qadi was an order. To disregard it would surely bring dire consequences upon the rabbi's flock. To try and meddle in the decisions of the Almighty, on the other hand, was a sin that could not go unpunished either. Nevertheless, Rabbi Nathan accepted. Arriving at the cemetery in our blue prayer shawls we could see him from afar, his thin old frame balancing back and forth over the grave of our great Rabbi Jacob Slama.

According to his last wish the bones of this eminent light of the

Talmud were resting under an old thorn-apple tree, his tomb marked only by a mound of fieldstones. One might ask how famous Rabbi Slama came to be buried amid the bones of the Jews of Nabeul? Many years ago the ailing scholar had arrived in Nabeul from the capital, hoping to regain his health in the breezy air of Cape Bon, but instead had died there, far away from his disciples. "At least let us pay our teacher our last respects," they begged the Almighty. The mourners' wish was granted. Winds were dispatched to pick up a cloud and blow it from Tunis to Nabeul, where it floated gently down upon the cemetery to deposit the whole company straight in the middle of the funeral.

Now it was our own rabbi who, fervently praying over the sage's resting place, was pleading with his long-departed colleague, maybe asking him to intercede for another miracle—a magic rain cloud. Here I must add with regret that the Jews of Nabeul, going against the express wish of modest Rabbi Jacob Slama who did not even want a simple tombstone, had built a mausoleum in his honor. This fake tomb, so to speak, had been erected not far from his real grave. It is there I went to pray and as the vault itself was crammed with supplicants I was reciting psalms on the outside, my forehead pressed against the marble wall. Behind the cemetery gate all the Jewish women of Nabeul, my mother among them, stood crying and lamenting, urged on by hundreds of Arabs watching the proceedings from every rooftop in the vicinity.

"Hear us, Lord of the Universe, please, send clouds . . . send rain, rain, rain," they wailed into a sky stubbornly clinging to its immaculate blue. To be nearer to the Almighty, Rabbi Nathan had climbed a hillock and as he stood there swaying all alone, his outstretched arms imploring heaven, a black wall rose on the horizon, growing with frightening speed.

The rabbi's prayer shawl was flaring up in a last awesome yellow light. The hill, the tombstones and the praying Jews had turned to shining lead. Then everything was blotted out by darkness. All at once the clouds let go, lashing down upon us like a waterfall that drowned our shouts of joy and thanks in its thunderous noise. Rain and tears biting in our eyes, soaked to our bones, we had to wade home through mud and puddles where only minutes before the road had been as hard as stone.

"Allah is with the Jews!" Everywhere we passed jubilant Arabs hailed us with compliments, with drumbeat and songs; our neighbors, Mahmood, Kasham and Abdel Kader came with their parents to bless the rainmakers, showering us with presents. Though the rain had eased, a steady drizzle continued to come down throughout that memorable day and night of celebration. Spirits were running high—

until the next morning when our town, shrouded in a sackcloth of rain and mud, awoke to the news of Rabbi Nathan's sudden death.

A great wail sprang form one Jewish home to another, followed by choking stillness. Guilt over the old man's death gnawed at everybody's heart; there was no need for words. We all knew what had happened. It was clear that our Rabbi Nathan had made a deal with the Almighty. Having offered his life in exchange for rain, he had taken upon his frail shoulders the wrath meant for a whole town.

Purim Magic

Early in February, when the north wind turned westerly and birds arrived to build new nests in our walls, but not before the morning Rabbi Parienti asked us to open our Bibles to the first page of Esther, would I be sure that spring had come. It also meant that Purim was around the corner, this merriest of Jewish holidays, the shining crown of an otherwise drab school year. When have I ever leafed as eagerly through pages as those telling the story of our exile in Babylon? Never would the rabbi catch me dozing through the streets and palaces of faraway Shushan.

Thinking back to those lessons I still marvel at that capricious old Purim scroll, masquerading as a Persian town and the ease with which the rigid Hebrew alphabet lent itself to disguise: when I stared hard enough at the characters, the tall *lamed* (ל), always first to change, would grow into a tower, the thickset *mem* (מ) became a palace, the fat *shin* (ש) a harem. All at once a whole line might link up into a wall with gates and turrets, the city wall of Shushan, ancient capital of Persia. Here the king is throning on a *gimel* (ג); one row below, riding on the *tsaddik* (צ) comes Mordehai—or is it Haman?—difficult to make out. Peering at me from behind the iron grille of an *aleph* (ע) Queen Esther modestly hides from view as the three viziers sit huddled in the middle of the longest word, plotting and scheming; then, just before the ringing of the bell a band of belly-dancing concubines pops out of the harem *shin*, spilling all over my Bible.

A thorough teacher, Rabbi Parienti would go through every detail of the scroll which begins with the banquet King Ahasuerus, mighty ruler of Persia, is giving for his ministers. His queen, the haughty Vashti, summoned to join the drinking party, refuses to appear, so infuriating the king by her snub that he decides to repudiate his wife and look around for a new one. With millions of pretty maidens to chose from in his one hundred and twenty-seven provinces his choice falls on no one else but on Esther, the niece of Mordehai, the Jew. Had Esther been less lovely, had the king taken time to check up on her family—who knows, he might have thought twice before taking a Jewess for wife. Instead he rushes headlong into the marriage with Esther, and as the kings of Persia always were the richest in the world, the wedding feast lasts for several weeks.

Amid all that happiness and merrymaking, however, a worm is slowly eating its way through the apple. Haman, great vizier of the king, blames the Jews for every ill befalling Persia. To believe him, dry weather, earthquakes, frost, heat and epidemics were all brought on by our people, and if for once there was no trouble, Haman would promptly invent some, as for instance an imaginary Jewish plot to overthrow the king. Whom else can Ahasuerus trust if not his great vizier? On the other hand still in the dark about the origins of his new wife, the monarch decrees that every Jewish subject in his one hundred twenty-seven provinces, man, woman and child, shall be put to death.

Sitting it out quietly inside the harem, Esther could have weathered the storm quite easily, yet decides to reveal to her husband the truth about herself, risking her life in an attempt to make him change his mind and save her people. Listening to the counsel of her wise uncle Mordehai she dresses in her most beautiful dress to go before the king. So persuasive is she that Ahasuerus does a complete turnabout. Now it's Haman, the scoundrel, and his clan who are condemned to die in place of the Jews! He and his ten sons are still hanging from the gallows as Esther's uncle Mordehai is nominated vizier in his stead, Ahasuerus showering him with honors. Clad in sky-blue and gold, Mordehai is led through Shushan mounted high on the king's horse. Jubilant Jews line the streets, thanking him, God and Queen Esther for their deliverance. The story ends with everybody going home to celebrate and bake sweet Haman's ears for their first Purim feast.

I know the Bible. I heard about the indignities our people suffered in exile and saw with my own eyes what came to pass in Hitler's time. If once or twice in a few thousand years the Jews got lucky, it calls for a big celebration.

Exactly one week before Purim, his arms overflowing with rolls of colored paper and a box of scissors, Rabbi Parienti would push open the door to our classroom with one elbow.

"Guess what the *comité* has sent for you rascals? Must have too much money . . . seems to me they have lost their mind. . . ." Playfully, our ordinarily caustic teacher held up the shiny sheets of paper, bright yellow, grass-green, blue, purple and scarlet, destined to be cut out into the main characters of our Persian adventure. Older boys taught us the trick: fold, cut, unfold, and a paper miracle took place. Haman, the scoundrel, and his ten beturbaned sons stood up before me, each with one mean eye in the middle of his head, their little arms stretched heavenward to implore mercy.

Time and again I exercised my skill on the members of that doomed family, cutting them out of newspaper until, the figures turning out neat and shapely, I would at last go over to use colored paper. Lemon yellow as a rule, perhaps because that color, reminding me of bile, seemed the most suitable for anti-Semites. Next I would make a prison for the company—a big, airy net cut out of purple. Extented to its full length by the weight a stone, the net's wide open mouth was now ready to receive my prisoners. Suspended from the wall behind my seat, ten one-eyed yellow faces would glare at me through paper bars for the rest of the week. Every time we read a passage showing Haman and his family in a particularly shameful light I would turn around and whisper:

"Only wait, you Jew-haters, wait and see what happens on Wednesday!"

When Wednesday morning finally came around, every little boy in class arrived at school with the biggest, clubbiest stick that he could carry. Resplendent in the gold-buttoned, sky-blue waistcoat reserved for great occasions, Rabbi Haim Parienti was already waiting for us in the schoolyard. Was I imagining things or could I actually detect a grin in the thicket of his beard? Pulling a watch out of his breast pocket he let it dangle awhile from its silver chain before a wave of his cane set events in motions. At the signal we ran to bring out our paper cages, piling them into one neat, colorful heap on the pavement.

"Fallu, little good-for-nothing, do for once something worthwhile . . . fetch us kerosene and matches!" Proud to be singled out, I darted to the kitchen, then watched the rabbi dribble kerosene over the prisoners before striking a match. "Burn Haman, burn Haman!" we shrieked into the crackle of the flames and stamping our feet with all our might we each advanced in turn to beat the burning paper with our clubs.

For a whole year I had been waiting for this moment. Was it only hatred for the old vizier that made me burn his entire family with so much holy rage? Wasn't it also revenge for having been shut up in the rabbi's class for so long that made me kick, club and stamp until the last spark had turned to ashes? Whatever the motive, the burning of Haman, lively start of two days of festivities, always gave me deep satisfaction.

Back home from school I would find my mother all flushed, busily dropping threads and ribbons of batter into a pot full of boiling olive oil. Wiping her face she fished out one of the crisp honey twists. Cooling it off with little blows she pushed it into my hand together with my share of Purim money: "There you are, my dear. . . . Spend it in good health and wisely!" It was the one occasion of the year when I received some spending money and if it was to last me through the day, I had to stretch my sous carefully. Once more I tried on the paper mask I had made for myself. Intended to be frightening, it had turned out rather funny, but looked great anyhow. Now I ran to buy the other trimmings indispensable to a happy Purim: A wooden rattle, a whistle, cartridges and, if there was money left over, also a toy pistol. I was ready.

The stone bench skirting three walls of our synagogue was already glittering with little Persians, Mordehais and Ahasueruses as I took my place to the left of my father. Dressed in white from head to toe and beaming under his best tasseled tarboosh, he also had a son to show off, one more boy trying to look Persian.

One furtive glance at the stunning masks of my comrades, then I had to turn my attention to Rabbi Ghez reading the Purim scroll, hanging onto his words as if my life depended on the Hebrew pouring from his lips.

At every mention of Haman's cursed name it was my duty to rattle, stamp and whistle, and with all the boys trying to outdo each other as to who could make more noise, the uproar was shaking our little synagogue to its foundations.

"Parshandatha, Dalphon, Aspatha, Poratha, Adalia, Aridatha, Parmashta, Arizai, Aridai and Vaiezatha . . ." As the rabbi summed up the ten names of the Persian miscreant's miserable offspring, we went so wild that it took minutes before he could resume his reading.

The next morning was dedicated to endless rounds of cake swapping. Knocking at the doors of my uncounted aunts, I had to present each and every one with a variety of my mother's freshly baked cookies, then have my plate returned to me full of their own confections. On top of such a unique opportunity to gorge myself on sweets, coins were dropping in between cakes. Even my aunt Mazal, too poor to bake anything at all, had saved a few sous for me. My cousins had been just as busy trading cookie platters. Meeting at noon behind Kikki Tibi's grocery we turned out our pockets inside out to count our combined fortunes: two francs and twelve sous, too little to pay for a Purim ride.

"Five francs? Yah, Ahmed, is your heart from stone?" we tried to bargain with one of the Arab horse-cart owners who, knowing our customs, were standing by to drive us up and down the main streets. "How can you ask for five francs when all we have is one ninety-eight? Where can we take five francs . . . cut them out of our back-sides? Steal from our parents? The sin will be on your head!"

"Allah is my witness." Ahmed raised his arms and rolled his eyes. "My heart is soft as camel butter, melting at the sight of a dead fly . . . " he protested as he crushed with one slap a handful crawling over the ribs of his scrawny mare. "It's that damned bitch here who's pigheaded, doesn't want to budge without a bellyful of oats. . . . What do you say, Jameela," he patted her nose, "will three francs do for these Jewish gentlemen?" At long last we agreed on two fifty and spurred on by Ahmed's cracking whip, as well as our rattling and whistling, Jameela took off in a gallop. Hafzeah's herb shop flew past in a clatter, the prison, the blue mosque and the Hôtel de France. I was racing through heaven, prancing with my mask and shooting off my pistol every time we passed a cartload of cousins from some rival clan. Only after the last cap had exploded, Ahmed's whip was hang-ing limp and Jameela's spring reduced to a mere traipse did we finally jump off, shaken through and through but happy.

It was time to join the by now torn and crumpled masks pushing through the arched doorway into Sidi (Sir) David Tarbulsi's court-yard. All my comrades from Talmud-Torah school were invited. Shuffling worn-out sandals over the red and white tiles of our bene-factor's garden path, we shoved each other to where Sidi David, framed by the ripening fruit of his lemon tree, was welcoming his guests. There he stood in person, handing out Purim presents: tiny wooden carts, lacquered horses and jumping jacks from a huge pile of marvels. It was Thursday, my lucky day; Sidi David recognized me in spite of my disguise.

"Isn't that Hamus's boy?" he said, pulling at my mask as I tried hastily to wipe my nose on my shoulder. And with a smile as broad as his thin face permitted, he wound my sticky fingers around the handle of a tin trumpet. It glistened like pure gold, with a voice shriller than the trumpets of Judgment Day. What a prize! Spending every spare minute at the seashore, I must have owed this good fortune to my frequent encounters there with Sidi David out on his daily afternoon stroll. He and his cousin Baruch had become so used to my presence on or around the jetty that the pair would take bets on my whereabouts: a snuffbox of tobacco for Sidi David if he could find me at the beach. . . .

"I won, I won—there he sits, over on the green boulder. . . . How do the fish bite today, Fallu?" David would wave his spindly arms at me and leap up in triumph; then, readjusting his legs to Baruch's weighty step, he would go back to help his cousin take apart the assets of some debtor. For "David and Baruch Tarbulsi, Traders and Wholesalers" did not come down to the beach to discuss fishing, a daughter's upcoming wedding or even their well-oiled import business; they could do this much more comfortably over a cup of coffee at Café Sportez. Here, where only I, the fish or an occasional sea gull could snatch tatters of their conversation, they came to debate the commerce of their left hand—moneylending. In Nabeul a Jew's left hand, used to carry out the baser but unavoidable chores of everyday life like handling toilet paper, was considered tainted, unworthy to point out the words of the Torah. In the case of the cousins this prohibition seemed doubly justified as their left hand, giving out loans to Arab farmers at outrageous rates of interest, was dirtier than anybody else's. Whatever hand dabbles in usury, whether its victim be Moslem or Jew, these practices are strictly forbidden by the Torah, and the cousins knew it. What is more natural than making up for the shortcomings of one side with good deeds and plenty of charity by the other? Blessed by every needy old Jew, every widow and orphan in our town, Sidi David's bony wrist and Baruch's cushioned paw had been kissed more often than the mezuzah on their doorpost; especially so Sidi Baruch's, through whose chubby fingers ran the funds of the comité.

The office of this all-important institution, a dusty cubicle on the ground floor of his house, lay mostly deserted. Sidi Baruch Tarbulsi preferred to discharge his duties in the street. Mornings he would carry out his honorary functions drowsing in the shade of his own walls, but around noon the sun caught up with him. Collecting his backgammon board and briefcase, he would then pull the presidential cane chair beyond the date palm swaying in the middle of the square and seek shelter behind the barrels of Kikki Tibi's grocery. His paunch secured between the supports of the armchair, both thumbs stuck in the breast pockets of his French vest, Sidi Baruch, now wide awake, would scan Place Sportez through smoked glasses. Seated right in the heart of Jewish life, the comité was well informed of the goings-on. Its president would know who had bought what at the grocery, who charged and who paid cash, who played cards on the floor of Mookni's coffeehouse and who could afford a table at Café Sportez, the swankest Jewish establishment in town. Baruch Tarbulsi knew who had a steady job, who was out of one, who was too old or sick to work, who did not want to work and who was unable to make a living because he was a born schlemiel.

The black briefcase propped up against his chair was bulging with papers listing every needy Jew in Nabeul, the circumstances of every widow down to her last child, their ages and even the names of those who had died. All the funds contributed by the community were at Sidi Baruch's disposal. Some he allotted for repair work at the synagogues, some went into the upkeep of the Talmud-Torah school, the steam bath, matzoh baking and the burial society; the rest, stretched by substantial amounts from the president's private income, was given to the poor. If one forgot Baruch Tarbulsi's left hand safely tucked away inside his trouser pocket, one had to admit that his right with the golden signet ring on its plump little finger was generous and just.

"Sidi Baruch, may you live to a hundred and twenty in health, riches and happiness and may your sons reach to the stars, your daughters bear their husbands sages of the Torah. . . . If only you could see how the bones cut through my children's skin and how they look at others eating. . . ." Ordering the woman home, Sidi Baruch would change his dark spectacles for reading glasses, make a note in his lists—before an hour had passed a basket full of food was waiting on the petitioner's doorstep. Meanwhile the president had started the daily game of backagammon which helped him get through his long office hours. Basha or Filli were the partners he liked best because they knew the most horrible curses, but any other of our community's numerous simpletons would also do. Teased at every move of the game, they would elate Sidi Baruch and bystanders by going into fits, yet in the end he always let them win, compensating the poor fools with snuff or cigarettes for their trouble.

After school, when my belly felt as empty as my pockets and I was ravenous for a handful of peanuts or pumpkin seeds, I could make two or three sous working for Sidi Baruch. Rambling down Market Street in the direction of Place Sportez, duly averting my face as I passed by the church, I could see from afar that my services would be welcome. Upset at losing at backgammon, Michael, the madman, had just swallowed the second of the two dice and only his paunch prevented Sidi Baruch from keeling over with laughter. Gasping and gurgling with delight, he was slapping what little of his thighs stuck out of his rotundity. He seemed in urgent need of cooling. Without even waiting for a wink, I ran off to fetch the palm leaf with the peacock handle from his office and went to work on him. Fanned left, fanned right, the head of the comité was slowly regaining his countenance. A last tear of glee drying on his cheeks, a last oily drop of sweat dripping from his nose, his face would settle back on its three chins to confront old Gamara, a frequent visitor. One look into Gamara's eyes was enough to wipe the smile off anybody's lips, but what could you expect? A childless widow, her main source of income was lamenting the dead, thankless underpaid work for an expert of her mettle. How often had I watched her from a respectful distance as she was leading the circle of wailing women squatting in the courtyard of a stricken house, beating her legs and chest, her face bloodied from scratching. No matter whether the corpse under the red velvet cover of the burial society had belonged to a just man or a rascal, Gamara could convince even the Almighty that he had been a saint.

"Why did you have to take him from the bosom of his loved ones?" the old woman would sob and scream. "He never hurt a fly, O Lord! All his money went to the poor and to help his aged parents. . . . Have mercy on them. Look how crushed they are! Console his widow, left alone in the flower of her years, her children weeping. . . ."

Gamara had come with a request. She needed a new skirt. An intriguing arrangement of tears and motley patches, her old one was unworthy of the approaching Passover, she claimed. Who knew better than Sidi Baruch, financier of the burial society, that lately there had been few deaths to lament in our community. Asking for his briefcase, he gave me some respite from fanning as he wrote out a receipt in his round and orderly French hand. Then Gamara, proving that she was as good at bubbling forth blessings as howling wails of woe, was handed a five-franc note which she signed for with her inked thumb.

After all that exertion, Sidi Baruch felt ready for a nap. Sinking back into the breezy sphere of the palm leaf, he let the visor of his cap glide over the dark glasses, his lips, puckered into a rosy ball, parted into a snore, and the upturned toothbrush mustache on top stopped quivering. This was the moment of relief I had been waiting for. My arms were hurting, but no sooner did I try to let them hang down for a while than a snarl would steal among the snores, and I had to go on fanning for another half hour to earn my pumpkin seeds.

As I grew older and strong enough to carry three big chickens at a time, Sidi Baruch introduced me to a more important job than fanning. Teaching me how to blow a peephole through the feathers of a prospective Sabbath bird, he showed me the way to inspect its belly, making sure it was plump and clean of lice.

"Remember, Fallu," he would warn me before any such errand, "looking at a beautiful fat chicken, people might become envious. . . . You never know where the evil eye is hidden. . . . So don't let anyone peek into your basket and tell the busybodies you are carrying old shoes."

In matters such as these I was a fast learner. I now made five sous with one run on top of which Sidi Baruch's wife would invite me for a bite every time the terrified hens emerging from my basket were fat enough for her husband's liking. Had my father got wind that his son like a famished guttersnipe was accepting food from strangers, he would have beaten me black and blue. Smelling fish soup from the bottom of the staircase I ran up taking two steps at a time when the mistress of the house called my name from the balcony. I never could refuse a snack. The soup was appetizing enough with its piece of fishhead swimming in the middle of the bowl; vaguely aware that it would not do to enjoy it crouching on the floor and not used to sitting at a table, I ate it standing up. With the next dish I really got into trouble; the woman gave me macaroni and a fork, the longest, slickest macaroni ever, smothered in a tomato sauce that smelled like the Garden of Eden. How do you catch yard-long, eely macaroni with a fork when you have never held a fork before, having to stand upright in the bargain? It was a very frustrating experience and I thanked God when the kind soul at last turned to polish her silver spoons. Now I would use my fist: one, two, three determined grabs followed by wild chewing as the last of the noodles slid down my throat.

"For one Jew taken by the Hand of the Almighty," my patron would often sigh, "nine are killed by the evil eye." But today I tend to think that it was fat chicken rather than some devilish spell that brought Sidi Baruch to an early grave. With each new spring his armchair became tighter, his afternoon strolls grew shorter; all the blessings showered on him by the poor of Nabeul were not enough to keep him in our midst. The generous president of the comité died before his time, though not before having been robbed of most of his possessions by the German invaders and seen the rest swallowed by Bourguiba's revolution. But that story comes much later.

Passover Is Coming!

Passover preparations got under way the very moment Purim flickered out. As only four weeks separate Passover from Purim there was much to be done if we wanted to celebrate our feast of freedom properly and even children had to pitch in. School was closed so that our classrooms could be taken over by a crowd of matzoh bakers, men working in shifts day and night, preparing the mountains of matzohs needed to feed the Jews of Nabeul for a week. Small portions of unleavened dough were flattened out with sticks; patterns were punched through the thin discs with the help of ten fingers, miraculously transforming lifeless lumps of dough into large flowers and crisp wagon wheels. The oven did the rest. Boys employed alongside the men would be running all over the place carrying flour and firewood, while women and grown-up girls, unclean for reasons that are obvious, had to stay away. As those hand-fashioned matzohs were naturally expensive, our comité would distribute them to the needy free of charge; my father, however, always made a point of paying for our rations. It was not the price of the matzohs, though, that was his greatest worry. The house had to be whitewashed inside and out; new shoes and clothes bought for the entire family; plenty of eggs and vegetables for the traditional dishes. What is more, without the slaughter of a sheep Passover was unthinkable.

For months my father had saved every franc he could possibly spare, hiding his hoard in a spot whose secret was unknown even to my mother. He had become doubly cautious because of the misfortune which had befallen us the year before. Then, as now, our door had been pushed open by a big ladder followed by the Arab house painter. Then also, as now, he had shouted a cheerful "Aslama!" and proceeded to daub everything in view with sky-blue lime, the first step on the arduous road to a clean, kosher Passover. Then, just as now, my father had wanted to pay the painter with some bills taken from his hard-earned savings, the only difference being that last year he could not find them. The treasure had been hidden away in the half-broken chest which was our only piece of furniture, my grandfather's wedding present to my parents. Safely knotted into an old handkerchief with yellow dots resembling gold coins, it had wintered in a corner of the upper drawer. After some pushing and shoving, the drawer opened with a shriek that set my teeth on edge. In place of the handkerchief my father's hand came up with a pair of socks in need of mending.

"Where is the money, Meesha?" Slow and deep, the question seemed to come out of a hole in the ground. My mother's eyes grew black and round the way they always would at an approaching tempest.

"May the Almighty strike me dead if I ever touched it; I did not even look at it," she said in a choked voice. My father had yanked all three drawers out of the rickety skeleton. Crumpled books, chipped wooden spoons, candle stumps and broken buttons tumbled to the floor. Trying not to attract his attention I had stood stock-still, riveting my eyes on some bits of paper that had settled on my feet, my father's accounts written in strange Aramaic scribble.

"My God, why did I ever marry her?" he was now groaning. "Why did You let her round calf's eyes trick me into it? What good are they to me if she can't see? Last week she lets the cat steal half a pound of tripe from under her nose. Now she cannot see thieves on two legs either. Don't just stand there, staring like a cow! Move, woman, better find that handkerchief!" My poor mother did not say a word; tear after tear silently running down her cheeks were caught up in the chaste neckline of her blouse. Convinced that somehow she must be guilty and had mislaid the handkerchief unknowingly, she had started to turn every garment inside out, had opened the big mattress, unfolded diapers and blankets, but there was no trace of the dotted handkerchief.

Slowly though not calmly my father had realized that his loss was final.

"So that's it. For her I let the sun scorch the flesh off my bones. For her I let myself roast on the roads. . . . I have more blisters on my soles than she has bubbles in her washtub. I am breaking my back to feed her and her children! Has she ever given me anything in return but bad luck? How many of her sons are still alive?" For an answer big sobs came out with a flurry of flour. In her desperation my mother was poking through our bags with provisions, emptying the salted fish over the rush mat and searching my baby sister's crib.

"Here." My father had thrown her clothes at her. "Get out of my sight! Take your children and go back to that black star where you came from!" By now completely soaked with tears and still without a word, my mother had tied her few belongings into her own kerchief—the striped one which is the only keepsake she has left me. The bundle slung over one arm, she gathered up my sister with the other and in a valiant attempt to hide her shame before the neighbors, enfolded both in her big, white wrapper. I trudged out behind her.

"Don't ever come back here. Let your brothers feed you from now on!" my father had thundered as she turned for a last look from the threshold.

As she had always done on similar occasions, my mother's mother, bedridden and half paralyzed, would welcome us warmly with her one good arm. Also as usual, after a week or so of part exile, part vacation in my grandmother's house, my mother's brothers would negotiate our return with my father, asking for his forgiveness. Once more my mother hid the baby inside the folds of her shawls as we trotted home.

Here I must add that among Jews, temporary banishment was the most common punishment for undutiful wives. An erring Moslem woman was simply shut up in a room without food or water. An ordinary beating, a husband's bout of infidelity, would be accepted without much of a fuss. Only if he did not provide for his wife and children was the matter considered serious enough to bother the rabbi. If some woman, on the other hand, infringed religious law, having served her husband meat and cheese at the same meal for instance, then it was the rabbi's task to punish her.

Men could ask for a divorce for two reasons: if a wife had borne no children after ten years of marriage or if two reliable witnesses had found her in a flagrant act of infidelity. The latter, thank God, was an extremely rare occurrence in Nabeul, but it happened. If it did, the cheated husband would assemble his witnesses and go before the Chief Rabbi. Not to offend the saintly ear though, he would take off one of his shoes and turn it upside down to intimate the full gravity of the matter. If no fault could be found with the evidence, the man got a divorce and custody of the children. The woman was sent off to another town.

It is hard to believe how things have changed. Take my wife, Fortuna, for example. Thirty years ago in Nabeul, had I told her that the moon was falling and asked her to catch it for me in one piece, she would have murmured:

"As you say, my husband," and waited all night in the courtyard with an open basket. You should hear her now—talking back from morning till night.

"Why do you paint nothing but nonsense? Why don't you ask more money for your pictures? Why can only our neighbors have wall clocks?" (In the end I got her the ugly contraption.) I should not complain though. I know of many doves that fluttered shyly all the way from Nabeul, only to start throwing plates at their husband's head in Safed.

My mother, however, was of the old stock, thankful to be taken back in by my father, who, resigning himself to a meager Passover, had accepted that thieves also are the Will of God. My mother had done wonders with the eggs and vegetables her brothers could spare, while on my father's side it was Uncle Goliath who charged into our room like a wounded bull, shouting that slow death from starvation was much too good for careless squanderers like us, after which he disbursed twenty-five francs for a lamb and matzohs.

Here now was our family, assembled in the same room one year later, all set to strike that last Passover from the record. Once again the Arab house painter splashed away at the ceiling, painting it so blue that the sky behind the lattices looked wan and pale. I was in a cheerful mood as always when I sniff fresh lime. My mother was out on the terrace, making coffee for Aunt Kooka. My father, huddled in a corner, sat worrying over his new hoard as if counting and recounting the bills would add to them. I remember my little sister standing beside me, blissfully slapping blue lime on her curls with the thin palm leaf strips of an abandoned paintbrush, when suddenly shreds of paper, dirt and straw rained down upon us as the painter cleaned out a rat's nest holed in between the ceiling and a wooden beam.

"Thump," the rag had landed at my feet. Of such short build that her eyes are forever close to the ground, my aunt Kooka had already pounced on the bargain.

"What do you know, yellow polka dots. My sister must be swimming in money," she said pointedly, "throwing a perfectly good rag into the trash. Watch how I'll wash it into a towel," and picking up the mess Aunt Kooka started to shake out the dust. Her mouth fell open. "Meesha, a miracle, a miracle!" she cried as coins rolled in every direction and paper money fluttered before her nose. Over two hundred francs! My father's lost treasure in its entirety was falling out of the folds. Fondling the dotted handkerchief, now several shades darker and dirtier than it had been a year ago, my mother wept for joy.

"Thank You, thank You, dear God, for giving my poor husband's sweat money back to us," she murmured over and over as she pressed the crumpled bills to her heart, kissing them instead of my father. I never saw my parents hug or kiss in front of me, nor any other couple in Nabeul for that matter. A great deal of kissing was going on, but it was strictly limited to either one's own sex or grown-ups embracing small children.

That Passover we felt as rich people do the whole year round. Even my father, possibly bothered by the memory of my mother's unjust banishment, loosened his ordinarily tight fist and took us on a shopping spree. I became the only boy to tramp Bab Salah Street on real leather soles, while my father bought the violet-and-gold-striped skirt my mother was to wear for many years to come. After that he got hold of the fattest sheep he could find in the market. The thieving rat was never seen again. Maybe it went treasure hunting at a neighbor's or it may have fallen prey to the cat or the house snake. Its nest, in any event, remained bare of bedding and uninhabited from then on.

Whatever became of the rat, once our room had received its new coat of blue lime, Passover cleaning could begin in earnest. The short weeks still separating us from the Seder night were spent scouring, scraping and washing to make sure not the tiniest bread crumb, a speck of flour or anything else likely to ferment had been overlooked in our household. It is by refraining from contact with bread or other leavened food and drink that we try to relive the hardships our fathers suffered on their passage from slavery to freedom, from Egypt to the other side of the Red Sea over three thousand years ago. Rightly fearing that the Pharaoh would have second thoughts and pursue the builders of his towns into the desert, our people left in great haste. They had not even waited for their dough to rise, taking wafer-thin bread called matzoh with them on their flight. I have never understood why eating matzohs is considered a hardship. Those we crunched every year for eight days in honor of the Exodus were so delicious that our Moslem neighbors liked them better than any other of our holiday specialties, gratefully accepting every morsel we could spare.

For the moment, though, much remained to be done before we could recline at the Seder table eating matzohs. Anything movable in the house was taken apart for a thorough cleaning. Doors and shutters were taken off their hinges; all clothes, curtains and blankets were washed. My mother and her neighbors spent their days in the courtyard amid the soapy steam of linens boiling in copper vats, amicably chattering over the noise of water buckets rattling up and down the cistern. Patient and unruffled throughout the year, my mother became frantic during Passover cleaning.

"Fallu, fan the fire. . . . Fallu, fetch more green soap. . . . Don't run away now!" She would not give me a moment's peace. Then, early one morning, my father would harness his donkey to a rented cart, loading it with all our sheepskins and the heavy mattress. My mother added pails, brushes, soap and a basketful of food for the day, sat my little sister on top of everything and took us down to the shore. There I would help her unload everything on some mossy boulder, pull out the wool from the big mattress and drown it in the salty sea together with the bedbugs. While I was spreading out the washed wool to dry on the warm rocks, the beach was coming alive. The whole length of the shoreline was dotted with women and children rinsing wool, hides, doors and shutters. Mothers and daughters, bent side by side over the dripping sheepskins, carefully combed them out curl by curl so that no bread crumb could possibly get by, as the boys, told to watch the family belongings, would instead play the kind of games that build up an appetite. When the sea was aglitter, dancing with sparks and patches of white sun, it was decided that it must be noon and food and drink parceled out. From that moment on, the cleaning party turned into a lively picnic. Stories were told and the singing ended only after sundown when rows of donkey carts, piled high with clean wool and sleepy children, would slowly stagger homeward in the soft evening air.

The next morning was slaughter day at my grandfather's house. Grazing on whatever there is to graze upon in a bare yard, our beautiful fat sheep had been there for some time in company of three, four others belonging to my uncles. It was a dark little yard, shadowed on all sides by a wall taller than the house itself, a thick, crumbly white wall full of holes. Goat cheese, I called it.

The old family-fortress, wall and house, had been built by my grandfather's grandfather—the one they said had come from Italy. Only very old Jews would haltingly speak of those times—fearful times, when the Turks had been the masters of Nabeul. The strongest house had not been strong enough to protect our people from robbery, rape and murder then, they would murmur, pointing to a brown spot and rust-eaten iron ring beside the entrance to Rahamim's house. There the one knife the Turks had allowed for the use of Bab Salah Street's inhabitants had been chained to the wall, they said. The walls of my grandfather's house, walls wider than the space in between were the stony inheritance that had come down to us from our distant Italian ancestor. He must have brought some wealth from the other side of the sea to build this maze of narrow passages, uneven steps, and doorways with rooms so low a man must stoop to avoid hitting the ceiling. The fortunes of our family had long since dwindled and my grandparents, seeing their children stare at the naked walls with hunger in their eyes, had often wished the stones would turn to bread.

I loved the old house. Having known no true hunger in my childhood I liked the walls just as they were, full of holes and crevices. It was there my grandfather taught me to catch my first bird and how to recognize its eggs. There that I learned which snakes were harmless and which were poisonous and had to be treated with respect. Under the grapevine I would tame my pet mice; over by the well play yo-yo with big brown spiders dangling from their threads. Overgrown with moss, the well shaft was teeming with pretty, black, redheaded worms; its depths were alive with green frogs and, sometimes when I was in luck, a pair of golden eyes would stare at me from the bottom of the pail my grandmother was bringing up with water. Once in a while during a night at the old house I would wake up to deep croaks and low humming, while light from an oil lamp filtered through my closed eyelids. Opening them with effort, I would look up at an immense, shaggy shadow tottering all over the vaulted ceiling—my grandfather's bearded profile bending and straightening, as he read the Bible to the song of the frogs.

It was bright morning and in one more day it would be Passover eve. Rabbi Shushan, the slaughterer, was standing in my grandfather's yard, sharpening his knife. He did so for a long time, drawing the blade back and forth, back and forth over his stone until the blade was sharp enough to kill a sheep with one single, swift stroke through the throat. There are things of which an animal has more knowledge than man. The sheep were getting nervous, bleating frightfully. I had never quite forgiven Rabbi Shushan for what he had done to my rooster years ago, although I had with time accepted that his work was sacred and important, the more so since without his intervention I would not be able to eat meat. I had, however, learned my lesson, keeping a distance from those sheep, chickens and pigeons destined for slaughter, afraid that otherwise we might become too friendly. Rabbi Shushan was ready. My grandmother, praying for a happy Passover, was kissing the mezuzah as he gave the blade a last test on his fingernail. One slit—the blood gushed out and everybody tensed, breathlessly looking at the rabbi as he pulled the bowels out of the carcass. One blemish on the stomach, a blue spot on the liver, a tear in the intestine and our beautiful sheep would be declared unclean, barely good enough to be sold to a Moslem at half price. Only after Rabbi Shushan had blown up the lungs through the windpipe and had found them whole would he at last smack his bloody hand on the sheep's hind legs—his way of saying that the meat was fit for Passover.

With broad smiles, men's blessings, women's ululations, one sheep after the other passed the test. Proud that I could stand the sight of blood without crying, I plunged my hand into the red stream, then, held up by my grandfather, planted it over the gate, beside his own broad, furrowed print. Everybody was singing and joking, the men busily stripping skins, the women cutting meat and scraping the bowels that would be made into spicy sausages and other stuffed delicacies. My mother drove a red-hot nail into the severed head of our sheep, right in between the horns. Well-cooked with the help of this simple expedient, the animal's brains were a treat reserved for the family's firstborn, which is to say myself; they were supposed to make me clever. I have yet to meet a quick-witted sheep, but I certainly enjoyed the taste of this delicacy. Apart from teeth and hooves, not a morsel of the animal was thrown away. The meat, of course, was cooked or roasted, including the skin covering the head. The bones went into soups and stews. And if the sheep had been a ram, its horns were destined to become a shofar, to sound in the new year in the fall. The hide, smeared with salt and lime, was nailed to the door where it was left to dry skin side up until after the holiday when, well rinsed in the sea, it would make me a soft and springy new bed.

Around noon on that busy day before the eve of Passover my mother and I went back to our own house where Nisria, the mother of my three little Moslem friends, was already waiting to buy our *hametz*.

"God bless you, Nisria, what would we do without you?" My mother kissed our neighbor on both cheeks, then helped her carry over to her cave whatever was still left of our winter provisions: dried couscous, beans, flour—in short any food forbidden to us on Passover. Nisria was well versed in the game; making believe this was a true transaction, she paid us two sous for the whole bargain and left. But my mother did not have to worry: once the holiday was over Nisria would return everything untouched. Not a bean, a lentil or grain of couscous would be missing. On the contrary, Nisria would always add freshly baked bread for the whole family, a sudden taste of heaven when you have gone without it for a week. How avidly we always fell upon her bread and how thankful she was for our matzohs.

For the rest of the day and far into the night my mother was completely absorbed in her cooking. She and her four neighbors squatting on low stools behind the charcoal burning in their tripods were cutting vegetables, chopping meat, swapping recipes and spices to the sound of bubbling stews and brass pestles, lustily pounding sesame seeds and cinnamon. Munching lettuce leaves and carrot chunks, I flitted about among the pots, pestles and women, fanning fires to burn brighter and faces to cool off.

"Fallu, dear, a drink of water . . ." or "Fallu, pass me the spoon over there . . ." Unable to hoist herself off her stool, fat Lajla came up with one request after another. Her face, which looked ready to blow up any minute, was glowing hotter than the coals. Her formidable bosom was heaving and falling at the same pace as the lid of her equally formidable cooking pot, the biggest of them all. Full to the brim with giant pads of stuffed intestine, a thick sauce loaded with artichoke hearts, garlic and tomatoes was noisily sputtering over the sides. The only one among our neighbors to use a cow's bowels instead of the traditional, daintier sheep's intestines, fat Lajla's *otsbana* resembled overstuffed cushions rather than human nourishment. Always a little envious of her children, I could not for the life of me understand why they were so skinny, especially her daughter whom I loathed. Already at the age of four she was making eyes at me, but I steadfastly ignored her then, and for many years to come when she was not so skinny anymore. Even so, she loved to see me cringe in embarrassment at her advances. Although nobody could possibly see me blush in the heat of all that cooking, I ran off anyway, to help my mother find hiding places for the bread, I said. Custom requires that we conceal ten small pieces of bread in our home on the night before Passover.

Getting up in the morning our first thought was again for the bread. Carefully counting, we collected the ten pieces from under the

bed, the drawer, and from behind the water jug to burn them in the
yard. Our neighbors were doing likewise and after we had all
checked and rechecked the premises, convincing ourselves nothing
leavened had been overlooked, we broke into loud congratulations.

"Happy holiday, happy holiday—next year in Jerusalem!" The
women embraced as the sahruta, their high-pitched, warbling howl
of joy echoed from one yard to the other. Surprising us with some
last-minute shopping and the astonishing announcement, coming
from him, that "You can't eat money, can you? Passover comes but
once a year . . ." my father put a big bag of almonds in my mother's
hands. Then shops bolted their doors though it was still early in the
day, and while the Jews got into their new clothes Bab Salah Street lay
empty in the sun, lazily stretching out in her own festive dress of
freshly painted lime. Nothing more for me to do than wait, I thought,
as I sat in the shelter of three big red hands that had barely had the
time to dry, one just on top of me over the gate and one on each side
of the doorpost. Not even Mahmood, Kasham and Abdel Kader, my
three Arab friends, were out in the street; nobody to play with but the
mewing cats. Driven half crazy by the vapors of stewing lamb floating
from every window, the cats came at me with trembling, upturned
tails, furiously rubbing their heads against my legs.

"Patience, patience," I told them, waiting more ardently for the
first stars to show up and Passover to begin than I have ever yearned
for the arrival of the anointed one on his white donkey. Instead of
stars, prophets or messiahs, it was my cousin Gaga who appeared on
the horizon. As he hurried toward me on his short bowlegs, his broad
body swung from side to side on its stunted foundation. His naked
heels riding atop a pair of old black shoes made him look as if he were
shuffling along in slippers. He was coming from the direction of the
railway station lugging two big baskets.

"Goo, goo, goo!" he crowed excitedly as he caught sight of me.
Smiling back at the warm berry eyes so eagerly striving to unite at the
root of his nose, I noted with satisfaction that Cousin Gaga was unchanged. Tucked-up crumpled trousers, sleeves stopping short below, shirttails flapping in the breeze—there was still the same old
orphan look about him, the same French beret dangling precariously
over one useless ear. Deaf and dumb, my father's cousin was indeed
an orphan, fortyish, and the friendliest, most outgoing soul I have
ever met. Once a year the broom that helped Gaga sweep a living
together in the shops of Tunis would be put to rest as its owner took
the train to spend Passover with his family.

"Goo, gee, gack . . ." Overjoyed to see me he planted kisses
where they fell, on my nose, my chin, my shoulder, while I was
wriggling to get a look at the treats sticking out of the baskets. Faded

skullcaps, ill-matched socks, cheap perfume, underwear that had sprung a run and toys missing either a wheel, a tail or a few fingers—from one Passover to the next Cousin Gaga would collect a vast array of slightly damaged knicknacks from the shopkeepers, his employers; one present for every member of our clan.

Our cousin's week-long kissing spree had only just begun: first the mezuzah was, of course, embraced with great effusion, then it was my father's turn, wincing at the explosion of wet busses on his ear. My little sister was drowned in kisses, and my mother had a leftover smack blown at her from a respectful distance.

X

The Seder

By now three stars had finally appeared and we could cross over to our synagogue to usher in the Passover.

For a while even Cousin Gaga fell silent. The air was light and heady, tasting of Sabbath wine with soda water, the sky so limpid that had it not been for those few bluish puffs of clouds, I could for once have seen the Gates of Heaven opening on Seder night. After Gaga had gargled through the prayers with us and kissed everyone and everything in the congregation—the rabbi's wrist, the books, the embroidered curtain on the Torah shrine—we went at last to celebrate the Seder at my grandfather's house. We walked together, my parents carrying a basket full with pots and plates between them, I balancing a mountain of matzohs on my head, and Gaga in the rear babbling to my little sister. When we arrived, the family was already assembled. So as not to spoil the purity of the occasion, we all took off our shoes before joining the company in our stocking feet.

At least fifty people were squeezed into a long and narrow room, the biggest built by the Italian ancestor who, apparently, had not anticipated that many descendants: my grandparents, their four sons and two daughters with husbands and wives, all of whom had been blessed with numerous offspring. Women and girls were nestling close together on the rush mat at the far end of the room, men and boys reclining each on his sheepskin around a low table improvised from empty vegetable crates. Covered by sheets washed into blinding whiteness in expectation of Elijah (the white-clad Prophet, forerunner of the Messiah, was the guest of honor hoped for at every Seder), it seemed every bit a real table. Laid out with my grandmother's treasures—a pair of bronze candle-sticks and a high-stemmed crystal glass, stacked with matzohs and laden with glazed earthenware bottles full of homemade wine—it looked festive indeed, but where was I to put my cup and plate? All available space was so cluttered with dishes, flowers, myrtle branches and Haggadahs that I could barely find a spot for our pretty yellow Passover pottery.

Flanked by Uncle Goliath and Uncle Said, his two eldest sons, my grandfather was reclining at the head of the table, ready for the big opening. Leaning to his left, his arm propped up on a cushion and his right hand leafing through a well-thumbed Haggadah, he was radiant in a white silk kashabia. White was not only the color of my uncles', my cousins', and of my own garb, but also of the linen cloth concealing the five Seder symbols in the low-rimmed wicker basket in front of my grandfather. I could clearly see the shape of lettuce heads and the glass with bitter water outlined under the cover, the "bitter herbs," as bitter as had been our slavery in Egypt. Also bulging through the linen was the big shoulder-bone. Later we would all take a bite from its roasted meat, passing the bone from hand to hand in memory of the Passover lamb sacrificed each spring in our Temple in Jerusalem—that is, until the Romans burned it down. To remind us of this great disaster at a time of thanksgiving and celebration, there was an egg waiting at the bottom of the basket—hard-boiled and slightly singed, an egg of mourning, Rabbi Parienti had explained in class. It meant that we were forever yearning for our long-lost temple, and as everybody present—from my grandfather down to the unborn babies—had to get a taste of it, he had to divide one small egg into more than fifty parts! Why *haroset* (a paste ground together from dates, nuts, cinnamon and sweet wine) is supposed to resemble the mortar our people used in building the pyramids, I don't know; maybe because the stuff is so sticky. It certainly does not taste of lime, and I, for one, could never get enough of it. The fifth and last symbol was the *massajoo*, three thin extrakosher, extraexpensive matzohs that could only be obtained from the rabbi himself.

It was my grandfather who at that moment caught everybody's attention; helped by his sons he was slowly rising to his feet. The gathering was silent as he lifted his crystal glass: "Blessed is our Lord, God, King of the Universe who creates the fruit of the vine," intoned the brittle voice, and then we would sit down again to empty the first cup.

"Blessed is God, Who chose us among all people to seek holiness through His commandments," my grandfather went on to recite in Hebrew. "With love Thou has given us, O Lord, festivals for joy and gladness." His singsong, a little faltering at first, was gaining strength either from the wine or from the sanctity of the occasion. Leaning there at the head of the table, all white, his beard lit up by candlelight, he was no more just a shrunken old man leading us in prayer. . . . Moses must have looked so, I thought, when he had no strength left to go down to the Holy Land.

I shall never forget the night my grandfather died half a year later. It should have been a very festive night, a rare night on which the Sabbath and Sukkot eve were falling together. Instead of sitting in the *sukkah* in my grandfather's yard, however, under the beautifully patterned roof of palm leaves and myrtle branches braided by his hands in a last labor of love, the whole family was gathered inside the house.

Broken, murmured sentences came from the corner where the women were trying to comfort my grandmother, rocking and stroking her as if to soothe a terrified child. The men had formed a half circle around the stone bench in the wall which had been my grandparents' bed for a lifetime; on its thin straw mattress my grandfather lay dying. Not seeing any of us he was staring at the vaulted ceiling, but more than by his eyes I was frightened by the sound of his breath coming in slow, uneven rattles.

Uncle Goliath had called for Tsemah, a pious member of the burial society and a great expert in the knowledge of vital signs. I pretended to myself that I had not seen him shake his head. Barely perceptible, that faint shake had been followed by absolute silence, even the rattling was coming more seldom.

Then, all at once, a formidable din had started outside in the street. My grandfather was very dear to me and I was feeling very low, still, curiosity will grip me by the neck at some of the saddest moments. I bolted out of the room to see what was the matter. The night was pitch-dark, all of Bab Salah Street in turmoil. Every Moslem was up on his rooftop—men, women and children banging on empty oil cans, pounding copper mortars, shaking tin baking sheets, howling and screaming at the top of their lungs in an effort to frighten off the murky shadow gnawing at the moon. Crazily jumping at the sky, the big white Arab watchdogs that are unleashed on the roofs at night were barking at the steadily diminishing moon-slice till their voices collapsed. How was I to know that the black shroud was something called an eclipse which was going to fade from its own accord? I was stunned. I stamped my feet, shook my arms and shouted the most abominable threats to shoo the thing away. In the end the hullabaloo helped. Slowly the black beast released its grip.

As I saw the freed moon race off through the clouds I went back into my grandfather's house. I sensed at once that there had been a change. I heard suppressed sobs, words from a psalm my class used to sing at funerals. Then I saw the empty bed, the two candles burning on the floor, and the long shape under the red velvet cover in between. I began to weep.

"No, no, Fallu, don't cry." My father drew me to him, hiding my face in the soothing smell of tobacco and sweat of his bournous. "You mustn't be afraid, son. God has taken Grandfather to the Garden of Eden, you know. . . . He was very, very old. . . . he wanted to go there." It was hard to grasp for me how grandfather could at one and the same time lie under the velvet cover and walk in the Garden of Eden, but I wanted to believe my father. The noise from the street was dying down, a bang here, a dog's bark there; inside the house, sobs punctuated the psalms. Finally Tsemah lifted his beard and earlocks from the prayer book. To bring red-eyed Uncle Goliath, the new head of the clan, to his senses, Tsemah sternly lectured him:

"Now there will be no more weeping, do you understand? How many years of life does the Almighty accord man? Three score and ten: that's what is written in the Bible, seventy years. Each additional year is a gift from heaven, a gift granted the just . . . and your father, the most just of the just has seen nearly a hundred! You know as well as I do that all those years over and above had to be taken from the lives of younger men, surely worthy, but still much, much younger. . . . Do I have to remind you of Hakoo? (A sixteen-year-old cousin who had been killed by a stone thrown by another youth.) So don't let the Angel of Death hear any more sobs," Tsemah admonished. "Do you want to weep a calamity on a young head, God forbid? Give thanks to the Almighty!"

And with that he led us in the song of Rabbi Shimon Bar Yohai, a song of praise and joy we used to sing after the Sabbath meal. It made me feel a little better. Later at the funeral there was so much excitement I almost forgot what the bustle was about. A huge crowd accompanied my grandfather to the cemetery. Every devout Jew in Nabeul had come, even the rabbis, for who would not to pay their respects to a just man whom the moon itself had mourned? Six neighbors from Bab Salah Street carried the bier. Those unable to share in the privilege tried to touch at least the velvet cover, hoping to capture a tiny bit of my grandfather's merit.

They made a lot of fuss over me, patted me on the head, jerked up my chin, pinched my cheeks into flaming red peppers:

"He was the last of the just, a holy man, your grandfather Rafael.

You carry on his name, Fallu, don't you forget it!" they said to me. No question about it, I was now the grandson of a saint.

Who would have thought my dear shrunken grandfather with the needle teeth, always snipping away at twigs and branches when he was not praying, had been a holy man? Yet the signs were unmistakable. To be grabbed by the Angel of Death on a Sabbath eve and at that ripe old age points in itself to unusual merit. Add Sukkot eve and the blacked-out full moon and even an ignorant boy like myself could understand that he was no ordinary grandfather.

Sadly I sat among the leaves of his abandoned sukkah, remembering all the good times we had had together. How we had listened for chicks ready to break out of their shells, how he would bring home ears of corn to roast just for me, and how we would crouch motionlessly side by side to trap a bird under the couscous sieve. From now on nobody was going to smother my sobs with spiced broad beans and sugar lumps, every time the cat would get hold of my sparrow.

The next Rafael Uzan—an unwilling scion of a saint! I wanted to escape my new role. Maybe he had not been that holy after all. Maybe the moon had veiled its face with a black shroud simply because it had felt sad with me for my poor kind, old grandfather.

Inasmuch as we were still at the Seder table and half a year before these events came to pass, none of those present knew that this was to be my grandfather's last Passover. My little grandmother stood bent over him with the bowl and water pitcher, and after she had rinsed the hands of every male around the table, he uncovered the Seder basket to let us taste the first of the bitter herbs. Holding up the three massajoo matzohs, he read out the ancient words in Aramaic:

"This is the bread of affliction that our ancestors ate in the Land of Egypt. Let all who are hungry come and eat. Let all who are in need come and celebrate Passover. This year we are here: Next year in the Land of Israel! This year we are slaves: Next year, free men!" Word for word, paragraph after paragraph, my uncles translated the Hebrew text into our everyday Judeo-Arabic for the women, thus giving some respite to my grandfather. I looked at Gaga. Worse off than a woman who could at least say "amen," he could not understand anything at all. Beaming in the new white shirt Uncle Goliath had given him, he sat happily gargling throughout the proceedings, sniffing the exciting smells coming from the kitchen.

To be slaves, to eat the bread of affliction—what was the meaning of it all? I thought of Gaga sweeping his way through the shops of Tunis, sweeping the whole year round for this one week with his family in Nabeul. And then Michael the madman came into my mind—Michael carrying bread to and from the bakery for all the women of Bab Salah Street. God knows why of all nights I had to think of bread on Seder night! But I clearly saw Michael before me as I had seen him many times, standing in the street, stuffing his mouth with crusts of bread he had scratched off the empty baking sheet. Was this the bread of affliction?

By now we had arrived at the four questions: "Why is this night different from all other nights? On all other nights we can eat bread and matzoh. Why tonight only matzoh?" I sang the first question together with my cousin Mordehai. All went well until we began to waver on the third verse of the double dipping. Uncle Goliath's ferocious glance caused us to stumble to a miserable end over the fourth and last problem on whether to sit upright or recline. My kindly grandfather cut in with a flourish:

"Our ancestors were slaves unto Pharaoh in Egypt," he chanted in his highest pitch, "but God brought us out from there with a strong hand and an outstretched arm. If the Holy One, blessed be He, had not brought our ancestors out of Egypt, we and our children and our children's children would still be slaves unto Pharaoh in Egypt. So even if we were all wise and clever and old and learned in the Torah, it would still be our duty to tell the story of the Exodus from Egypt. The more one talks about the Exodus the more praiseworthy it is."

Here my grandfather put down the heavy, ancient Haggadah and rose to bless us. Gripping the Seder basket with both hands he held it high above the heads of his four sons:

"Yesterday we were slaves, next year in the Land of Israel!" We sang with him at the top of our voices, three times for every group of four so blessed. Now Uncle Goliath took over. Easing the basket out of my grandfather's arms he repeated the benediction, never stopping until the last person in the room, down to the little girls, had bent their heads under the wicker-basket. As it happened, everybody present at that Seder would later end up in the Land of Israel, apart from those few we had to leave behind in Nabeul's cemetery.

"Yesterday we were slaves, next year in Jerusalem!" We chanted for the umpteenth time. Then my grandfather fell back on his ordinary monotone to dwell on the long story of our four hundred years of slavery and hardship. Drawn out by my uncles' translations for the women, the account went on and on, slowly progressing from the building of Pithom and Raamses and to the incredible miracles God Almighty had to perform to get us out of the clutches of the Pharaoh. Only the rumblings of my empty stomach combined with my grandfather's sudden tremolos at every mention of the Holy Name kept me from falling asleep. As I tried hard to remain on my best behavior and all my cousins did likewise, I could not find diversion from that quarter either, except for Cousin Eli, as famished as myself, who made a furtive pass at the matzoh. A whack from his brother's wooden spoon and a short wail was followed by a more desperate shriek from the women's corner. Aunt Shmeha's youngest daughter had upset a bottle of wine, saturating her mother's new green dress. We drowned her cry of distress in a rousing:

"And we cried unto the Lord, the God of our fathers, and the Lord heard our voice, and He saw our affliction and our labors and our oppression . . ." I saw with relief that only a few more pages were separating us from dinner and that we had finally arrived at the Ten Plagues. Now we all knew what awful things can happen if the Ten Plagues are not recited amid utter silence, all but Cousin Gaga, that is.

Uncle Goliath took it upon himself to make him shut up. Stroking a long imaginary beard he bowed reverently and repeatedly in the direction of my grandfather, cupped and recupped a hairy paw over Gaga's mouth until his blackberry eyes lit up with understanding. Clasping both hands tightly over his babble lips he stared at the lines of the Haggadah upside down on his knees, then looked up for approval. My grandfather could begin:

"Blood—frog—lice—" Gravely he dropped one plague after another into thick silence. "Beasts—blight—boils—hail—" With each curse he splashed a little wine into the bowl my aunt Mazal held out for him. She in turn poured water on the plague, and to be on the safe side the whole company finished it off with a determined *"sim silanu."* But then, just as we had to pass through the three last and most terrible afflictions, "Locusts—darkness—slaying of the first-born," such odd, hollow gurgles were coming from behind Gaga's clasped hands that I had to press my face very hard into my sleeve.

Aunt Mazal, walking as if on eggs, went out into the street to empty the receptacle of so many curses far away from any Jewish dwelling. All the while, a muffled string of "Googoogoos" echoed eerily through our solemn wait. I was sitting bent in two, afraid to burst out laughing and come under fire from Uncle Goliath. At last Aunt Mazal, having got rid of the evil water, came back into the house. We could breathe again.

Second blessing, second cup of wine, drunk to our deliverance from bondage and to freedom. Sleepiness flew away as the first matzoh was shared, followed by the haroset and the egg. As my grandfather passed around the big chunky bone and fifty little packages of matzohs, each wrapped inside a lettuce leaf and dipped in bitter water, three words glowed at me from the bottom of the page: DINNER IS SERVED.

At last came the procession of pots: big brown earthenware pots blackened by charcoal fire carried in by our mothers, smothering us in a fragrant steam. Each family had brought its pot of meat, its pot of rice, and a platter heaped high with silky lettuce leaves, sliced carrots and radishes, garnished with lemon wedges and slender green onions.

Craning his short neck, his nostrils trembling and wide, Cousin Gaga's eyes were rummaging among the dishes, ferreting out the juiciest chunks of lamb, the thickest portion of stuffed intestine emerging from the sauce. Ringed in by artichoke hearts and fresh broad beans, these tidbits were swimming in a slick, peppery lake of olive oil, tomato paste and plenty of crushed garlic. . . . Ah, to plunge in with my big Passover spoon, fish out the fattest slice of lamb, the largest puff of otsbana . . . That belonged, of course, to my father, whereas I, the eldest son, got a share about half his portion. My mother's was again several sizes smaller, my sister's slab not bigger than a matchbox, and the unborn child in my mother's womb received a tiny thimbleful just for the taste.

"Smack, smack . . ." The noise of fifty pairs of lips smacking in tune heightened everybody's enjoyment to a point where Uncle Goliath, completely absorbed in chewing, did not even notice the broad rivulets of sauce running from Gaga's chin upon the new white shirt. My uncle had his hands full coping with his own otsbana. His round face crimson from the effort to master the biggest portion of them all, he outshone the kettle before him—the only copper one among the whole company of pots. Having eaten to my heart's content, I looked at Gaga whose happy smile was breaking up the coating of sauce on his cheeks into a crisscross pattern. Too full to gargle, he sank back as song wafted in through the open door, some neighbors now deep into the second part of the Seder. After the women had taken the leftovers to their corner to share them out among themselves and their daughters, we were ready to proceed.

My grandfather wiped his beard, filled his glass for the third time and made it tinkle; "Gentlemen, let us say grace. . . ."

"May the name of the Lord be blessed forever and ever!" we answered in choir. A long grace, at the end of which we were permitted to raise the third cup: "To peace!" By now my head was swimming. The river of Egypt was shimmering bloodred inside my grandfather's crystal goblet. Risking a side-glance at Uncle Goliath-Pharaoh, I saw him pouring wine into the cup of the Prophet Elijah. All evening the door had been kept open to prove that we had left the ways of slaves far behind in Egypt, having become free Jews and fearless men. But although the door was wide open, and though I could have sworn I saw the milky tip of Elijah's robe flash past, his cup in the center of the table had remained untouched.

"Pour out Thy wrath upon the heathen that have not known Thee, and upon the kingdoms that have not called upon Thy name!" My grandfather could still muster some thunder into his old voice— enough to shake my cousins and me out of our bloated drowsiness. As we reached the last part of the Seder, the narrow room rang with thousand-year-old hymns of joy:

"If our mouths were filled with song like the sea, and our tongues like the crash of the waves. If our lips could speak like the endless sky and our eyes shine like the sun and the moon. If our arms could reach like eagles' wings and our feet were light as the hind's . . ." Unable to read, the women were humming the tune only, the girls beat time with their wooden spoons, and Gaga threw his head from side to side in an independent rhythm of his own. Uncle Goliath, his deep base resonating below everybody else's, kept consulting his watch. Stopping short our chant in the middle of a verse he ordered us out into the courtyard, under the walled-in square of a black sky packed with stars. Precisely on the stroke of midnight the Gates of Heaven were going to open for the tiniest fraction of an instant and our chances to squeeze a request through were just as small. I stood ransacking my befogged mind, finding nothing more worthwhile to ask for than a fishing rod as I heard my mother whisper by my side:

"Please, dear God, let me bear one living son . . . one for the three you took back, only one, but strong enough to live. . . . Please, I ask for nothing more. . . ." I never got a fishing rod and had to make do with a piece of string for many years to come, whereas my mother's plea, rising from the depths of her soul, found its way into the ear of the Almighty. In what terrible, unexpected manner it was granted I will soon tell.

I don't remember much of anything that happened later on that night, after the fourth and last cup to the Temple in Jerusalem; I must have fallen asleep on my sheepskin. I can't even recall singing "The lamb my father bought for two *zuz*," my favorite song, the one that closes the Seder.

Next evening it was the same long ritual and the same festive meal all over again. For the rest of the Passover week I was free as a bird. Breaking in my leather soles, the pockets of my new pants swelled with almonds, I would stroll through Bab Salah Street or go down to the beach for fish and matzoh picnics. At the beach, my friends and I played endless almond games. First lancing, then catching some with one and the same hand, it was invariably nimble-fingered Dooha who emptied everybody else's pockets. Good-naturedly, though not without a little prodding, he would in the end share them once more and all of us feasted together.

Having been invited to each of his kinsmen's houses, Cousin

Gaga bathed in the sunshine of his clan. Passed along from table to table, he was filling out around the edges, quite in contrast to the moon which, full on Seder night, was rapidly slimming.

On the eighth and last day of Passover my father and I got up before sunrise, dressed in white and went to join in the prayers at the seashore. The fallahs were out early. "Hey-y-y - hey-y-y - hey-y-y . . ." they banged and shouted away in the cornfields. A cloud of birds shot up into the dawn, soared, then disassembled, falling out like fireworks on Bastille Day. Now we were pushing upstream through a goatherd with hundreds of pale yellow eyes questioning on all sides. The Arab shepherd knew where we were going.

"Good morning, good morning!" he beamed, waving his staff. The more often the Jews went to worship the better the Moslems liked it, for was there not one heaven stretched over Nabeul and the sea, and could they not but profit from our prayers?

We were walking alongside Rabbi Ghez and others from our congregation when the prickly-pear path left the cactus hedges to open upon a strange sight. Where the beach used to be, a thousand red tarbooshes were bobbing like fishing tackle on the milky stream. Clad in their whitest kashabias, all the Jews of Nabeul were standing there facing the sea, each congregation rocking back and forth in prayer. Washing our hands in the surf we joined in their song, the song the Children of Israel had sung to the Almighty as they stood on the shores of the Sinai watching the last of the Pharaoh's warriors drowning in the Red Sea.

Hoosha, the barber, had worked out a way of his own to attain merit: on the day we commemorate the dividing of the waters, he would brave the waves in his Sabbath clothes, praising the Lord and Moses with chattering teeth as he walked up to his armpits into the sea. Until he left for Israel many years later, he used to do so every Passover. However, when Hoosha settled in Ramla, a landlocked dust bowl east of Tel Aviv, the barber was run over by a car. (If I mention him here in the middle of the song of Moses it is because the dead barber's shadow is still mixed up in my married life. Lately Fortuna will not let a day pass without sighing for Hoosha whom she claims to have jilted for my sake.)

Straight from the commemoration of the crossing of the Red Sea, the great miracle that had saved us from the pursuing chariots of Egypt, my father and I would go to the market to search for a head of lettuce. The Arab farmers, well aware of our customs, had kept their biggest, greenest lettuce for this day. Returning home with an immaculate, leafy beauty we wrapped it in a wet rag to keep it fresh. Later in the afternoon we plucked its leaves one by one to decorate our room. One leaf went on top of the chest, two on the bed; others were attached to the bread basket, the oil lamp, and the lattices in the window until only two leaves were left. From the roof of the synagogue we watched the sky for the three tiny silver specks which were to announce the end of Passover. After the service my father stuck one of the leftover leaves behind his ear, the other behind mine. Together we passed before all their green sisters in our home, chanting: "*Shanta hadra, shanta hadra* . . . a green year!" the ancient plea for prosperity.

A Pilgrimage to Testour

French School and Little Girls

Passover was over, my beautiful vacation gone. Something new in store for me. My father took me to the barber, the pious Hoosha who used to pray immersed up to his armpits in the sea and whom Fortuna pines for to this day. That she would have been widowed twenty years ago had she married him instead of me does not seem to bother her. When I was but a schoolboy the barber, already in the flower of manhood, would shear off my hair with the same fervor with which he would chant hymns standing in the water. My baldness, covered by a blue beret, made me ready for French school where a well-shaven head with no place for lice to hide was the first condition for acceptance.

It was my closest contact with the West so far. Monsieur Mauricet, *le maître*, looked extremely distinguished to me, tall and thin in his light-colored suit of European cut and his dark red tie. The latter hue, echoing back from his high cheekbones, came to full bloom on a prominent, sharp nose as purple as Algerian wine. To let my eyes wander above this point was embarrassing since my new teacher, who was of the Christian faith, went through life bareheaded. Monsieur Mauricet spoke only French.

"*Bonjour,* young man, sit down," he said, assigning me a seat behind a real school-desk. Apart from a blackboard, the like of which

I had never seen, plenty of chalk and the raised desk of le maître the room was just as desolate as my class at Talmud-Torah school. In one corner stood an old, battered cupboard whose uses I will soon describe. It was here, bent over a slate, I was supposed to spend my mornings from now on studying French, arithmetic, geography and history. In the afternoons I would continue my religious education with Rabbi Parienti. Since I was required to go to synagogue once before and twice after school I obviously had to cheat on something if I wanted time to play.

Trying to be evenhanded, I cheated on le maître, Rabbi Parienti, and the Almighty in equal proportions. Rapidly becoming expert at playing truant, I whiled away whole days in the fields and at the beach. Since the majority of students at French school were Jewish and the rest were Christian of mainly Italian extraction, the Saturdays and Sundays were days of rest. I regretted the rule that Moslems, whom the French authorities tried to keep illiterate, were not admitted to our school. Otherwise, we would have had Friday off too.

I managed. One sou would do the trick if I felt either like fishing or bird catching in the middle of the week. For that sum, an older student more advanced in French was willing to write me an excuse about a fever or a belly ache which I adorned with the name of my mother and a flourish. (My poor mother could not sign her name in any language.) After an absence of a day or two I would present the note to Monsieur Mauricet who, probably sorry that I had come back so soon, accepted it without question. How I learned to speak French under those circumstances, and even a smattering of orthography, remains a wonder.

In contrast to Rabbi Parienti, responsible to a higher power than any ordinary ministry of education, our teachers at French school took little personal interest in their students. They followed, on the other hand, a more methodical approach. Whereas Rabbi Parienti would fly into a rage, hitting out left and right with his myrtle cane, le maître, well-versed in a wide range of punishments, coolly meted out the penalty according to the gravity of a culprit's offense. To retribute chatting, for example, outstretched fingers were rapped with a ruler. Hands folded in the back, wrongdoers had to stand face to the wall, usually with the additional requirement to keep one foot dangling in the air. During any ordinary lesson, a row of at least three or four such storks, lined up near the teacher's desk, would have their drooping legs promptly revived by a slap of the ruler. Nevertheless I preferred standing on one foot for chatting to being shut up after class for laziness. All alone with my French history and a copybook, I would have to reproduce whole pages of bizarre events and silly dates in order to regain my freedom. Besides the recollection that all

French kings with the exception of Napoleon were Louis, I remember but one obscure sentence of those hours of drudgery. I must have written it a hundred times:

"Vous êtes le premier en histoire de France, eh bien, parlez-moi de Vercingétorix, que fût l'année de sa naissance, sa mort? Repondez-moi oui ou non." The gibberish made no sense to me then and it does not now, yet here it is, engraved in my mind forever.

I have already mentioned the old cupboard that occupied one corner of the class. But for a few books and the maps for our geography lessons, it was completely empty; having spent many a morning in its peaceful, musty-smelly belly I should know. Used mainly as a prison to punish boys caught at theft or serious fighting, I would sometimes be singled out for the latter category.

On the whole, my years at French school were a happy, carefree time, much of which I spent outdoors catching fish and birds. It was also the time that I tried out my first but not at all timid feelers toward girls. My contact with members of the other sex having been restricted to the family circle, I was slowly beginning to take notice of the nimble-footed creatures in long aprons crossing my path on their way home from girls' French school at the far end of town. Budding aspirations to manliness can manifest themselves in the strangest fashion.

In the habit of instantly gulping down any sweet that came my way, I would now save them up instead, plastering my pockets with chocolate, honey balls, licorice and rubber bands. The moment I met some pigtailed beauty walking by herself I would bar her way, push the sticky mess under her nose and command her to take it. If the frightened girl refused, as she almost always did, then I would pull her hair, kick her and run away.

One of my victims was Fortuna—how would I know she would one day become my wife! She was plump and round-faced between two thick braids, really cute as she was trotting home from French school in her long-sleeved black apron with white collar and red buttons. Shyly glancing at the proffered sweet, she turned up her little nose, her wide brows meeting disapprovingly. Lifting first one shoulder then the other, she averted her face, blushed and in the end accepted. That is my side of the story. Fortuna's version of the incident is different. I had threatened her, she says, with a dirty pink peppermint stick, grabbing her by one of her pigtails as she tried to flee. Then, the moment she opened her mouth to let out a scream, I shoved some kind of glue into her mouth. In any event, rumors about the mad knight errant were whispered from ear to ear. It did not take long before little girls would accept my sweets, often with a smile.

My Mother Bears Twins

At home I had to spend more and more time helping my mother who was pregnant and nearing her term.

"What's new . . . has anything happened?" My father's first question would be for my mother as I ran to welcome him and the donkey back home from their weekly peddling tour. He even forgot his customary inquiries about the number of my visits to the synagogue. A few years earlier, when my little sister had come into the world, it had been the same.

"Anything new?" he had shouted from afar and I had nodded. "A boy or a girl?"

"A girl," I had said. Turning his wide-brimmed straw hat this way and that in agitation, my father had walked up and down the yard, swallowing his disappointment in silence as befits a good Jew. Then, having regained his composure, he entered as always to greet my mother, ignoring the cradle hanging from the wall. His dignified conduct had been unlike that of some of our neighbors whom I heard bitterly cursing their wives in similar circumstances, as if their mates had brought a girl into the world to spite them. True, girls had to be fed and sheltered for long years before they could finally be married off at great expense. Nevertheless, that first anger at having fathered a daughter would almost always turn into affection later on, as was the case with my father who prefers my sister Esther to me any day.

Although I was still a child when Esther was born, my mother had to rely on my aid at the time of her delivery and lying-in. As soon as my mother felt the first birth pangs she sent me running to my aunts and to Meah, the midwife, and I had helped carry the pierced chair to our house. In the meantime our neighbors had already lit a fire and put on water to boil; linens were readied and candles were lit while prayers were offered for a safe delivery. I saw my pale, sweating mother installed in the chair, her hands clutching its arms so hard the knuckles stood out white. She was groaning and as Meah spread my mother's knees wide open, I was asked to leave the room. Amid all the women milling about, praying for help from Rabbi Meir, Rabbi Shimon Bar Yohai, the Patriarchs, Prophets and of course the Almighty, I had barely been noticed.

"Shout, my dove, scream your heart out!" I had heard my aunt Kooka encourage my mother as she held her head. "By the grace of God you will bear a beautiful son. . . . All of us will come to his brit milah, his bar mitzvah and his wedding!" Screams, awful screams coming from our room, followed me into the homes of our neighbors and out into the yard where more women, assembled under our window, were clamoring for assistance from above. Seeing our rabbi praying in their midst, my heart had sunk, for only when a birth was taking a bad turn would his help be sought to intercede with heaven. I don't know how long I stood there, begging God to make the screams stop. Night was falling when at last there came a lull, everybody cutting short their prayers to listen for the first cry of the child, as feeble as a kitten's. Rousing thanks had gone up to the sky until, the air still vibrant with sahrutas, a series of fresh screams hushed the celebration.

Completely mixed up by now, I heard people say that my mother was giving birth to twins. After she had fallen silent for the second time, however, there was a great stillness—no thin wail, no shouts of joy followed. Talking to each other in muted voices, the last of the women were dispersing into the night when I saw Meah the midwife traverse the yard carrying a bundle. With a queer feeling in my stomach I watched her put her burden on the ground, covering it with an upturned washtub.

Apprehensive of what I was going to find in our room, I stood in the dark trying to puzzle out what had happened. Soon my Aunt Kooka came looking for me. Taking me gently by the hand, she showed me something red and wrinkled whimpering in the crib, my new baby sister. So as not to disturb my mother resting behind the curtain, I was to lie down on my sheekpskin very quietly, Aunt Kooka said; but instead I crept out into the yard again, drawn irresistibly to where our copper washtub, closed over Meah's secret, glimmered dully in the moonlight. Taking a deep breath I lifted up one side. A tiny baby was lying on the cold stones before me, half covered by a swaddle cloth. I could see it quite clearly. Eyes tightly shut, it was peacefully asleep, keeping very still save for some slight twitch. Feeling with certainty that this was the brother I had been waiting for, I was outraged. How did they dare treat him like an outcast? My mother's need for rest mattered little to me as I stormed into our room.

"What did you do to my brother?. . . . Why is he out there on the stones?" I shouted, angrily tearing at the bed curtains. "Bring him in at once or I will tell my father!" My mother had turned her face to the wall. Aunt Kooka drew me to her lap.

"You have a sister, Fallu. Your brother was not strong enough to live. He went to the Garden of Eden to play with your other brothers."

"He's not, he's not," I cried hysterically. "Under the washtub in the yard, that's where he is. I saw him move!" And before anyone could hold me back I ran out again. Looking longer and harder at the infant than I had done the first time, it seemed to me as if the little hand sticking out of the linen wrap was moving up and down.

No one followed me. The neighbors and Aunt Kooka were afraid to investigate too closely a baby said to be stillborn. My poor mother was too weak to think straight, let alone get out of bed. So I decided it was up to me to carry my brother inside. I hurried back to find a blanket but the women at my mother's bedside joined forces to prevent me from slipping out again. In an effort to calm me (and with fat Lajla blocking the door) they patted and kissed me to distraction and told me to stop rebelling against the will of God. They also said that Meah had never been mistaken in these matters. Aunt Kooka stroked my confused head until I finally fell asleep.

The burial society members were early risers. The next morning the copper vat was hanging from its hook as always. Aunt Kooka had taken it down to do my mother's blood-soaked wash as if the vat were just an ordinary washtub and nothing had happened.

Fifty years have passed since the day my mother gave birth to twins, and though I was but a small boy at the time, pitted against a whole bunch of frantic, superstitious women, I still cannot forgive myself for having given in. Through all those fifty years a little hand, its feeble flutter, has haunted me. Tiny fingers brush the strings of my memory ever so lightly, bringing back the screams and prayers of that night—the image of my mother's bloodied linen and of one more brother who never grew up.

And Another Brother Arrives

Several years later my mother was with child again. My parents, going to extraordinary lengths to try and ensure the birth of a healthy son, made a pilgrimage to the tomb of Rabbi Fraji of Testour. It was a many hours' drive from Nabeul. Reputed for countless favorable intercessions with heaven on behalf of women who had trouble with pregnancy and childbirth, that kind rabbi's spirit was said to be especially well disposed on his birthday. That is why, on the Sukkot holiday, and in partnership with a couple of other families in need of Rabbi Fraji's help, my father and mother set out before daybreak in a hired carriage with two horses, taking me along.

Driving into Testour at noontime, we headed straight for the cemetery which was already ringed with carts, mules, horses and donkeys from every corner of Tunisia. Some nabobs even arrived in motorcars to plead with the good rabbi. Crying at the graveside of a sage of the Torah is prohibited on the day of his anniversary so the crowds were milling about the cemetery in a hopeful, festive mood. On every patch of burnt-out grass not overgrown with thistles, in the meager shade of every little shrub, big-bellied women were squatting at their husbands' side, picnicking to the music of drums and tambourines, while wives, as yet flat, warmed up at the sight of so much jolly roundness.

Smoke trembling in the hot noon sky led us to the famous tomb itself—a plain mound of fieldstones, not even shaded by a tree as was the burial place of our own Rabbi Jacob Slama back home. I have already mentioned how the Jews of Nabeul, cleverly circumventing the great sage's wish for a modest resting place, had built a big marble shrine at some distance from his real grave. Possibly still humbler than his counterpart, Rabbi Fraji's remains had successfuly resisted any such attempt at trickery. In back or in front of his tomb, whether made from stone or from marble, any monument his disciples tried to errect in memory of their beloved teacher would cave in the moment it was finished. In the end they had given up.

Hundreds of candles were burning on the mound in honor of the saintly rabbi's birthday as we approached to light three of our own, pressing kisses on the dripping, reeking stones. Choking with smoke, we had to wait until the guardian rabbi of the tomb finished supplications on behalf of a woman swooning and moaning as if she were about to give birth on the spot. So as not to see how many coins were passing from his pocket into the rabbi's hand, my father turned his head, then pushed my mother forward.

"This here Meesha, daughter of Abraham, wife of Hamus," he explained, "promises the great and merciful Rabbi Fraji that if she will give birth to a living son she will name him in honor of the rabbi." While the guardian of the tomb stood swaying back and forth, mixing my parents' message into Hebrew prayer, my mother added a plea of her own—the same I had heard her whisper on Passover eve:

"Please help me, dear Rabbi Fraji," she begged, spreading her arms over the unborn child. "Please, ask the Almighty to let me bear one more living son . . . one for the three He has taken . . . that is all I want. . . ." One should not try to force the hand of the Lord of the Universe. My poor mother was to get exactly what she had asked for. Soon I will tell at what price.

There at Rabbi Fraji's birthday party, however, things to come still lay safely hidden in thick white folds, my mother becoming dreamy-faced at every kick of the unborn inside her. The view of so many others who had come with babes in arms to thank the rabbi for his mediation filled my parents' hearts with hope, spirits rising even higher after a lunch of hameen and a dessert of dates and almonds. Having emptied our last bottle of wine, we joined in the general merrymaking, still somewhat inebriated and still singing when we arrived back home in the small hours of the night.

From that day on my mother looked forward to the approaching birth with calm and confidence. Inevitably it came; this time though, as I ran for the midwife, her pierced chair and the tiny copper bathtub, no rabbi's intervention to speed up the delivery was needed. When before long the angry cries of a newborn male filled everybody's ears, the sahruta greeting his arrival lasted for at least five minutes. Coming home on the following Thursday and seeing the talismans pinned to the bed curtain—the paper fish and the hands with the five outstretched fingers—my father understood at once. In case he still had any doubts, they must have vanished at the smile my mother flashed him from her pillow.

Though he could embrace his ruddy new son, he had to keep his distance from my mother for a period of forty days during which he was not even allowed to accept food out of her hand. In the meantime, we had to celebrate my brother Fraji's brit milah, a big affair consuming all my father's resources besides necessitating a shot in the arm from Sidi Baruch's comité funds into the bargain. My aunts kept bringing in mountains of sweet pastry baked in olive oil, huge bowls of broad beans powdered with cumin, and on the tottering heirloom chest a row of bottles would clank against each other every time I tried to open a drawer. Still confined to bed, my mother, all smiles, was enthroned behind the half-drawn bed curtain, her earrings dangling from the folds of a new headscarf of such generous proportions that the knot over the middle of her forehead looked like a bird with spread wings rather than her ordinary butterfly.

My grandfather having departed for the other world, it fell upon me to provide myrtle for the blessing as the day of the circumcision was dawning. I was also to help Mimmesh, the *mohel*, carry the Prophet Elijah's wooden armchair to our house. Ready to receive a new Jew on its velvet cushion, it stood propped up against the wall, the two lions carved on the back squinting maliciously at my brother's cradle. With all those novelties, our room seemed hardly recognizable—even the smell was odd, a festive combination of myrtle, fresh pastries, diapers, and the overwhelming aroma of very ripe tangerines, the gift of our Arab neighbors.

Among the first guests to arrive was Sidi Hushhash, the impatiently awaited godfather who, having slipped an envelope into my father's hand, went to occupy the seat of honor—Elijah's chair. Now the ceremony could begin. Without an inkling of what lay in store for him, tranquilly sleeping on the velvet cushion, my brother was now deposited on Sidi Hushhash's lap, from where, at the most critical moment, he hit the mohel with a beautiful, high arc of piss. Having dried himself, Mimmesh circumcised him anyhow, little Fraji bellowing with so much strength throughout the proceeding that the admiring guests could not find words enough to congratulate my father.

"A true lion's cub, Hamus, that son of yours. . . . May he grow into a light of the Torah!"

The child, a powerful eater from the start, ceased fretting the moment it was given the tip of a wine-soaked rag to suck. The same sweet wine also acted on my father whom I have never again seen as happy as on the day of my brother's circumsion. Hugging even me in the process, he embraced every one of the well-wishers with the exception of the women. Then, growling a lullaby, he actually danced a few steps, cradling little Fraji in his arms. In the end, forced to sit down on the ground, he kept throwing kisses to the sky, softly muttering things to himself while I was busy with the food, looking out for Elijah's white robe in between mouthfuls. Finding no trace of the Prophet, I watched instead Mimmesh take up his mohel's plate and rub the foreskin in a small heap of ashes. After my Aunt Kooka had buried the mixture in the yard, Mimmesh proceeded to auction off the tools of his trade.

"Five francs for this exquisite silver-plated vessel . . . who gives a better price?" Uncle Goliath did, making the highest bid. Then came the turn of the forked silver holder and the blessing on the wine. Sidi Hushhash purchased his own seat in Elijah's armchair. Naturally these only fake transactions where the buyer got thin air and my father got the money—a much needed push to restart the family cart charged with an additional passenger.

Here I must mention my brother's navel cord, safely buried several days before his circumcision. Not to have done so would have been extremely dangerous: otherwise any barren woman could swallow it, become pregnant and bear a child, thereby condemning the first baby to die. As far as we, the family, were concerned, everything possible had been done to protect the newborn. Elijah the Prophet, however, eagerly awaited guardian of newcomers to the fold, had not come to the celebration. Having watched out for him throughout the proceedings I can say with certainty that, though he is said to have put in fleeting appearances at many a circumcision, he did not show up at this one.

Growing rapidly into a robust toddler it took some time before we became aware that my brother Fraji was not like other children. He learned to walk, he could hear and see as well as anybody else, but he had yet to babble his first word. Always hungry, he would stuff anything he could lay hands on into his mouth; but the day he burned his lips with a live coal my parents became worried. Very slowly he learned to half talk, half mumble. When the time came, he was even unable to hold his own among the blank-faced, snot-nosed innocents at the end of the bench in Rabbi Parienti's class. He never rose beyond the reasoning of a two-year-old, taking more than thirty years to get somewhat toilet-trained.

Misery and heartbreak. The blows and kicks my mother had to suffer brought her to an early grave. My brother Fraji has not known a day of sickness to this day. His greatest pleasure is eating bread, a whole loaf at one sitting, drowning it with enormous quantities of water—more than I have ever seen any other human being drink. He nevertheless has a strange fear of water, gulping it down without looking. When someone tells him what to do, he can push wheel-barrows, carry loads, and, in his youth in Nabeul, he made a little money serving as live bobbin to a weaver. Here in Safed he works in the graveyard. My old father, still taking care of him, has a hard time to make him wash because of his fear of water. This is the living son my mother had so yearned for. After him my parents had no more children.

XII

Wine, Birds and Other Passions

The same fall my brother was born, news of the sudden death of Aunt Shmeha's husband reached our family from Tunis. Hastily putting up my little brother and sister with Aunt Kooka, my parents rushed off to the funeral in Tunis, leaving me behind to watch our home.

Shocked by the news and pressed for time, my father had nevertheless remembered to open my Bible to the portion of the week, enjoining me to read it thoroughly. Needless to say that, my parents gone, I was soon looking out for another occupation. Keep your eyes open, they had said. What was I supposed to watch in an utterly peaceful room where everything was standing or hanging silently in place? The sole intruder was a woodworm ticking in the heirloom chest. Never having seen one I prepared to catch it, but however softly I crept toward that drawer, the clever worm stopped ticking the moment I came within range.

What was in the drawer anyway? My father's fairy tales, in shreds and printed in a script I could not make out, prayer books in slightly better shape, torn phylacteries, two Roman or Phoenician coins my grandfather had once found in the myrtle wadi, empty snuffboxes, a broken oil lamp, three single socks with heels resembling sieves and a corkscrew. Though the inventory of the first drawer was not very exciting, the corkscrew prompted me to explore the storage hole under my parents' bed where the yield was more promising. Right in front, behind two unopened bottles of red wine, I found eggs, more of them gathered in one basket than I had seen since Passover! My father must have bartered them for a length of cloth. Figuring that with so many eggs it ought not to be too hard to make an omelet, I got a fire going on the tripod. That was easy, as it was to let the eggs, one after another, slop into a lake of sizzling olive oil.

"Bock—bock—bock." They were terribly noisy eggs, bubbling and sputtering into a green-brown mess because of the olive oil— much less appetizing than I had anticipated. They would have to do, I thought, as I climbed on an upturned cooking pot get at the bread, suspended in a basket from the ceiling in order to discourage hungry mice. To round out my meal, I gave the corkscrew a trial on one of the two sealed bottles. The cork, however, instead of slickly popping out as it would for my father, crumbled into the wine in bits and pieces.

Cork crumbs could be spat out. Deciding not to let such details spoil my lunch, I took draught after deep draught of the good red wine to wash down the green eggs, trying my hand on the second bottle when the first was half empty. Its cork broke into only two parts which, for some reason, made me very happy. Taking gulps from the second bottle made me feel even happier—so wonderful that I started singing—softly at first, then louder and louder in an irrepressible outburst of joy. Mistaking my jubilations for distress signals, our neighbors, who knew that I had been left alone, burst into our room, giving me barely time to hide the bottles. My shouts of joy reduced to incoherent mumblings, I fell flat on the rush mat as they stood worriedly consulting in one corner, concluding that loneliness paired with sorrow for my uncle's death had thrown me off my tracks.

"Fallu, dear, Mother will be home in the morning . . . come, you can sleep in my room . . . I have licorice. . . ." Fat Lajla rocked me on her bosom, the smell of sour sweat being the last thing I took in before dozing off.

I slept for twenty hours. They must have carried me to my sheepskin, for that is where I awoke to the faint light of dawn, feeling awful and thinking it was evening. But seeing that our room was getting lighter all the time instead of darker I finally dragged myself to the well where a few cold splashes of water on my face brought back my memory.

Soon my parents would be home. What was I going to do? First I filled the bottles with water. Since they were dark green glass, nobody would guess the red wine inside had turned into a weak rosé. Working like an ant, I somehow managed to retrieve the stoppers from spat out bits of cork. But to replace the seals was another matter. I tried tomato paste. I tried to mix red pepper pulp with candle wax. I begged the jinn to come up and help me. It was hopeless. Any moment now my father might open the door. At least I should get rid of the excess of omelet sticking to the rush mat and sweep the bread underneath, mangled as if the cat had got its claws into it.

That gave me an idea. Smashing the two bottles on whose appearance I had worked so hard, I equipped myself with a broom and a fishtail, using the latter to lure in the cat, the former to frighten the poor animal into a mad jumping circle. Trying to outdo each other, howling and screaming, I chased it from the bed to the windowsill, from the chest into the wildly swinging cradle, up the lattice and down the wall, the uproar bringing back fat Lajla as fast as she could waddle.

"Look at that . . ." I sobbed, pointing to the broken bottles. "My father is going to kill me. . . ." To make Lajla feel sorry for me, I put both my hands over my backside. Before the cat somehow escaped through Lajla's bulk blocking the doorframe, our neighbor had witnessed the last round.

"Don't you worry, Fallu, count on Lajla. . . . Haven't I seen with my own eyes how you went after that crazy cat? Must have got mice in that room, you know. . . .

My father's hands twitched as he saw the mess. Only Lajla's staunch protestations and my mother's silence in the matter of the missing eggs saved my hide on this occasion.

Busy bird catching or fishing, I would frequently arrive too late for evening services at the synagogue. Hearing my father's steps, my mother would hurriedly take out my prayer book, putting it on top of the chest.

"Where is Fallu?" were always his first words.

"Can't you see?" My mother would point to the book. "After synagogue he went out again." More and more I had to rely on her help to find time for my newest pastime, bird catching and bird breeding, soon to flare up into an all-consuming passion. In later years neither women nor painting, gardening nor antiques hunting, ever claimed as much of me or gave me as much in return as did my two great loves—birds and the sea.

It started when Cousin Kakoo let me have a pair of pigeons in a wooden cage in return for a damaged silver earring he made me filch from my father's peddler's pouch. Thoroughly disgusted with myself for robbing my own father, I was nevertheless unable to resist the pigeons' round stare, their shimmering little heads, and the feel of their soft, plump throats. Theirs was the first of many cages to cover the wall by our window.

Kakoo was aware that where the silver earring had come from there was more damaged jewelry. To tempt me, he would dangle visions of red robins, crested larks, sparrows, finches and Egyptian dwarf roosters before my avid fancy, many of which he had caught himself. After I refused to go along with another dirty deal, he agreed to teach me how to set traps and nets in exchange for a final fee.

Birds now became the center of my life. I knew no greater delight than to roam the fields or lie long hours in hiding, waiting for some songbird to land in my net. Fortunately, my father was away ped- dling most of the week; resolved to suffer my new craze in silence, he hoped birds would lead me into less mischief than my other friends.

My mother did not mind the peeps and chirps, the cooing and the trills, the hopping, fluttering and incessant scratching of tiny talons. Slowly the blue wall by the window was disappearing behind a patchwork of cages. To protect my birds from the mean and hungry cats prowling the terrace, I had to lodge them inside. There were pigeons, larks, quails, robins, finches and my great pride—a pair of yellow canaries. I regarded them all as friends and guests rather than prisoners. Patiently I learned the habits of each species, found out what grain or seed it preferred, which worms and insects I had to catch for it, what stuff it needed to nest and breed. Fondest of the vegetarians among them—so much cleaner and friendlier were they than the flesh eaters—I felt in time that I understood their language, knew what they wanted or had to tell each other.

Here is how I would procure mates for lonely singles: a wild bird of the same kind as my captive would fly over our house, hear a familiar call coming from our window and flutter down to follow it. Quickly hooking my bird's cage with its baited trap out on the terrace wall, I then hid behind the window. Desperate for a companion, my bird would keep calling, warbling so hotly that the stranger, unable to resist, would hop nearer and nearer, finally entering the trap. To reward my old bird for its help, I sometimes set it free, letting the newcomer take its place.

Bird families are very close. All those I observed in the wild would stay with a single mate for life. Only in captivity could I trick a male into accepting two females in his cage, or, if he had absolutely no other choice, a female of another species; even then, however, she had to be either a grain eater or a worm eater according to his own preference.

Best of all I have always liked finches and sparrows. On the closed balcony that is part of my flat in Safed, I have made a little studio for myself. There I paint my pictures under the reddish stare of a pair of finches.

I wish some of our Israeli architects who plan those huge, monotonous apartment crates, dividing and subdividing them into identical boxes, would watch the birds building their nests. To see how inventively swallows, hummingbirds and finches exploit their building site, how skillfully they will transform the simplest materials into pretty, comfortable homes, our planners might come up with something less dull than cubes and cubicles of poured concrete.

Here again the finch stands out as the most refined among bird builders. At mating time, prospecting for a proper site, the couple would fix their choice on an elm or an olive tree. Loudly claiming ownership, the male would then fly off, leaving the female to her own devices. Losing no time she went about her task, first hopping over the refuse heaps of the neighborhood in search of hair—long black hair from the head of a woman. If none was available then a horse or donkey would have to do. Once I even saw a finch holding on to a donkey's tail, tugging at the owner's hair until some of it came loose!

Neatly coiling her treasure to form the bottom of the nest, the female enlarged it into an outward winding circle with thread pulled from rags and sacking before weaving a wall from blades of straw and grass all around her. Only after the little bird had convinced itself of the solidity of its construction would it fly out to assemble the luxuries that make its nest soft, sweet-scented and pretty. Padding the bottom with cotton wool and feathers, the bird flew out once more, gathering aromatic thyme and the fragrant pink and yellow petals of wild flowers to scatter on top of everything, then hopped up and down, flattening its bed. The male, chirping encouragement, now arrived on the scene to survey the proceedings from the upper branch. The moment the female was ready, he fluttered down to inspect the lodgings, singing his approval. Cooing and billing her around the eyes, he finally entered the nest to make love to his mate.

Not always did things turn out that well, however. It sometimes happened that the male, either displeased with the nest or with the female, left again, in which case the poor thing had to tear everything apart and start from scratch. On the other hand, it was the male who worked to feed his female all through hatching time, listening for the first soft "tss-tss" of the young, jubilantly trumpeting the news from the treetops when he was at last able to hear them. Teaching them how to fly and how to feed on thistle and nettle seed also was his job.

After the young were fully fledged, the parent birds would leave to choose a building site for a new nest large enough to bring up a new family. This was done twice each summer or even three times if sufficient food and water were to be found in the neighborhood of their tree. This circle of events repeated itself for five or six seasons until the finches grew old. The pretty red feathers on their heads would thin out, their round eyes narrow to pinpoints, their beaks become crossed. In the end their little claws grew so long that they sometimes closed up in circles and I had to trim them to prolong the bird's life.

So much about finches which are so neat that even baby birds will not leave droppings in the nests, but try to spurt them on the top of the straw wall. Sparrows, on the other hand, are downright dirty. Generation after generation of young birds will sit on their own excrements in the same filthy nest, yet I love them. Besides being firmly convinced that sparrows have religious feelings, I admire them for their cleverness and their close-knit family life.

In Nabeul they used to construct their large, somewhat clumsy-looking nests inside the hollows between roof tiles and rafters or the numerous cavities of the uneven, lime-washed walls. Together the couple built their nest. Together they brought up their young. If one of them were to be caught by the cat or by a snake, as often happened, then its mate would sit brooding in the lonely nest for a period of mourning. At last stretching its wings again one sunny morning, the bird would fly out in search of a new companion, courting equally lonesome singles until it found one ready to share its nest.

At the end of a long summer afternoon, precisely at the hour I was supposed to be praying *Mincha* at Rabbi Hai synagogue, I would instead often go sit under the old carob tree by the blue mosque. High up from the minaret, through the four holes opening onto the four quarters of the heavens, the *muezzin* was calling Moslems to worship. Nibbling on a sweet black carob pod, I would watch the faithful of the Prophet shuffle over the domino slabs of the walled yard and take off their shoes if they were wearing any to wash their feet before entering their carpeted house of prayers.

It was not curiosity about their divine service, God forbid, that brought me here, but rather a desire not to miss the nightly assembly of sparrows taking place in the large crown of the carob tree above me. The sun was slowly setting, its light filtering through the dark foliage flaring up in a last blaze of golden yellow before softening into the rosy glow of dusk. The third and last *"Allah Il Akbar . . . Allah Il Kebir"* was still echoing from the minaret as the first sparrows already arrived. Soon they were flying in from every direction, hundreds of them settling like dust on the gnarled branches. Chasing away outsiders such as starlings and finches with energetic pecks and flaps, they kept changing places in a continuous turnover of hopping, the whole tree undulating under their gray waves.

"Toui-tee-bit, toui-tee-tee." Turned west to the fading light they all joined voices in a rousing twitter, now and then letting their chant die down so that only the voice of their leader should be heard mounting to the firmament. After a while the whole choir would set in again, the birds continuing in the same manner until nightfall.

In the darkening sky behind the minaret one, two, three silver specks were beginning to twinkle, right above the large pointed star embedded in the copper crescent. At that moment the leader whom I would like to call the bird priest, silenced the assembly with a single "Tiou-tiou-tiou," followed by complete silence. As if frozen to the spot, all the sparrows remained—each one on its branch. Each hid his head under one wing and went to sleep. At dawn, the bird priest reawakened his flock with a sharp "Sss-ttt-sss," after which they assembled and took off for the day with a great deal of flapping and twittering. Those sparrows that had arrived in pairs also left together.

At sundown they were all back again. The last fledglings had left their nest, freeing the adult birds of breeding cares. The nightly tree-top rallies were to continue for the rest of the summer.

So often did I come to the blue mosque that the Arabs returning home from prayers were beginning to wonder. Seeing me gnaw on carobs while they were looking forward to a dinner of sour milk, bread, and olives, they would make fun of me.

"Aslama, Raful (my name in Arabic), what mischief have you done again that your father has you feed on carobs, same as his donkey?"

The last Moslem had left the mosque. The birds were fast asleep. The tree stood black and silent. Finally, I got up to wander back to Bab Salah Street in an unusually pensive mood. Stopping awhile at the watering place on Rabat Square to look at the animals drinking, I caught sight of old Rabbi Bishlino trotting home with a load of corn ears in the hood of his bournous. His bearded head modestly lowered, his eyes half-closed as if he were walking past so many women, the venerable scholar was making his way amid a group of mules and donkeys lustily rolling in the dust to kill their fleas.

I have never been bashful.

"Peace be with you, Rabbi Yitzhak," Lightly I touched his shriveled hand, then pressed my lips to my own wrist, throwing him the kiss. "They say the rabbi knows everything . . . every word written in the Torah . . . the Talmud, the Mishna, and the Gemara. . . . May I ask the Rabbi a question?"

"What is troubling you, my son? Go ahead and ask." His wise old eyes were looking into mine.

"It's the birds, Rabbi Yitzhak . . . do they pray to the Almighty just like us?"

"You are quite right, child, they do. Remember the story of the flood? All the animals had boarded the ark when Noah, about to close the door, noticed that a pair of birds were missing. Seeing them praying on a tree, he waited for the two to finish. . . . And now you would do well to do the same as these birds. Run, son, you will be late for *Maariv*. . . ."

I went straight home to fetch my prayerbook. I felt proud that I had followed the rabbi's advice; I had also avoided doing my French homework.

Bab Salah Street

Rabbi Hai Synagogue

Whereas ancient synagogues, graceful and stately relics of the past, are the most highly prized jewels of their community, ours was just plain old, resembling an outsized, disproportioned beehive rather than a gem. Standing across from our own home on Bab Salah Street, Rabbi Hai synagogue was nevertheless invisible from the street, its one room completely swamped by randomly built smaller chambers, the outcrop of its holiness.

To enter this stronghold of learning great scholars, kabbalists and Wonder Rabbis had humbly stooped under the antique doorframe. Its walls, thickened by countless layers of lime, had seen the joys and sorrows of more than a dozen generations, looked on mysterious happenings and somber events. Silent witnesses to several pogroms as well as a miracle or two, the stones themselves were full of secrets, treasures and trickery.

In times of persecution long ago at the hands of the Mamelukes and later under Turkish rule which was not much better, the congregation would seek shelter in the synagogue, the richer among them bringing their gold to bury under the floor or in the thick walls. The danger they were in must have been very great, for some of them never retrieved their prized possessions. However, no matter how many holes later generations dug to get at the hidden gold, no Jew ever laid eyes on a single coin. Incensed that His own people had dared bury their money in His sanctuary and judging that there would have been less of it to hide had the rich given a share to the poor, the Almighty had put a curse on it. Jews, digging their fingers to the bone, would never see a trace of gold, while Arabs hired to do repair jobs on the site would suddenly disappear from Nabeul to reemerge shortly afterward as rich effendis in another town. They would not even finish their job, and I have seen with my own eyes the tools and the broken pitcher one such lucky devil had left behind on the spot.

Wealthy members had long since died. I could not think of anybody belonging to our congregation who, at the time of my youth, still had gold left to worry about. Poor invalids who had nobody to take care of them, like Yedida, the blind storyteller, were lodged in the tiny rooms bordering the synagogue's cobblestone yard; the rabbi and his family occupied part of the upper story. From a completely bare balcony opposite the latter's quarters, women wanting to participate in prayers could watch the men through an open hole in the sanctuary's ceiling.

Next to the women's balcony was the room where Rabbi Hai had once taught his disciples. Since the great kabbalist's death a century earlier, that room remained closed and untouched by human hands.

It was said of the Wonder Rabbi that, having cured the Bey of Tunis from a deadly sickness, he had refused an award of gold and precious stones, requesting instead a favor that would profit the whole community. Seeking permission to own a house, Rabbi Hai obtained the same privilege for his fellow Jews; from the day his wish was granted the Jews of Tunisia were allowed to buy houses and later, even land.

After the death of Rabbi Hai, the congregation of Bab Salah Street was left with his empty yeshiva. Over the years, one narrow chamber after another was added to the original little synagogue as well as schools—upstairs, downstairs, on the roof, and to the sides—to enable as many Jews as possible to live in the holy man's shadow.

Every now and then, stealing away from prayers, I used to climb the steep steps leading up to his room and press my face as far as possible through the rust-eaten bars of the window. Gradually my eyes would adjust to the dimness. As no one ever dared to enter, risking the wrath of the deceased kabbalist, Rabbi Hai's yeshiva had been taken over by spiders whose webs hung over the room like a profusion of gray curtains.

Partly visible through tears and holes in the ragged fabric of the webs, was the true attraction of the room—the rabbi's slippers; dust-covered and lonely they stood on his desk, their toes pointing heavenward. Recreating the kabbalist's image, I would start with the saintly slippers from where he rose in a long white robe not unlike that of the Patriarchs of my dreams; his face, however, radiant with a flaming beard and piercing eyes, would invariably resemble Uncle Goliath.

Of Rabbi Hai's famous candlesticks I never saw a trace. Hard as my eyes would strain through the gray, I could not find them. Here is their story: One stormy winter night, the rabbi sat at his desk, poring over his books by candlelight when the same door that was now closed forever flew open. Two thieves burst into the room, making straight for the candlesticks. As they seized the rabbi's most precious possession they suddenly stiffened. Their limbs frozen to the spot, neither one could lift a finger from the heavy silver lampstands. They cursed and begged and pleaded but the rabbi would not honor them with so much as a glance. Drawing mysterious letters, numbers and signs on the parchment before him, he kept calling every known Archangel, and running out of names invoked fallen ones, of a much more sinister nature. Flanked by his two involuntary candleholders sputtering invectives and blasphemies throughout the night, Rabbi Hai remained seated between them until dawn. The next morning, he went out calmly to call the sheikh; he did not release the thieves from his spell until the arm of the law had put them safely into chains.

Flights of worn-out stone steps, dark little vestibules and narrow passages led to the synagogue proper—a windowless vault, large only in comparison with the other rooms. Only through an opening in the domed roof could light and air stream in. By day a luminous round lid, at night a gaping black hole, the skylight would on winter mornings turn into a gray source of cold. Gales of wind would sweep in rains that caught us on our stone bench by the wall. These walls, ranging in color from sky-blue in dry spots to rich ultramarine in damp corners, were forever peeling, and bare save for the mirror that had once belonged to Rabbi Hai, encased in a carved frame that at the time of my father's youth had still born traces of gold leaf. The mirror had long since let go of the brilliant reflections of kabbalists and Wonder Rabbis. It had slowly dulled and become pockmarked with mildew.

The many oil-lamps suspended from the ceiling, on the other side, were clear glass but dusty. They had been offered by grateful members of the congregation to mark the birth of a son or a deliverance from sickness. Some of them, bearing nameplates, had been hung up in memory of dead relatives. After they had lit up our sabbath evenings for a year or a little longer, the *shamas* would discreetly take them down, first one lamp, then another, and replace them with new ones commemorating more recent events. One row of oil lamps, though, always remained unchanged. Suspended in front of the Torah shrine, they were engraved with the names of saints and sages, Rabbi Hai's lamp hanging in the middle not far from my grandfather's, right in front of the embroidered curtain. It was a gold-embroidered velvet curtain covering the niche in which our Torah scrolls were standing upright in their cases.

Handwritten on flawless parchment, the Torahs were the most precious possessions of our congregation. They were housed in colorfully lined, embossed and carved casings, some of copper, some of wood. Shining above all others, one of them was clothed in filigree silver with a crimson silk lining, and silver pomegranates and silver leaves sprouting from its crown. Whenever my father had a franc or two to contribute to the upkeep of the synagogue, he would in return be honored with the reading of the weekly portion from one of the scrolls. I would remain on my feet throughout, kissing his hand as he returned proudly to our seat on the bench.

In summer it was not hard to get up in time for morning prayers; in winter Sahar's voice, booming through the dark, would raise me from my sheepskin. Like Yedida, the storyteller, blind Sahar lived in one of the rooms belonging to the synagogue, earning his bread with the help of some inner clock. It was his business to wake the Jews of Bab Salah Street for *Shaharit*, for *Slihot*, or for any other early-morning business. By the feel of a doorknob or handle, he could tell the houses of his clients. He could tell the time with the help of a clock lodged somewhere in his head. More precise than Uncle Goliath's pocket watch, this clock never stopped ticking:

"Four thirty-five, Laloo." He would bang on the candlemaker's door. "The train for Tunis leaves in three-quarters of an hour." "Up, up, Hamus—twenty minutes past six, the rabbi is waiting for his *minyan!*" He would rap his cane on our lattice window.

Crime and Justice

On Saturday my father and I used to return to synagogue after breakfast, and it was on such a peaceful Sabbath morning that we were standing in a group around Rabbi Ghez patiently answering our questions, explaining why locust is kosher while shrimp is not. Having treated his attentive listeners to a glass of arrack and wanting to offer them a bite as well, he sent his wife up to the kitchen to bring food for his guests.

Tumbling down the stairs, she was back in a jiffy, empty-handed.

"Thieves, thieves!" she squeaked, landing on the last step. "May their entrails burn hotter than my peppers!" She had spent all of Thursday cooking the rich hameen for her family. It had disappeared together with the pot. Neighbors came telling how they had wondered why three fallahs were seated on the roof of the synagogue, ravenously eating out of something. . . . It was on the roof that the pot was found, empty but for a "thank you" of a nature I would rather not detail.

These three fallahs had gotten away with it, but woe to a thief caught red-handed! To begin with, he was only cursed, maybe knocked about by his captors. Soon, however, he would be roughed up by a crowd, women taking off their wooden clogs to give him a good lesson. By the time the *shwaishes,* the sheikh's policemen, finally arrived, the wretch would be ready to confess. The shwaishes, colossi clad in turquoise-colored pantaloons, tunics with golden tassels and carrying curved swords, looked much more frightening than the French gendarmes decked out with mere pistols. Moreover, they rode horses which, harnessed with plenty of brass-studded leather, were no less awe-inspiring than their masters. The tarboosh set straight over their ferociously black brows, one flash of a shwaish's eye was enough to prompt any wrongdoer into surrender, tender his hands to be chained and trudge behind the horses to be brought before the sheikh.

Responsible only to the *Qaid,* highest instance of local autonomous government, it was Sheikh Tlatly who kept the peace in our part of town. Justice of the peace Sheikh Tlatly was the most distinguished Moslem of the neighborhood who, even in his own house, always behaved like a gentleman. Running errands for him I have entered his home more than once, and so I know of what I am speaking. That any man could speak so politely to his family filled me with wonder.

At mealtime his low table would be set with a great variety of dishes which he ate not only in company of his sons, but in that of his wife and daughters too. While our ordinary Arab neighbors simply knelt around the pot to eat their dinner, Sheikh Tlatly's family took theirs cross-legged, the same as Jews. Refined manners can be impressive, but the perfume emanating from everything and everybody in the house was outright perturbing; it made my head swim. From the jasmine flowers scattered over the magistrate's bed to long rows of bottles exuding orange blossom scent, the house was full of gifts competing for his favors. If one knew the right price to pay for his goodwill the sheikh was easygoing on top of being polite.

From a fallah, he expected only produce. Had, for instance, Yussuf and Ibrahim come to blows over a donkey, each claiming to be the rightful owner, then it fell to Sheikh Tlatly to decide which one was the thief. As sure as the moon was going to rise over the sheikh's roof, a shadow would be seen dragging a basket through the dusk, stop at the threshold to his house and knock. A lace curtain would move ever so lightly, the door slide open, just enough to let pass the basket filled with fresh fruit, vegetables, eggs and a hen or two.

"Kindly tell the Sidi Sheikh that Yussuf Abu Amar has brought a little present for his honor," whispered the shadow. After Yussuf left Ibrahim's basket would not be far behind.

Next morning at the appointed hour both warring fallahs would sit on the floor of the sheikh's office who, weighing the evidence presented, would naturally let tip the scales of justice on the side of the heavier basket. If, on the other hand, a man who had been robbed or injured wanted to make sure that his assailant sweat it out in prison, then he had to pay cash.

"In the name of Mohammed . . . I swear on the Koran, I never touched him, a stone fell on his head. . . ." The hands of the accused were entreating the ceiling. "May Allah kill me with the same stone if I ever hurt this man!"

Throughout the accused's earnest protestations the sheikh's dark glasses moved back and forth from the wildly waving hands of the defendant to the nervously drumming fingers of the plaintiff. Stopping the drumming, the plaintiff slowly raised two fingers, meaning:

"Twenty francs for you, Your Honor. . . ." The defendant was still only emptily gesticulating, Sheikh Tlatly decided that he had to be the culprit.

"Liar!" the magistrate thundered in the defendant's direction, then turned to the plaintiff hidden under bandages. "Look at the poor fellow . . . nothing but a nose to speak to . . . Three months in jail will teach you to club heads!" Too late, the accused raised three fingers, at last countering the plaintiff's proposition.

Writing down the sentence, the sheikh sealed the envelope. Entrusting it to the shwaish who led the condemned to jail, he told him to deliver it to the warden. Together with the sentence, the sheikh must have slipped a bill into the envelope, for a few days later the prisoner had vanished from his cell. His disappearance was kept secret while he was sent off to the countryside on an extended vacation. After three months, the jailbird would fly back to Nabeul, not nearly pale enough, but with the sheepish airs befitting someone freshly out of prison.

It was a system which made everybody happy: the injured party got his satisfaction, the offender a vacation and Sheikh Tlatly and the warden a supplement to their lousy salaries. Only a wretch, too destitute to scratch twenty francs together, had to serve his term, and generally having to endure a caning on his naked soles in the bargain.

In the calm Nabeul of those days, serious crimes were seldom committed. To the inhabitants of Bab Salah Street jinn, spirits, devils, demons and the evil eye were more threatening than some miserable thief and seemed more real than an occasional robber from out of town.

Neighbors

If Jews and Moslems lived in peace together it was largely due to Sheikh Tlatly's stick of authority wielded from the other end of Bab Salah Street. To my boyish eyes he was the embodiment of refinement itself. Just to meet his children on their way to Moslem school was an inspiration! Neatly dressed, his daughters' faces were hidden behind small lace veils from the age of five or six. Both boys and girls walked in clouds of perfume.

I never dared to force candy or chocolate on Arab girls. Seldom leaving their homes unaccompanied, they were even shyer than their Jewish counterparts. Only from afar would I watch them play their favorite games in some yard. Mostly it was "wedding." Forming a circle around a stiffly seated little figure wrapped in shawls, supposed to be the bride, the others would invent never-ending verses to some high-pitched, nasal tune, drum on tin cans, and politely pass refreshments, dishes full of pebbles.

Things were changing between me and my childhood friends—Mahmood, Kasham and Abdel Kader. Now when I went to visit their home their growing sisters would quickly cover their faces on seeing me and leave the room. A close-knit Moslem family, the father had contented himself with only one wife, generous, warmhearted Nisria, my mother's good friend. Most of the time her room looked neater than our own; her kitchen, though, was as any other fallah's: a raven-black hole where every pot and pan, every utensil was covered with soot from the open fire. In her black oven she baked heavenly *pitta*, but would never offer me food forbidden to Jews when she invited me to eat together with her sons.

The family was well off. Beside two cows, several sheep and

goats, they owned a number of fruit and olive trees and a few narrow plots of land where they grew corn and vegetables. They were very hardworking people. The children helped with the farming from an early age. But harder workers than anybody else were the two cows. Tied to long ropes, they would patiently stamp up and down a steep path for days on end, hoisting numerous pails of irrigation water from the mudhole which was the family's greatest asset.

My three friends were growing fast. Gone were the days when Mahmood's sleeves were forever shiny with snot or Kasham's trousers, tied under the knee, sagged with fruit filched from his father's trees. Lately they had begun to look cleaner, almost dignified, and they had become more secretive. When I congratulated Mahmood on the occasion of his thirteenth birthday, he blushed. As important an event as our bar mitzvah, it was their time of circumcision, very painful at this age. It was the Arab barber who performed this operation.

Although Mahmood was ashamed to talk about the intervention, it was nevertheless impossible not to notice what had taken place. Mahmood was nowhere to be seen for about a week. Reappearing after that period in brand-new clothes and setting his feet wide apart, it was obvious what had happened.

Not all our neighbors led the well-ordered life of the family of my Moslem friends. Take Tabou, for instance—a Jew dwelling with his wife and children in a sadly sagging hovel propped up on the back wall of our house. From Sunday morning to Friday afternoon Tabou would trot from one end of Nabeul to the other buying and selling used clothes; his sour face, half hidden under a mound of rags, seemed to be everywhere at once. Nobody could say that he did not try. Tabou's star, if he had any, did not shine over trade. One of the poorest Jews on our street, he would come home every Friday with two bottles of wine, regardless of how little money he had earned during the week.

Every Friday evening, at the precise moment my father was chanting the blessing to receive the Sabbath in our home, the hullabaloo started.

"Enough, enough, you camel's paunch . . . you will finish eating the head off your neck!" Tabou's wife could be heard shouting at her husband, who resembled a mean, starved Bedouin dog rather than a camel. His appetite whetted by the wine, he had fallen upon the hameen she had used all her resourcefulness to put together and would not leave off.

"You monster, may your belly burst . . . will you rest only after you have seen your children die from hunger?" she screamed at

Tabou who was cursing drunkenly through his full mouth. Vainly trying to wring the pot from their father's hands, his sobbing sons begged him to stop eating. Every Friday evening it was the same—screams, sobs, curses, and recriminations. When the uproar was finally dying down, doors could be heard opening and closing and the sound of footsteps as the neighbors sent their children, myself among them, to discreetly deposit some of their own Sabbath food at Tabou's hovel.

Saturday morning at the synagogue, scrutinizing Tabou's hollow profile, I would wonder how in the world a whole potful of hameen had entered that scraggy body. Too proud to beg, his wife kept the family going by her wits. I used to watch her at it with great interest. When her door gave a little squeak, I knew she was looking out for a victim. The moment some well-dressed Jewish matron passed by she ran into the street, dragging several of her children behind her. Pouncing on the unsuspecting woman, Tabou's wife spat over her shoulder:

"Poo, poo, poo—Why do you stare at us—haven't you ever seen starved kids before?" she shouted. "Aren't we miserable enough without rich snobs rubbing salt into our wounds?" The stunned woman in vain tried to protest; the exchange turned from sour to acid. Faces flushed and before long two deadly anagonists stood hurling invectives at each other as a circle formed around the contestants. Whether the scene made you laugh, pity Tabou's wife or feel ashamed before our Arab neighbors, "grinding" was a spectacle nobody wanted to miss.

Grinding was our women's very own way of quarreling. Like sparring roosters, they would hop forward, straining their necks until they came face to face. The match would begin. Spitting into her left hand, each woman would rub her right fist round and round in her upturned palm, thus grinding her opponent into an ever mounting rage.

"Staring at others." Tabou's wife was now at it. "Why, haven't you looked in a mirror lately? It's plain to see for everyone that you haven't set foot in the steam bath for a year, you fleabag!"

"Look who is talking!" Although ferverishly grinding, the insulted passerby was not quite capable to keep up with an expert of the caliber of Tabou's wife. "Clean your kids before you open your big mouth. They are crawling with lice. . . . Your husband is the worst drunkard in all of Bab Salah Street!" she retorted a little lamely.

"And yours then . . . who can blame your husband for running after whores if your stinking bed is black with bugs?" (As far as I know there were no Jewish whores in Nabeul.) Strands of hair loosening up over their heated faces, they were going on and on, punctuating the grinding with their wooden clogs and ending up by cursing each other's family. It was time to intervene, but Tabou's wife, tearing at her adversary's opened braid as if to scalp her, had worked herself into such a frenzy that nothing could stop her now, not even the fear of the Lord.

Pulling the kerchief off her own rumpled head she cast it to the ground.

"Look upon me, God, Almighty . . . wherever You are, look down upon my tears and my distress. . . . Pay back the one who caused it!" This was really serious. To stand bareheaded under the heavens calling down malediction could mean sickness and death for the other woman's children and who knows for whom else. People were not laughing anymore, they were afraid. Angrily they turned against the well-dressed woman.

"See what you got for putting Tabou's wife in such a state?" They closed in on her. "Make up with her if you don't want something awful to happen. . . ." The woman, as pale as she had been red earlier, needed little prodding. Fearing for her children's lives she was already imploring forgiveness from Tabou's wife, arranging for a peace offering of milk, eggs, barley bread and chicken to be brought to her attacker's home. Tabou's wife relented. She lifted the curse, and the incident ended in the street as suddenly as it had begun, with both women publicly embracing.

"May your children give you nothing but joy, dear, and my the Almighty forgive both of us!" Tabou's wife blessed the stranger and rearranged her hair.

Tabou's next-door neighbor, widowed in early womanhood and lacking the audacious spirit of Tabou's wife, had brought up her children with the aid of the comité. Her sons were grown now, able to take care of their mother. They had also managed to find husbands for their sisters, for all but Juliette, the oldest. In Nabeul a girl of fifteen was considered of marriageable age. Juliette, with her twenty-seven years, had practically no hope left that someone would still lead her to the *huppa*.

This seemed unjust, for she was neither uglier nor sourer than the next, her reputation being absolutely blameless. So blameless, in fact, that it might have frightened some suitors off her doorstep; not everyone knows how to appreciate a girl who never throws sideways glances, never chats with strangers. Instead of using cheap tricks, she had tried spells and magic to attract a husband, but apparently in vain. She had finished by shutting herself up in her mother's room bemoaning her fate, tears welling up in her eyes every time she looked at her sisters' children. Between her slowly withering breasts, half a dozen charms and amulets were hidden, and others were pinned to the wall. Yet, in spite of all these efforts, no fitting suitor appeared on the horizon.

Every morning at six o'clock, black-frocked Bedouin women would drive their full uddered goats down our street, shouting:

"Milk, milk . . . bring out your pots!" This was the signal for Juliette to rise from her lonely bed.

"*Majali ya koom—majali ya koom—majali ya kooooom!*" (May my new fate rise with me!) Three times her desolate, drawn-out cry soared high over the clanking of the bells, neighing of donkeys and the shouts of fish and vegetable vendors.

Reuben was a distinguished bachelor—an accountant so sought after by his clients that he had found no time for courtship and marriage. On his way to work early in the morning he would sometimes pass through Bab Salah Street at the very moment Juliette's plea was mounting from her window. Neighbors had long become accustomed to her three shouts, taking them as much for granted as the morning crows of their roosters; Reuben's solitary heart, however, was touched by the depth of despair in Juliette's voice. He made inquiries, met her brothers and was invited to the house. In brief, they got married.

The whole street was happy for Juliette. As a wealthy, well-educated bachelor like Reuben would have been an excellent match for any girl, the more so for a twenty-seven-year-old spinster. A little strain of miserliness running through his otherwise fine nature hardly mattered. If he measured his wife's weekly oil and sugar ration, shutting the rest away for fear she might give some of it to her mother, this was only to be expected from an accountant; anyway, Juliette, fondly stroking her swelling womb, took it with a smile.

The good fortune which had at last come to Juliette had bypassed the home of Kraim and his wife Fatmah, an Arab couple living just one house farther down the road. In spite of every precaution, Moslem prayers combined with Jewish magic and Arab witchcraft, their babies had died one after another, leaving Kraim ready to grab at anything, any straw, any stratagem to deflect the eye of fate, even a black pot. Black being the color of bad portent, no Jew would have done what Kraim did, not even as a last resort, but the Arab in his distress put a giant black pot over the entrance to his house.

I cannot imagine where he had found the monster. Hideous and sooty as if it had come straight out of a devil's kitchen, it loomed on the white wall above his door, freezing the glance of passersby with its stark blackness. It was precisely what Kraim had intended when he put it there, to draw people's attention away from his home and his family, catching it in the pot instead, together with the evil eye. I can recall how later new babies were crawling in the yard behind the pot, though I usually looked the other way when I came near Kraim's house.

I was nevertheless mixed up in the vendetta of Bab Salah Street, an event that took place under Kraim's very window. An Arab hawker by the name of Haha would make the rounds of the neighborhood every fortnight, banging on everyone's door to offer earthenware for sale. Although relations between Jews and Moslems were good at the time, ranging from the hard bargaining in shops and markets to the cordial visits between neighbors, there were even then quite a few Arabs who could not stand us. Haha was one of those, of the bony-faced, yellow-skinned kind who could hardly hide their hatred of the Jews, ironically their best clients.

Unlike his master, Haha's donkey was an exceptionally friendly beast, thankfully pushing its muzzle into any hand giving it a pat or a stale crust of bread. Haha did not like it when my friends and I fed his donkey or talked to it.

"Keep away, Jew dogs . . . filthy breed of dirty Jew bitches, I spit onto your faith!" he once hissed through his long, yellow teeth, believing we were out to steal his pottery. Stung to the quick, we walked away in silence. We did not tell anybody about the incident, but resolved to avenge the honor of our mothers and of our religion in our own way.

When Haha entered Bab Salah Street a fortnight later we were prepared. Our friend, the donkey, was trotting in front, carrying two broad baskets full of pottery.

"Bowls, cups, pitchers, strainers. . . . lids for every pot. . . . Pots for every lid!" Wrapped in the hot afternoon haze, the street lay empty; nobody seemed interested in Haha's pots and plates. The only one to open the shutters of her window was Fatmah, Kraim's wife. Seeing that she could not make up her mind between a water jug, a glazed bowl and a painted camel, Haha gathered up all three pieces, passing under the black pot to do the serious haggling in the shade.

My friend Dooha and I had to act fast; getting out of our hiding place, we went to work on the donkey. While I held up its tail Dooha smeared its backside with pepper pulp, which he pushed in with a broomstick. Neighbors continued to bake behind closed shutters; only green flies, buzzing but discreet, were braving the heat; we retreated unseen, waiting for events to take their course.

We did not wait long. Soon the donkey felt the first prickings. It pulled on the rope, neighed and kicked, then, the pepper stinging deeper, threw all fours into the air. Haha came running just in time to see the animal go mad, but with the slow fire at its rear end now blazing, no one could have restrained its fury. Throwing its weight from side to side it broke the rope, smashing the baskets full of earthenware against the walls. With potsherds clattering in every direction and heartrending "he-haws," the donkey danced crazily through the length of Bab Salah Street. Cursing Haha raced behind, leaping like a demon to snatch at an exploding pitcher or wildly wobbling dish. It was no use. Not before every piece of pottery had been broken did the tormented beast finally calm down.

I must confess that Haha's contortions, his horrible curses gave me so much satisfaction that I forgot to feel sorry for the donkey. In any event, the pair never again set foot on Bab Salah Street, Haha telling all over town that it was haunted and how he had seen tiny devils flying amid his jugs and bowls. While in his case the identity of the devils was well known to me, stranger things were happening in our neighborhood, less easily explained.

Sabbath of the Jinn

Shlomo, a Jewish fishmonger, and Rashid, an Arab farmer, had both disappeared in mysterious circumstances, never to be seen again. It was whispered that, lured underground into the dark domain of the jinn, they had married two she-devils, staying downunder of their own free will. Looking at Shlomo's wife now selling the fish in his place the story seemed credible enough. As for Rashid—who knows? He had been a bachelor.

Personally, I have never met a jinni, but my friend Palmidi who once had the opportunity to see one cross his room gave me a good description. It was a small fellow, he said, not higher than a footstool—his body, arms and legs resembling sticks, his head shaped like a prune. Shooting out of a crack behind his parents' bed, he had run to the opposite wall and disappeared through it without a sound.

Having the touchy creatures living their shadow life under our very feet, we had to be careful, especially at night when they were on the move. If at bedtime I sometimes forgot myself, letting drop a shoe or a schoolbook—any heavy object—I would hurriedly apologize.

"*Ha shakum smalah!*" (In God's name, watch out!) was the traditional formula to warn them. Animal or human blood dripping to the floor or worse yet, boiling water, injuring some prune head could infuriate the jinn beyond warnings and apologies. The perpetrator of such gross negligence was in danger of being tricked down into the underworld never to be seen again.

Be that as it may, so long as we kept our jinn well disposed we had nothing to fear. Ready to go to any length to ensure her family's safety, my mother knew how to please those little people. Every Thursday afternoon, rain or shine, she would send me over to Hafzeah's shop to get two sous' worth of incense. Throwing it on the hot coals after sundown, she would then swing the tripod very slowly, letting the sharply scented smoke thoroughly penetrate into every corner of our room. It being Sabbath eve in Ashmedai's kingdom, my sister and I would on those Thursday nights be constantly reminded not to shout or laugh out loud so as not to offend his people.

It also was the night my mother spent in the kitchen cooking the hameen, and my father came home from five days of wanderings to prepare for our own Sabbath. He did so at the steam bath where the Jews of our neighborhood, sprawling amid the hot vapors, came to sweat out a week's dust and toil and unburden their troubles to each other.

Before leaving for the bath my father used to hand me his peddler's pouch, telling me to sort out his earnings. Lately, however, he had conferred this honor more and more often on my little sister. Outraged and unhappy, I felt that an important privilege had been taken from me, the firstborn son, to be bestowed on someone who, besides being a girl, was also much younger than myself. To add insult to injury, he also let her have some pocket money, while I had to rub my eyes with raw onion to squeeze out the tears that might bring a few sous out of my softhearted mother's pocket.

The missing earrings and silver coins, those I had swapped for birds with my cousin, must have caused my father's change of heart, a fact I would not easily admit.

Anyhow it was now my sister who was emptying the contents of the pouch, lovingly counting bills and coins, piling them into little heaps, separating broken chains from single earrings, anklet parts from colored gems. Jealousy was choking me—to hell with my father's money, to hell with the Sabbath of the jinn! Starting a war dance, howling and making faces, I whirled my sobbing sister's neat little heaps and piles into a mess, the uproar bringing my dismayed mother running in from the kitchen.

She was still pouring groats and sugar in the corners of our room, trying to appease our invisible guests, when my father returned from the steam bath, all pink with drops glistening in his reddish hair. Lying facedown on my sheepskin, he asked my mother to give him a massage. It was the one thing my mother disliked doing for him, the more so since for only a little extra money he could have gotten a more professional one at the steam bath.

"Please, my husband, have a heart . . . I had my washday. Fraji is teething . . . I had to carry him around all afternoon . . . with the cleaning and the cooking my arms feel like iron . . . my legs like butter. . . ."

"Fallu will have to do then," my father grumbled into the sheepskin. "Come on, son, tread . . . trample . . . step it up!" My bare feet treaded the muscles of his back, then I jumped up and down on his hairy calves. The harder I tried to hurt him the more my father seemed to enjoy it. "Harder, Fallu, harder . . . can't you do better for my tired back?" Letting all my weight come down in a furious jump I could hear the bones crunch, but still no moan. "That's a little better, not bad, not bad . . ." was all the response I got for my pains.

Hugging his knees with satisfaction, my father sat up. As always when he had had a good week, he sent me over to Nisria to ask whether she would let him have a rose from one of the bushes she grew in empty oil cans on her roof. Sticking the bloom behind one ear, he then pulled a bottle from under the bed and poured himself a glass of wine.

"I am going to tell you a story, a steam-bath story." He turned to my sister and me. "One that really happened. What did your mother say just now when you made a racket?"

"Shhh . . . they can hear you from Tunis to Rades!"

"Right, listen then. I will tell you what the saying means.

"Many years ago, maybe a hundred, a big woman came from Rades to Tunis and started working at the steam bath. They called her Leah. Strong and healthy, she rubbed, patted and kneaded her clients so thoroughly that she was soon in favor with the greatest Jewish ladies of the capital.

" 'You wait and see,' she would say in her pleasant, deep voice as she wrapped some grateful lady in her towel, 'The day Leah dies there will be an outcry—such a cry people will hear it from Tunis to Rades!' The ladies, of course, would try to be gracious.

" 'Why, Leah, you should not talk like that . . . you will live to a hundred and twenty, . . .' but aside they would mutter: 'Who does she think she is, King Solomon's daughter?'

"For over forty years Leah worked on the finest ladies of the capital, the wives of rabbis and big merchants until, finally dead of old age, she was brought to rest in her hometown, Rades. Imagine everybody's consternation when during burial rites it was discovered that Leah was a man! Like fire in a storm the news raced from Rades to the capital; the cries of shame and outrage could be heard from Tunis to Rades.

"Now you know where the saying comes from and can sleep easy," my father finished with a yawn. "Shhh . . . don't laugh." He pointed to the floor and with that last warning retired to his own bed.

Once or twice a month word went round that Bahla, the wife of Shooshoo, the shoemaker, would give a performance in the evening, cordially inviting all her neighbors' children to assist and to bring their mothers. At nightfall dozens of boys and girls would push each other into Bahla's house where her daughter, Kockeena, was assigning the guests their seats on the floor. After everyone was seated, Grandmother Hadara would serve dried melon seeds to those who behaved.

Some mimic gift drove the irrepressible shoemaker's wife to spend her days improvising costumes and her evenings rehearsing endlessly. Ready for a show, she would stretch a sheet over the dirt-plastered arch separating an alcove from the main room of her house, placing a kerosene lamp in such a way that the audience in the dark part sat facing an illuminated screen.

"Silence, silence. . . . First act," Kockeena announced into the cracking of the melon seeds. "Friday morning at the market."

The parade began. A donkey neighed past, wriggling long ears, the shadow of a camel swayed by in proud silence; then came a monkey noisily eating peanuts, curling and straightening its tail, the snake charmer playing the double flute to the undulations of his rattlesnake. Wild applause forced Kockeena to declare an intermission, even though the most thrilling number was reserved for the end: a shaggy-haired giant, swaggering on stilts, was growing over the whole length of Bahla's sheet.

"Roola, Roola!" some of the smaller children screamed, running out into the street as the beast's shadow fell upon us, grunting horribly. The rest of us—shouting, stamping and clapping so hard that we would return home with hoarse throats and sore hands—were the most appreciative audience that Bahla, as a true actress hungry for acclaim, could wish for.

Bahla's theater was a marvelous pastime for winter evenings; hot summer nights, however, were spent out in the open. Packed close together, our low-ceilinged houses would store up the afternoon heat to turn to ovens in the evening, driving their inhabitants to seek relief in the street. On footstools, doorsteps or simply squatting on the ground, Arabs and Jews sat chatting together in the dark, hoping that a little breeze might waft in from the sea. Moonlight smoothing out the walls made the stones look much cooler than they felt. Clustered in the brown shadow of Bahla's doorway, the women were exchanging recipes.

"Two cups of rye, half a cup of olive oil, three spoonfuls of honey and a handful of raisins . . ." My mother's gentle voice was giving away her golden rule for raisin cookies while whispers and quickly suppressed peals of laughter came from the dead end of the alley where girls were confiding secrets to each other.

The men were seated in the middle. The Jews among them were boasting of big sales and incredible bargain buys which they had made in bygone days, while Arabs spoke of tomatoes grown to the size of watermelons and hens that would lay eggs with golden nuggets. At bedtime they had got around to fearful stories about ghosts and a string of miraculous escapes from the clutches of the demon Obeita. The women, on the other side, would rather hear tales about less ferocious spirits, the little jinn, and devils guarding vast treasures in the entrails of the earth.

Here is the story of the Jew Moshani's adventure with the devils as remembered by his granddaughter Hadara, Bahla's mother. Stretched out on the warm ground covering so many secrets, I was counting the stars as her brittle voice captured my attention.

Many years ago when the Turks were masters of Nabeul, my grandfather Moshani used to live in the old house behind Ibrahim's olive press. My grandmother, who was with child, felt one evening a strong urge to dip her bread in olive oil. Everybody knows how children can be marked for life if their mothers' fancy for some snack during pregnancy was not promptly satisfied. Hurrying to oblige his wife, Moshani spilled a few drops of oil and tripped on the slippery liquid. The heavy bottle hit the floor, breaking into pieces. A poor Jew, my grandfather was so upset at the sight of his precious olive oil seeping into the ground that he completely forgot to apologize to the little people underneath.

Half an hour later Moshani was getting ready for bed, sadly reciting the *Shma Yisrael,* when someone knocked on the door. An elderly Jew stood outside, well dressed and pleading urgent business.

"Sidi Moshani?" he inquired. "Excuse the late hour, but I have to leave Nabeul early in the morning. Since your wife may need new shoes I wanted to see you first. Thought you might take a look at my collection of embroidered slippers, the prettiest any woman ever set eyes on . . . they are in my suitcase around the corner. . . ." This being my grandmother's first pregnancy my grandfather, still very much in love, followed the stranger to a nearby courtyard. He had never noticed it before. He was then led down a steep flight of steps into a dimly lit, seemingly empty cave. Only then did he grow suspicious. Wanting to turn back, my grandfather Moshani found to his consternation that the entrance had disappeared.

"Where are you, Sidi Jew, and where are the slippers?" he asked into the gloom.

"No slippers for you, impudent earthling. . . . What do you expect, a prize for clumsiness?" a voice croaked near Moshani's knee. "Have a look at my head . . . see what you did to me?" The little voice was whining now. Rubbing his eyes Moshani saw to his amazement that in place of the distinguished merchant a tiny devil stood beside him. Lifting a lantern he pointed to a big bump on his prune head.

"Throwing bottles around without so much as an apology . . ." the creature hissed through a slit serving him as a mouth. "Well, we shall see what the king will have to say to this . . . follow me!" Sheepishly my grandfather Moshani trailed the devil and his lantern through a succession of tunnels, too dumbfounded to get out a single word of justification.

Gradually the tunnels were opening up into underground thoroughfares, brightly lit by candelabras wrought in the strangest, most intricate loops and meanders. A town came into view, its tiny houses shining in every imaginable hue of metal, inlaid with enamel designs of a kind my grandfather had never encountered anywhere. The geraniums, the trees and bushes in the garden were all grown from colored glass. Ruby lanterns suspended from ropes of pearls were strung over the market where he- and she-devils on their sticklike little legs were scurrying among the booths. "Everything was glittering and gleaming," my grandfather used to mutter when I kept asking what wares were laid out in that market, and how could he set in words things, shapes and colors nobody had ever seen before? Anyway, he would add, he had to keep his eyes on the ground because those little people were running between his feet. All he needed was to crush one of them. Didn't he have trouble enough with that devil with the bump?

Walking on, my grandfather Moshani and his captor arrived at last at the palace of Ashmedai, king of the underworld. And what a palace! It was crystal with a gate guarded by two black beasts with tongues of fire. My grandfather was so blinded by the diamond walls in the throne hall that he was still blinking when he was brought before Ashmedai.

"Hey, over here, Jew Moshani!" ordered the king's second in command. "Let's open the trial. Of what crime do you accuse him, Kafkafuni?' he asked, turning to the devil who had been holding his prune head from the moment they entered the hall.

"Your Honor," he whimpered, "this Jew Moshani almost killed me . . . dropped the heaviest bottle in all of Nabeul on my head and did not find it necessary to apologize," said Kafkafuni, his thin voice rising with self-pity.

"Moshani, this looks serious . . . what have you got to say for yourself?" King Ashmedai's left eye was twitching, the other kept my grandfather transfixed. Realizing that if he wished to see again my grandmother and the light of day he had to speak. Moshani opened his mouth with effort, but no words came out.

"Here, drink, Moshani. Maybe it will loosen up your tongue." Feeling sorry for both the frightened Jew and wounded Kafkafuni, King Ashmedai offered my grandfather a cup of coffee, nodding encouragement so vigorously that his crown tottered on his horns. "Sidi Jew, we mete out justice according to the law. If you are innocent and tell the truth, no harm will befall you."

Sipping the coffee, Moshani began to mumble until the words came rushing out like water:

"Your Honor . . . Sidi Ashmedai, Your Majesty . . . believe me, in the name of God Almighty you have got to believe me. I did not do it on purpose! My wife is pregnant, grace to God, and wanted bread with olive oil. I was afraid the child would be marked with an olive, or even several, God forbid. . . . In my hurry to pour the oil I spilled a few drops, slipped . . . and dropped the bottle! I am a poor Jew, Your Majesty, and that cursed bottle should have lasted me to the brit milah. The sight of all that good oil going to the devil was too much for me. . . . I completely forgot about your people! It never crossed my mind that someone else might have been injured in the accident.

"You have no idea how it hurts me to see that terrible bump on your head, Sidi Kafkafuni," my grandfather now turned to his accuser, "I am deeply sorry for the suffering I have caused you, please forgive me if you can. . . ."

Touched by my grandfather's obvious sincerity and remorse, King Ashmedai wiped a tear from his evil eye. Even dried-up little Kafkafuni looked somewhat mollified.

At this point Bahla coming from the kitchen with a steaming kettle, interrupted her mother's story.

"Well, what next . . . how can we go to sleep if you don't tell us what happened to Moshani?" We insisted on hearing the end of the story as Bahla stood pouring sweet black tea over mint leaves in everybody's cup. It was too dark to see the smile on Hadara's old face, but there was a chuckle in her voice.

"Can't you make up the end yourselves? Had Ashmedai not released my grandfather then I would not be here to tell you this story, my daughter Bahla could not have treated you to tea, and my granddaughter Kockeena would not be sitting over there giggling.

"The unborn child of the story was my mother's oldest brother whose birth brought luck to his parents. Not only was he born without birthmark, but with the gold that King Ashmedai gave my grandfather as a parting gift he later built the house in front of you—the one I still live in with my family."

Satisfied with the ending, we dispersed for the night. Lying down on my sheepskin, skin side up for cooling, I turned very softly on my stomach so as not to hurt anybody's feelings in the underworld.

Approaching Bar Mitzvah

Next morning on my way to school I met Dooha, Palmidi and an orphan called Reuben. Friends since the days Rabbi Parienti had tried to drum the Hebrew alphabet through our thick heads, we had gone on to French school together, sharing the same interests. These were seldom connected to our studies, although all four of us were bright enough, even inventive when it came to devising tricks and adventures. This morning Dooha had come up with a plan. He was fed up listening to grandmother stories. He wanted to bring some life into our evenings.

After dark, as the men were grouping for their nightly chat and the women, hands still wet from dishwashing, were venturing out on their doorsteps, Dooha and I stole silently away. It was feeding time for the hungry cats of our neighborhood—the hour after dinner when they went prowling over the refuse heaps at the end of the alley, searching for fish heads.

Our ropes were ready. We were lucky; the big black male we had set our hearts on was busily cracking bones, so noisily that he did not hear us draw near. With the first throw I caught him. He clawed and scratched like a demon. Still we managed to fasten the long rope around his neck, tying a rust-eaten, discarded oil can to the other end. Then we let him run.

The only way open to the frightened animal was the access to Bab Salah Street filled with Jews and Arabs quietly chatting in the dark, sipping after-dinner tea. Fur bristling, green eyes blazing through the night, it shot howling past the stunned assembly, jumped madly up the walls with the can clattering behind. As screaming women rushed into the nearest houses, the men unashamedly bolted the doors from the inside for what was the use of standing up to a demon? This one ghost at last either found an exit or had broken the rope. Calm soon returned to our neighborhood which for many evenings afterward lay deserted. The "Roola" of Bab Salah Street became the talk of Nabeul—evidently a Roola of the most vicious kind with long black hair and eyes as big and green as unripe lemons. Dooha and I kept quiet, knowing full well that, had we been discovered, our prank would have earned us the beating of our lives.

Although nobody ever got wind of my worst plots, there came a period in my life when I got one thrashing after another. The older a culprit at venerable Talmud-Torah school the harsher was his punishment, and I belonged now to the big boys.

I had learned to read Hebrew fluently, knew by heart prayers, psalms and long portions of the Scriptures, still my thoughts would mostly dwell on food during our lessons. One day Rabbi Parienti caught Dooha and me eating bread we had filched from the kitchen. Since there was no time to invent a story, we were made to confess. Rabbi Haim Parienti flew into a rage. Assembling our class to witness the retribution, he sent for two tall students of the Gemara, sixteen-year-olds, to bring out the *fallaka*—that ancient scourge of Nabeul's thieves. Grinning, the pair let the gracefully curved wooden bow dangle before our eyes, then made us lie down on our backs. Forcing our kicking, wriggling legs up, they each grabbed one of our feet, pushed them together between the wooden bow and horsehair rope, and began to turn it. Unmoved by our moans and pleas, they twisted the fallaka until the rope cut deep into our flesh—at which point Rabbi Parienti took up the old myrtle cane.

It was I who screamed loudest, I remember, being of heavier build than my friend Dooha. Since my foot stuck out more than his, I got to feel the full brunt of the two dozen strokes dispensed on our naked soles. Was it the shame of it or the pain? From that day on, trying to avoid the fallaka, I never stole again.

My father's punishments were less refined. Every time he would catch me cheating on prayer time or skipping Torah lessons (French school by contrast could not matter less to him), he would simply and soundly thrash my backside with his belt. He did so with the majestic leather belt fitted with pockets and studded with copper nails he had bought for his wedding. To this day he does not know it was I who caused it to disappear. Naturally I had taken that belt into deep dislike. Every time I found it lying around I spat on it if nobody was present.

One morning I saw my father take off his mark of authority, hang it on the wooden wheel over the well and disappear into the stinking shed that served our neighbors and us as a toilet. Having fed our chickens at the far end of the courtyard, I stood leaning against the wall, right next to the long pole we used to take our wash off the line. It gave me an idea. Silently and from a safe distance I poked the belt at the wheel until it gave a little, sliding slowly to a point of no return—plop—into the well. My triumph was shortlived; my father went the same day to buy himself another belt which, if less imposing than the old one, was just as damaging.

It was a few weeks later at the height of summer that my father and I were returning home from Sabbath morning prayers. Though I felt an irresistible urge to run down to the seashore, it appeared that he had other plans for me. As I was now in my thirteenth year, approaching bar mitzvah, he wanted me to spend the holy day of rest (which had never seemed as hot and sticky to me as that day) in the bosom of my family, reading the Torah portion of the week.

Opening the Bible for me, he prepared to take a nap. Yawning, he took off the new belt and his Sabbath slippers to sprawl out over the big mattress.

At first I dutifully read aloud part of the weekly portion—the story of Balaam's ass complaining about the unjust beatings by its master. Soon, however, I was softly talking nonsense to my crested lark, keeping one eye on my father's tired face. The moment he seemed to have dozed off, I grabbed my fishing string and sneaked toward the door. When it came to anticipating my intentions, my father's senses were incredibly sharp.

"If you try once more, Fallu, I will make you see the Sabbath stars at noon!" he promised without opening his eyes. Deeply sighing, he turned over. But not before the first gentle snores began to part his lips did I take another chance at escape.

My customary luck did not smile on me that morning. Opening with a malicious creak, the door made my father jump up, furious. To make things worse my mother, who sometimes would try to protect my exposed backside with her own body, was visiting my ailing grandmother. Though my father used the belt without restraint, nothing lasts forever; he tired and his rage subsided. Having made me kiss his hand and ask for his forgiveness, he barred the door with the big wooden bolt, then lay down again, this time determined to stay awake. After a while the heat and his great weariness got the better of him. Worn out from a week's wanderings on hot and dusty roads, haggling from morning till night with stubborn peasants, he fell profoundly asleep.

Having at last learned my lesson, I had become more cautious. Bent over the Bible I bided my time, patiently watching a fly on my father's skullcap. It was crawling toward a bushy brow amid beads of perspiration, paused to rub its tiny legs one against the other, then crossed over to the broad-bridged nose. My father did not stir under the tickling touch, giving me fresh hope. The fly meanwhile had ventured onto his mustache where it was blown up and down by a series of snores so powerful they tore my father's mouth wide open.

That plucky little fly steadied my nerve. As quietly as possible I unfastened the bolt and opened the door. Once outside, I put my knife through a slit in the wooden panels. I could tamper with the bolt which I pushed back to its original position; once more the door was closed from the inside, seemingly untouched. Running down to the beach as fast as I could I joined my friends. The wales on my sore backside burned fiercely at the first contact with the water; soon however, playing in the waves, I put any thought of the homecoming in store for me out of my mind.

Returning home at noon my mother, my sister Esther, and little Fraji, finding the door shut, knocked and shouted.

My father arrived to pull the bolt, satisfied that it had remained in the same position he had left it in. Still, as the family assembled around my mother's weekly masterpiece, the tureen with calf's foot, chick-peas and tomatoes steaming on the rush mat, I was missing.

"Where is Fallu?" my mother wondered. "Wash your hands, Fallu, darling. The hameen will get cold," she called into the court-yard.

"Better seek him under the bed, that's where your darling son is hiding," my father mocked her. "Gave him a sound beating. Had to put him under lock and bolt, the infidel . . . soon to be bar-mitzvahed and wants to run off fishing on the Sabbath. Grace to God he still has a father to keep him on the right track. . . ." Having talked himself into a fresh rage, he threw aside the planks covering the pantry under my parents' bed.

"Don't you worry," my father said, "he will come out soon enough . . . would to God he were as ready to give thanks for His blessings as he is to eat them!" Furiously groping through the dark space in between bags with beans and sorghum and behind pots with pickled fish, he came up with empty hands.

I seemed to have vanished into thin air, but there was one more possibility. Was I hiding in the deep nook above the heirloom drawer behind the Passover dishes? In his rage my father forgot how much good money he had paid Haha for the crockery stacked up in the niche, the precious utensils we used once a year only during Passover week.

Gripping his measuring rod, he raised himself on his toes, thrusting it among the clinking dishes as my mother tried to check his hand. Even now he did not swear.

"Fallu," he shouted. "If you don't come out immediately I will break every bone in your body. . . . With these my own hands I will hang you head down from the ceiling! What sin have I committed, oh my God," he ranted on, poking deeper amid cups and plates. "What have I done that You have given me that mule for a son, jumping like a mule, eating like a mule?" The sound of shattering dishes was the only answer. Now even my father was beginning to worry. "Enough is enough, Fallu. . . . Come out now and I promise that I will not punish you. . . . I give you my word on Rabbi Eliahu's holy name that I will not touch a hair on your head!"

In the silence following my father's plea a frightful thought had begun to take shape in my mother's mind. Shut up, beaten and humiliated I must have looked for an escape, any refuge away from my parents' home. Since the door had not been unlocked where else could I be but with the little people from down under? Finding more human kindness with the devils than with my own father, I might already have sold them my soul, resigned the sunlight and disappeared forever!

At first my mother froze, then she began to scream.

"What have you done to him . . . where is my son?" She shook my father, out of her mind with fear. "I want my son back . . . give him back to me!" she wailed throwing herself to the floor. Beating her breast, tearing her hair and scratching her cheeks in wild mourning, she was scaring my father to death. Standing before her, helpless and stony-faced, he must then and there have made a vow for my safe return. From that fateful Saturday on, in any event, he never again raised his hand against me.

With my mother screaming and moaning and my father praying, neighbors alerted my uncles who arrived in all haste. One of them, Uncle Said, had seen me playing leapfrog on the beach. I had even asked him for a drink of water, he said. His words did not seem to sink in, so he took my father's arm, drawing him in the direction of the shore. Dusk was falling and he was running in a stupor when an all-too-familiar figure entered his field of vision—a boy with caked curls, shirt and pants standing stiff with salt and legs green with seaweed.

My first impulse was to run. Instead I remained riveted on my boulder, amazed to see my father closing in on me with open arms and sobbing.

"Blessed be the Lord, King of the Universe, who showers His debtors with kindness!" he prayed, hugging me tight. Throwing kisses to the rising moon and a few pale stars just becoming visible, he wrapped me in the folds of his Sabbath mantle, and so we walked home, close for once.

My mother received her reborn son as if I had come home from years of wanderings and starvation. At dawn she ran to light candles on the tomb of Rabbi Jacob Slama whom she believed responsible for my miraculous return. How I had passed through a bolted door remained a mystery. Whenever I was questioned on the matter I gave myself sleepwalker's airs, saying that I could not remember.

When my bar mitzvah was imminent, my father, in an attempt to double his resources, lost all his savings.

From sure signs in the weather and the behavior of various animals, Arab farmers had predicted a drought. Tootoo the seer also had found in her water glass strong indications for a rainless season. Because of these omens, my father and my mother's brothers speculated on an apparently foolproof dry winter. Putting their money into a joint business venture, they bought beans, barley, wheat, corn and dried peppers, waiting for prices to rise.

Something nevertheless must have gone wrong with the interpretation of the signs or else plans in Heaven had to be changed at the last minute, for in September clouds were beginning to drift inland from the sea. In October they towered brownish-gray over the leaden waters, the sky discharging itself in a continuous downpour from the beginning of November to the end of February. Wheat and barley, competing for which was going to sprout faster, shot out of the rain-drenched soil. Peppers and tomatoes grew like trees. Prices fell and so did my father's face.

Ordinarily coming home from a week's work with a jasmine sprig tucked behind one ear, a bottle of wine under his arm, even smiling if he had closed a good deal, my father was now always moody, finding fault with everyone. He took my mother to task as if she were answerable for the rain or for the attitude of her brothers who laid the blame for their losses on my father's mistaken drought predictions. The family squabble acerbating, my uncles did not even assist at my bar mitzvah.

By contrast, it was my father's brothers who helped us. Uncle Said bought me a shirt and trousers, Uncle Moshe gave new shoes, and Uncle Goliath, the rich man of our clan, paid for my prayer shawl and phylacteries—the most expensive items needed to be initiated into manhood. The ten francs my good Aunt Kooka had saved for the great event I used to invite my younger cousins to an outing on Ahmed's horse cart, treating them to sweets and cigarettes. Boys, even small ones, who were guests at a bar mitzvah were allowed to smoke. A tail of snot-nosed youngsters followed me for the three days of celebration wherever I went, begging for halvah and cigarettes.

They were just kids, I thought. Putting a distance between them and myself, I felt very grown-up after a ceremony that had given me a somewhat premature place among the ranks of men. Rabbi Hai synagogue had been cracking at the seams with well-wishers, packed with bearded men in prayer shawls who had come to hear my first reading from the Torah scroll. Uneasy with so many eyes on me, I had held on to Rabbi Parienti's silver Torah pointer; the stiff index finger of its tiny hand wandering from word to word steadied my mind. I read so well that my mother, outside on the women's balcony, shed tears of joy over me, and my father's broad breast swelled with pride.

Promises
Kept and Broken

After three days of reveling, no cigarettes were left. My little cousins dispersed, while for me adult life began in earnest. No more French lessons, no more Talmud-Torah school. I was asked to choose a trade.

I made up my mind to become one of Nabeul's many Jewish shoemakers. Their sewing machines had always seemed more impressive than those of the tailors. Passing by old Huani's shop, I liked to listen to the rattle of the chain, look at how he cut and hammered leather into shape. Before going into peddling which was more lucrative, my own father had been a baboosh maker. Pleased that at least in the choice of my craft I wanted to follow in his footsteps, he went to make an agreement with Huani. My apprenticeship was to last three years during the first of which I would solely be nursemaid to Huani's five small children, outcrop of his second marriage to a much younger wife. Any arrangement seemed better than school. Also, Huani, experienced in his craft, was a good master. Rearing several generations of children had made him a patient man. The grandchildren from the first set were older than the five sons and daughters his young wife had given him!

His small ones were from now on in my care. Besides watching them play in the street I had to feed them, dress them, wash their faces and wipe their noses. On the whole they were nice children, and we became very attached to each other. Building castles from mud and pebbles we spent many pleasant hours together until one of my charges disappeared as happened regularly. Rushing off in hot pursuit, I would find one or two of the others missing when I finally returned with the lost sheep.

Since food was not included in our arrangement, Huani and his wife never once invited me to their table. I was, however, welcome to finish what was left over in the children's cups and bowls. In addition, the baker would let me have six brioches for the ten sous Huani gave me every morning to buy five, the sixth consequently going down my gullet. My master's grown-up children and their offspring constantly dropping in, the shoemaker had found a simple way to nourish the whole clan. Twice a week, year in, year out, he used to bring a cow's head from the butcher's which, cleaned and axed into fractions, made a great variety of stews and soups.

At home it was my mother who saw to it that I did not go hungry. But since I was growing fast and spending my days running after my charges when I was not at the beach, my naturally healthy appetite had become bottomless.

"Eat, my son, eat," my mother would smile at me, marveling at the amount of hameen I was able to get down. "May you rise as the evening star, high above the crowd. . . . How happy we will be at your wedding. How proud to bless your son at his brit milah. . . . Poo . . . poo . . . poo . . ." she added, spitting seven times over her shoulder to ward off the evil eye. Installed on the far side of the Sabbath tureen, cross-legged, dignified and too full to swallow one more bite, my father was meanwhile watching me clean out the pot in silence. Seeing that I was not going to stop eating of my own accord, he finally cut short the meal by reciting the blessing, then stretch the leftover bread and his right hand for my sister Esther and me to kiss. (My brother Fraji was still in the cradle.)

Since the bedeviled Saturday when my parents had believed me lost forever, my father was trying hard to keep me in the fold by other means than beatings. His efforts redoubled after my bar mitzvah.

"Who was officiating at prayers tonight, Rabbi Ghez or Rabbi Yitzhak?" He would examine me before letting me have my dinner. "Who besides you was laying phylacteries at Rabbi Hai synagogue?" he would ask me in the morning, having me spell out the names of nine other Jews who had prayed with me before inspecting whether the imprint of the phylacteries' leather strings was still visible on my forearm.

His suspicions were well-founded. The promise I had given Rabbi Parienti to go to synagogue at least twice a day was long forgotten. My working hours left me only the very early morning or very late afternoon to roam the beach. I felt pent up. Although I still kept birds, my little feathered friends were powerless to rival my old flame, the sea, holding me in the grip of a renewed and boundless passion. Had I not rested my eyes on the moving immensity of its waters, not filled my ears with the rushing of the surf for a whole day, I could not fall asleep for longing.

To skip working hours with the flimsy excuses of my school days was now out of the question, so I had to cheat on prayer time for my needed recreational forays to the shore. It did not take long to improvise a set of tricks allowing me to change synagogue for the sand dunes whenever I felt like fishing, swimming or just sea gazing. At the hour other Jews would take their prayer books out of the drawer, I would kindle driftwood on the beach, licking the grilled fish sticking to my fingers as the sea swallowed the last of the sun's orange wedge. Rolling up the string I used for fishing, I then turned homeward, passing by one of the synagogues in town to inquire after the names of those who had just finished praying there.

"At what synagogue have you been praying . . . who was there with you?" my father greeted me with the usual questions.

"Kikki, the grocer; Menahem who sells guts; Shooshoo, the shoemaker; Tabou, the glutton; Abraham, the greengrocer; Harera, the stutterer; Laloo, the candlemaker; Moshani, the pepper merchant; and Boodmah, the fisherman. They were the minyan at Rabbi Hai synagogue, Rabbi Ghez officiating . . ." I spilled them all out in the same breath.

With the first rays of light, my yearning for the sea awoke with me. Putting on my beret I would pick up the embroidered bag with my prayer shawl and phylacteries and left as if to go to synagogue. Farther down the road, however, I would hide the bag in a nook of an old wall, running to the beach for a morning splash. Wiping seaweed from my legs and pulling at my beret to conceal strands of wet hair, inside an hour I was back in Bab Salah Street carrying the bag I had recovered from its hiding place. Then, before returning home for the fatherly inspection, I wound the phylacteries so tightly around my arm that they left a deep mark.

My father was puzzled. Somehow my tanned countenance, sunbleached hair and ebullient mood did not seem to fit in with the kind of life I was supposed to be leading. The less he could find fault with me the more suspicious he became.

Through most of the day while watching Huani's children, I would dream about the sea. What color would I find her in the afternoon? I would wonder. What fish, fixing me in round-eyed surprise, would be dangling from my hook? Changing from pink to orange and to blue, octopi would make love with entangled arms, porpoises laughingly jump over each other. Why should I pray in a dark, stuffy synagogue, I asked myself, where only words written on parchment and the narrow skylight reminded me of God, when a thousand marvels were waiting for me in the waters? Wishing a good evening to Huani's wife, I directed my steps straight toward the sea.

A springtime thunderstorm was in the air, a battle in the making over the horizon. Like a ruffled canary, the sun was glaring through the sulfur-colored edges of the clouds. In imminent danger of being swallowed, it was splashing the blackness of the waters with a harsh gold and yellow trail. As I came down to the beach all the gold was gone; a few last spatterings of red and the first lightning flashes were taking over from the drowning sun.

Fish bite well during an approaching storm. From the moment I had thrown my line it would not stop jerking. Standing in the twilight on my favored boulder I pulled in one fish after another, oblivious of the rumbles above me or raindrops thick as chick-peas bursting on my skin. Only after it had become so dark that I had to wait for lightning streaks to see what I was doing did I finally set out for town, wet and happy, the fish threaded on a piece of string hanging beside my prayer bag.

By now it was pouring. When I arrived at Rabbi Hai synagogue I saw to my consternation that it was closed, the congregation having long since finished the evening prayers. Luckily I found a housewife ready to buy my fish for half their worth before hurrying home, soaked through and through.

"Where have you been, Fallu?" my father asked out of the dark end of the room.

"Where should I have been? At evening prayers . . ." I bluffed, dripping water all over the floor. "Had to wait for the rain to stop. . . ." As he, however, questioned me more pointedly than usual, I smelled a rat as I gave out a list of fictitious congregants.

"A pity to waste your spittle . . . keep your dirty lies inside your godless mouth!" my father cut me short. "Rabbi Ghez has not set eyes on you for three weeks . . . same story everywhere . . . and I, fool that I am, running through the rain to look for you in all the synagogues of Nabeul! But let me tell you one thing, Fallu . . . If I have vowed not to lay a hand on you I did not promise to feed an infidel! Upon my life, Meesha," he raged on in the direction of my mother, "if I catch you giving this faithless animal one single morsel of bread, I will cut your tresses to the roots! Let him scrape leftovers from the plates of Huani's children like the dog he is."

I must say I felt like one. Just like a wet and hungry mongrel with bent head and pinched tail I went to lie down in silence. In the warmth and comfort of my sheepskin's curls I reviewed the evening behind closed eyes: rain clouds eating a fierce canary-bird with yellow feathers, lightning zigzagging on black, oily waves, flashing on the scales of my silver fish. Forgetting my hunger I fell sound asleep.

Awaking to a cloudless, clean-swept sky, whiffs of north wind whistling through the lattice window aroused fresh yearning in my empty stomach, only partially calmed by the breakfast my good mother brought for me to eat secretly in the donkey shed.

"I will yet make a good Jew of that faithless dog . . . and if I have to drag him by the ears to synagogue . . ." my father muttered through his teeth as he pushed the bag with the prayer shawl and phylacteries into my hands. For several days in a row I went docilely to morning, afternoon and evening prayers, until the following Sunday when my father had to leave for his peddling tour.

Looking back upon my childhood, I now can see why my father, tirelessly trying to make a good, observant Jew out of me, has so little to show for his efforts. Having the fear of God knocked into me with so much determination I had become more fearful of my father's fist than of that from above, and on this occasion, as on many others, I took to my old ways as soon as he rode away on his donkey.

XVII

Moonlighting
on the Waterfront

Three Friends

My friends had also quit school to be apprenticed: Palmidi with a carpenter, Dooha with a barber, and Reuben, the orphan, with a shoemaker like myself. Unable to stay inside four walls for more than a few hours at a time, we would slip away to the beach whenever we could make it, meeting by the railway station at the old water-pump. A small treasure lay hidden under the grille covering its gutter: all the coins that had fallen out of the pockets of overzealously pumping fallahs and camel drivers. The gutter had helped finance most of our childhood sprees, though lately only Dooha's fingers were still thin enough to push through the rusty bars, fishing out a few sous or even francs to buy us drinking water at the beach.

A simple mode of communication kept the four of us informed of each other's movements. The muddy liquid oozing from the gutter into an irrigation ditch was clogged with cactus leaves upon whose thorns we used to stick our tokens. Seeing for instance Dooha's or Palmidi's stone pinned between the spikes I knew that they were already on the shore, waiting for me.

A slender sandstone splinter of nondescript hue was Dooha's mark, pointing as obliquely as my friend's thin nose. Always doing as he was told, quiet Dooha got tips as a barber's helper, the first among us to jingle honestly earned money in his pocket. The last time I heard from him, he had a barbershop somewhere in southern Israel where he lived with his family.

Red, round and speckled, Palmidi's stone was but a pale reflection of my bosom friend's true coloring and dimensions: he had flame-colored hair, a freckled, blue-eyed countenance and a belly so formidable that no belt could contain it. Puffing and gasping for air, he was forever slowing down our pace. Yet so much unexpected strength was hiding behind all that fat and gentleness that Palmidi's favorite pastime was to break planks with his bare hands. The Palmidi clan were powerful eaters; his father had to hold two jobs, working as a customs' man by day and watching a factory at night.

Palmidi had a whole bunch of sisters, and in later years he would nudge me to marry one.

"Fallu, go ask my father for Habiba, she swoons every time she sees you passing," he said at least a hundred times. "My father has promised her a cupboard, a table and two chairs for her wedding and you know my mother loves you since you were a child." As much as I would have liked Palmidi for a brother and as much as kind, blue-eyed Habiba reminded me of him, I could not bring myself to take her for my wife. As it happened I was to marry Fortuna who, although unreasonably jealous, is a good wife and after every child got her figure back. On the other hand the Palmidi sisters, so sweet and tender, knew no limits in their outward spread. Most members of the family died in early middle age as did my friend. Having emigrated to Israel he made such a good living as a carpenter that he ate and drank himself to death.

With Palmidi's premature departure, I have come to Reuben, our leader, whose end was to be still sadder. His token, a black flintstone, was sharp and many-sided. In his dark way perhaps even handsomer than myself, Reuben was also smarter, a wily, wiry tomcat always landing on his feet. Had he been born under a luckier star I am sure he would have become an inventor or a politician—maybe a great party-boss. But instead, a curse seemed to hang over his life right from the start.

His father died when he was in the first grade, leaving his mother with five small children and the impossible task of bringing them up on the pittance that the comité doled out to needy widows. So Reuben, the oldest, at an age when other children warm the school bench and play games, had to feed and clothe a family, which he did with the aid of stealing. It was uncanny how during all his years as a provider he was not caught once; the lucky beggar could wiggle out of any scrap, but when it came to important decisions, like choosing a wife, for instance, then Reuben's star stood always over hell.

Although the story of his marriage is for later, let me just say that he was trapped into wedding a loose woman. Only one daughter and great shame resulted from this union. With his next wife and more daughters, Reuben settled in Israel where he became a heavy drinker. His eyesight was affected, and when he had gone completely blind he ended his own life by throwing a live wire into his bathtub.

The Prickly-Pear Path

Meanwhile, roaming the beach together, we were too busy enjoying the present to think much of the future. The rotting cactus leaves in the ditch had found their use; day in, day out our tokens would be pinned between their thorns, my own, a piece of mulberry wood shining smooth and brown among the three stones of my friends.

Behind the ditch the leafy gate opened to my private Garden of Eden, a narrow dirt path closed in on both sides by a mile or so of prickly pears, running in a straight line to the sea. Once inside, surrounded by its humming, crawling twilight world I felt free, out of reach of fathers, rabbis and Huanis. Throughout spring and early summer, the cactus hedges were in bloom; their thorny leaves with graceful yellow tulips soon turned into an unending supply of fruit that although sweet and juicy, was dangerous to handle. To pick it while the sun stood high would have been folly since the hot fruit, falling off easily, might shower the picker with a profusion of tiny, penetrating darts. With my hands protected by a rag, I would pluck them only early in the morning, cooling them in seawater before peeling off the skin and refreshing myself with the core at the beach.

The path was teeming with insects buzzing my ears, whirring by on their way to collect nectar from the cactus flowers. Getting stuck in the sap of decaying leaves, they were easy prey for the fork-tongued lizards shooting in and out of the tangled growth. Sun rays finding a passage through the tall, dense hedges lent sudden brilliance to the blue-, white- and lemon-colored wings of butterflies caught in their milky stream. The prettiest I would catch and later press them between the pages of my copybooks where they continued a dried-up existence spread out over French exercises and multiplication tables.

Better than butterflies I liked the songbirds nesting in the gray-green jungle, fluttering from thicket to thicket. What could be cuter to look at than their young seated in a row on the edge of some large, fat cactus leaf, noisily demanding to be fed? One parent, trying to avoid the hair-thin darts on the fruit's reddish skin, would cautiously peck a hole through the pointed end of a prickly pear while the other would push chunks of flesh into one gaping beak after another.

Here and there where the hedge thinned out a little, an Arab became visible, working his vegetable patch or cornfield. Asked politely for a tomato, a pepper or an ear of corn, he would usually let me have one. It also happened that I helped myself to some produce with only the permission of his scarecrow. Redisappearing behind the hedge, I continued my advance amid the sweetish smell of honey and rotting fruit until the path suddenly ended. The cactus walls got lost in sand and I took a deep breath of salty air.

Ramoo the Innkeeper

The sea—one day a gray-blue mirror, the next bitingly green with snappish little snow-white crests—stretched out before me. In stormy winter weather it turned black, hurled itself hissing on the rocks in front of Ramoo's beach café, froth sputtering as high as the house. The only building on the beach, Ramoo's place was intended mainly as an inn for fishermen since bathers with money to spend were a rarity in these parts. On those days, high seas made the moss-covered rocks too slippery to throw our lines from. In hot weather, hungry and thirsty after swimming, we went to work for Ramoo.

His paunch making it hard for him to bend over, he was always glad to let us sweep the floor, stack bottles, carry groceries or wash the dishes. Our pay consisted of bread and water, first and foremost plenty of water.

"Shhh . . . shhh . . . beat it, you rascals!" He would at first try to shoo us away. "All day swimming in the sea like *goyim*, eh, and when you are hungry, you remember Ramoo . . . but I am not the comité, you know. Here one has to work for one's food. . . ."

"We want to work, we want to work," we cried, one seizing a broom, another beginning to peel garlic.

After an hour or so of drudgery our thirst, mainspring of all that zeal, having become unbearable, Ramoo would at last set an enormous water jug before us, ordering us to drink it up to the last drop.

"Want to eat me out of house and home, eh, and the hair off my head into the bargain . . ." he grumbled, adjusting the skullcap on his bald pate. "But first you drink!" Not before the jug was completely empty would he bring us some bread with olives and tomatoes. Who could get them down after all that water? As usual we got the better of Ramoo, letting the liquid trickle in the sand the moment the innkeeper's eye was turned on a paying guest, burying the traces of wetness with our toes.

Amid clouds of flies, vapors of fish fried in garlic, and smoke of grilled shish kebob, the diners were seated around true tables, Ramoo's pride. Pushing a stool under a client's backside with the authority of a maître d'hotel, he would then shove a table right under his nose with bravura and a lot of screeching, put a hand on his shoulder and whisper about a very special dish he had reserved for a patron of his importance. Guests knew they had to enter the game if they wanted to eat well.

"Whatever you propose, Ramoo . . . your cooking is *manna* from Heaven . . . in Tunis they talk about nothing else . . . They say that your restaurant is the choicest on Cape Bon. . . ." Beaming with happiness from one pink, fat ear to the other Ramoo would wrap a slightly soiled towel over a bottle to reward the flatterer with a glass of wine.

Those liking entertainment with their food could make a fool of him.

"Have you heard, Ramoo . . . how awful . . . have you heard what Dadoosh has been trumpeting in the market?" Someone trying to play a joke on Dadoosh was needling Ramoo. "Donkey meat, he said you serve . . . rotten fish and watery wine . . ." Ramoo's face turned dark. When innocent Dadoosh, having walked all the way from town in order to eat a good meal, appeared in the doorway he did not even let him enter.

"Son of a son of a bitch, seven times cursed liar!" he received stunned Dadoosh. "Enter here and I will kill you. . . . Who do you think you are, you nobody, you double-tongued slanderer? The like of you I can buy any day and without notice, together with your dirty rags, your squint-eyed wife and all your mangy breed. . . ." The comfortably installed eaters were choking with laughter as poor, hun-

עיר נאבל

ארם זולה במחשבות של שדים עושים לי חדרה מזמינים
מביאים יהודי עם חליל ותוף מסובבים עליו ראשי מכאים הרבה אנשים
פהם ויצמים כל מיני בשמים ויוצא עשן מכל הצבעים ומזמרים כן על
ומזמינים בחדרה שרוקרת על יד המיטה בריקיר ומזמרים על
ושערותיה יורדת על פניה ולמחרת האדם רועש
מהמיטה כריא בלי מחשבות קם

אשה זונה ביער נאבל שמה חפסיה בת שמונים נמוכה והולכת עם מקל
מוכרת בחנות קטנה כל מיני בשמים ותרופות מעשבים יונים בתוך
צנצנות בקבוקים וקפסאות יש לה דברים של מזלות ושל חתונות
גם מבקרת חולים ועושה מסושים עם מלח
וישתיה של עשבים נותנת לחולים.

Warding Off Evil by Rafael Uzan

ערב פסח: מנקים את הבית, שורפים את החמץ, אופים מצות
שוחטים כבשים ומתכוננים לחג, ובליל הסדר יושבים אל שולחן
ערוך במצות ויין, אומרים עבדים היינו לפרעה מלך מצרים:
וירדפו מצרים אחרי בני ישראל ויט משה את ידו על הים וישובו המים ויכסו את הרכב וההפרשים לכל חיל
פרעה ובני ישראל הלכו ביבשה בתוך הים ויכוים להם חומה מימינם ומשמאלם ויראו את המצרים מתים:

The Seder by Rafael Uzan

Moonlighting on the Waterfront by Rafael Uzan

The Camp at Menzel-Temime by Rafael Uzan

The Prickly-Pear Path by Rafael Uzan

gry Dadoosh, vainly clamoring his innocence, had to retreat with empty stomach.

Being of generously proportioned build and loving to cook for others as well as for himself, one would think Ramoo was open-handed; he was, on the contrary, one of the most tightfisted men in Nabeul, stingier still than my own father. Besides his pocketbook he had one more sensitive spot—an inordinate fear of anything reminding him of death. Anyone wanting to tease him had only to mention a funeral or recite some line from a psalm to make him furious.

One day some steady patrons, irked by Ramoo's bragging and diminishing portions, decided to play a trick on him. The tallest among them sneaked into Ramoo's private room. There the prankster lay down on the floor, setting up two candlesticks brought for the occasion, one near his head, the other by his feet as one does for dead bodies while his companions kept Ramoo busy in the front room. He then lit the candles and, covering himself with a white sheet, stretched out stiffly on his back.

Ramoo, needing to go to the toilet, had to pass through his room. As he opened the door there was a short silence followed by a great howl as he banged it shut again. Still screaming he ran out of the house and into the dunes.

"How did he get there . . . how did he get in . . . how can a dead man walk through a closed door?" He was so upset they feared he was going mad. His patrons had to pat his back and fan his face for half an hour until Ramoo was composed enough to tell what he had seen.

The "dead" man in the meantime had left as he had come, through the toilet window.

"Come on, Ramoo, be a man and have another look, you must have been dreaming. . . ." The guests brought him back into the house. "Me dream, when did you ever see me dream? I tell you, I saw him lying there stiff as a stick the same as I see you . . . but how, for God's sake, did he get in there?"

"If it was no dream then maybe you went a little bit crazy, just for a moment . . . it happens, you know . . . Open the door and you will see, the room is empty . . ." the men led him on.

"I am no crazier than you are, never have been and never will be . . .I tell you I saw him with these eyes," he repeated obstinately, with both forefingers pulling down the lids of his black goggle eyes to make his point. Each of the men had a hard time to keep a straight face.

"We bet you five hundred francs nobody is in there, no dead and no living . . . Let your help go in if you are afraid." Ramoo accepted the bet, sure of winning. The door opened on an empty room. As he was born a Frenchman and had served in the French foreign legion, the innkeeper paid his debt of honor like a man: five beautiful, crisp one-hundred-franc notes. But the winners, honest fellows, did not take the money. On the other hand, they were not brave enough to tell him the truth. Our colossal cook and hero of the foreign legion had an extra entrance built to his toilet to avoid entering his room!

After having gained some experience in handling Ramoo, my friends and I would keep him boiling—or simmering—over a low flame according to the circumstances: whether we were hungrier for food or amusement. Seeing him fumble with his large key in the money drawer, we crept up behind the counter to startle him.

"Here they are again, the hungry pigs . . . why must they always come to me? Why can't they feed on pebbles?" Letting him ramble, Reuben and I, keeping our voices low, were meanwhile gravely talking to each other.

"What do they want, those dogs? . . . Ramoo has a heart of gold, why do they say such things?"

"What, what . . . who says what?" Ramoo interrupts us, greatly troubled.

"You see that fishing boat?" Reuben pointed to a tiny blob on the horizon. "There are three men on board. Yesterday they broiled some fish here on the beach, cursed you with every bite . . . couldn't repeat it. It was too horrible! But we gave them such hell they won't dare to set foot here again. . . . Don't let them in if they come to your place. . . ."

Grateful for having intervened on his behalf, Ramoo gave us some food, swearing as he sliced a big cucumber:

"Dirty dogs . . . come here to drink my wine and afterward they go and spit into the bottle. . . . May they never come back from out there!" Looking out over the open sea he shook both his fists.

Having eaten, we were once more ready to tease:

"Have you heard the news, Ramoo? No, you haven't? How is that possible? The whole town talks about that poor young million-aire . . . his name has slipped my tongue . . . died suddenly this morning, never was sick for a single day. . . ."

"What . . . what are you saying?" Ramoo did not want to understand at first.

"He died!" we now shouted into his ear. "That young million-aire . . . He died this morning!"

"Go to the devil and remain down there . . . out . . . out I say, may you go to the same place as that confounded millionaire!" Naturally we were back at the restaurant the next day, hungry and thirsty, chanting the praise of Ramoo's golden heart as we cleaned his terrace.

Sometimes, when we had stayed at the beach until late, we would see a carriage draw up, Ramoo run out, bowing deeply as he furtively led some sheikh or effendi in flowing white to the inn's upstairs room. Because the Koran forbids the drinking of alcoholic beverages, Jews and Christians were not allowed to sell arrack, wine or beer to their Moslem fellow citizens. But for the rich, of course, one made exceptions.

The Fishermen

Ramoo's steady guests, however, were fishermen, most of them Arabs, a number of Italians and here and there a Jew among them. To me all of them looked alike with their skin tanned to leather by sun and salt—features as thick and crumpled as my father's peddler's pouch. The wooden bottoms of their boats, burning sand and wet boulders had pounded their feet into giant squares, toughened their soles into boards which they liked to show off walking barefoot over broken bottles. Ready-made shoes were never big enough for them, and as the fishermen could not walk either to mosque, synagogue or church on naked feet they had to be fitted with sandals cut out of outsize slabs of rubber tied with leather straps. Strutting barefoot into the beach café they were treated like royalty so long as they paid cash, indulged the owner's little whims and showed their appreciation for his hot cuisine.

Downing fried mullets with pepper stew, they quenched the resulting fire with a deluge of arrack, their elbows propped up on Ramoo's tables. Staring straight through you and beyond the wall, their eyes were forever fixed on some remote horizons and endless waters full of fish. Silent people, they were Ramoo's best listeners, never interrupting his tall stories. If they did sometimes talk it was of nothing but the sea, the weather and the fish. There was no fisherman who had not at least once narrowly escaped drowning. No year passed without the sea taking a victim to avenge her plunder. Still I have never seen one of them turn his back on her or the treasure hidden in her green depths, holding the same fascination for them as does a deck of cards for poker players.

"Once a fisherman, poor to the end of days," they said in Nabeul. How often, before sunrise, had I helped them push out their wooden boats into the surf—some setting sail, some having to rely on only their arms to row them out on the open waters. Sounding their dreams for good omens, they would start out buoyed by hopes that by evening had mostly turned to bitterness and curses when they landed with half a dozen fish in their net, not even enough to appease their hungry families.

All of that they took in stride, awaiting the one great day when the miracle happened—when they came in drunk with excitement, their small boats almost sinking under a load of jumping silver. For a few days they behaved as if they were the richest men in Nabeul, bought casks of wine and cans of oil, distributed bread and cake to all their friends, including me. After a week or so of lavish spending they would go back to being poor men, cursing the sea and waiting for their luck to turn.

My friends and I were on good terms with the fishermen. Wading through the shallow water with the boat's rope tied around our waists, we used to help them tow along the shore, receiving some of their catch for these and similar services. Each of us contributing the ear of corn, the pepper or tomato from the fields, we would gather driftwood to light a fire, the smoke attracting some fishermen to join our circle.

The fish, delicious without so much as salt and pepper, were crackling in the flames and darkness was falling. Having spat the last fish bone into the sand, Tony crossed his legs and, putting both arms around his knees so he could rest his head, made ready to tell a story. The son of Italian parents, he was more talkative than ordinary fisherfolk. Staring into the dying embers he began:

Once there was a poor fisherman who caught few fish. Bringing in his net on a stormy afternoon, he found it to be heavier than usual: a big fish with brilliant colors was wriggling in the mesh, beautiful enough to be fit for the table of a king. Stringing the fish on a raffia rope, he heaved and pulled until he finally arrived with his load at the palace gate where two tall eunuchs barred his way.

"You, fisherman," shouted the king who had observed the scene from his window. "That fish over there, is it a male or a female?"

"I don't know and I don't care, haven't yet opened it," answered the fisherman. "Only want to sell it." The king ordered the man in, and as the fish was opened on the marble top of the royal table, they found its belly to be full of eggs.

"It's a female!" exclaimed the king. "I'll take it . . . ask any price you want. I will have it prepared for my queen of whom I am so jealous that I let no male fish or poultry reach her table. . . . She rides a mare, all her servants are women and her guards are eunuchs."

"Hee, hee, hee," a thin giggle rang through the kitchen. The fish, greatly amused, had begun laughing. The king was not amused.

Indignant that a dead fish dared mock him, he turned his pique on the fisherman:

"Either you tell me on the spot what it is I said that is funny enough to make a fish laugh or you will die!" he hissed through his teeth. "All right," he added as the fisherman remained silent, "I'll give you one month's time, but if you don't come up with a good explanation before four weeks have passed you will have to choose between the rope and the sword."

Deciding to withhold the sad news from his wife and their only child, the poor fisherman walked home with hanging head, too depressed to be alarmed at a certain change having taken place in his daughter's appearance during his absence. Alas, after a few days had passed he could not help noticing her altered shape, understanding to his horror that she was with child.

"Oh, God," he cried. "Is death not punishment enough for my miserable sins? Must I also see this shame?" Sobbing, his daughter claimed her innocence, swearing on her mother's life that she never had so much as kissed a man.

Innocent or not, her womb grew by the day instead of by the month. Not until her birth pangs had started did she remember the pink powder, which she had once tasted, in an old box on the shelf.

"That's it," she moaned. "It's the pink powder that has made me pregnant. . . ."

Out of all her roundness she bore the tiniest son, not bigger than a man's hand. Swaddling the newborn, the fisherman's wife almost fainted as he sat up on the table and began to talk:

"What's the matter with this family? Why does everybody look upset? . . . Why are you so sad, Grandfather?" The tiny boy turned to the fisherman, cowering in a corner. "Maybe I can help you?"

"Nobody can help me, least of all a newborn baby," sighed the fisherman. "How would you, of all people, know why that blasted fish had to start laughing? My four weeks are almost up. I thought about it day and night and cannot find the answer." At last he poured his troubles out before his family, trying to prepare them for the worst. Again the newborn intervened:

"Grandfather, I have an idea," he said. "Don't worry, I will save you. Hide me inside the hood of your bournous and take me before the king."

What more have I to lose? the fisherman thought to himself. He put on his bournous, took the child and went to the palace where the king was waiting at the window.

"Got my answer?" the king shouted as he saw the fisherman approach.

"Not me, I am not good at words, but I brought someone to talk in my place." With these words the fisherman reached into the hood of his bournous and to the king's amazement came up with a baby in his palm.

"Sit me on the table in front of you and take off your crown," the little one addressed the king, who was openmouthed and nearly toppling from his throne with wonder. The crown, much too wide for the child's head, came to rest on its shoulders. Nevertheless, the tiny boy seemed satisfied.

"I will tell you the fish's secret now," he smiled, "but first you must take me to the queen's bedroom. Give me your hand. . . ."

Hand in hand the king and the tiny boy passed the honor guard saluting a crown seemingly walking on the floor. When the two arrived in the queen's bedroom, however, they found it empty.

"Roll back the carpet!" commanded the little one's voice from behind the crown and lo and behold if they did not find a trapdoor concealed underneath the pile, a secret boudoir underneath the trapdoor. . . . And who do you think was in bed there?

Almost finished with his story, Tony rested for a while, looking out at the moon's broken sickle rocking on the waves.

"Well, it was the queen, of course, with one of her many lovers," he continued. "Although very upset at first, the king knew at least why the fish had laughed so hard. Making the little boy heir to the throne, the king married the fisherman's daughter . . . and lived happily ever after. . . ."

Tony fell silent. It was too late for another story, but he promised a still better one the following night if we agreed to come early the next morning to catch some cuttlefish for him; their many arms, cut into pieces, made the best bait to attract bigger fish. Picking up our wet clothes, the four of us regretfully retreated through the dunes to where the crooked leaves of the prickly pears lined the way back to town.

Marvels from the Sea

Gone were the songbirds, butterflies and bees of my lighthearted afternoon walk in the sunshine. Jutting tall and forbidding through the darkness, the cactus walls now looked downright unfriendly. One way or another I had to get home. With only the new moon for a lantern and here and there a firefly, I slipped back into the gloomy tangle, glad to have my friends for company. More company than I had bargained for: on one side frogs welcoming us with dismal croaking, on the other, crickets exercising their hind legs in strident unison. I wondered how the birds in their nests and lizards in their holes could sleep through it all. Stronger than the smell of fish and smoke still clinging to my body, the night scent of the cactus flowers combined with the honeyed perfume of overripe prickly pears made my head feel heavy.

Shadowy rabbits were hopping through the dark. I could make out spikes, then a whole hedgehog, watching out for its old enemy, the snake.

"Sheikh bait, sheikh bait . . ." Reuben called out a warning, pointing to a viper poised motionlessly with its little head held high, ready to pounce on a field mouse. Snakes had never attacked me; I was more uncomfortable with the hollow "hoo-hoo" coming from a nearby tree.

"Look," whispered Palmidi, and there it was, sitting on the branch of an almond tree—a white owl with black specks shining through the night. Pulling him with me, we ran until my heavy friend was panting so hard we had to stop and let Dooha and Reuben catch up.

"Did you see it?" I heard myself breathe. Ever since I could remember, my mother had told me to be wary of owls.

It seems that a very long time ago a young girl, unaccompanied by her mother, went to the steam bath and was raped. In her grief and shame, she would not return home. Wandering around in despair, she prayed for help from Heaven.

"Dear God," she begged, "change me into an animal and let me take revenge!" Her plea was heard by the Almighty. Answering her prayer, he changed her into an owl and gave her back the pretty white dress she had worn to go to the steambath. Showing herself only at night, she will fly out to seek revenge, singling out little boys to poison with her deadly spittle or by default she would deposit her venom on their clothes. To keep her away my mother used to seal broken lattices with rags. No one in his right mind in Nabeul would leave a baby boy's diapers to dry on a clothes line after nightfall.

The owl we had seen sitting on the almond branch must have been a male bird, for we arrived home safe and sound, only very late. My mother (my father was away on his peddling tour) was waiting for me in the street.

"Fallu, my son, what did you do so late at synagogue, was it hard to find a minyan?" She put an excuse into my mouth. "Come inside now. I kept your dinner on the coals."

The next day a series of soft knocks on the lattice window woke me before daybreak, Dooha signaling me to get up.

"Where are you going in the dark, Fallu?" came my mother's voice out of the big bed. We were a fortnight before New Year.

"To say the prayers of forgiveness," I lied, proffering my prayer-shawl bag through the bed curtains in an effort at sparing her feelings. "I shall be back in time for work."

Hiding the bag as fast as I had pulled it from the drawer and equipped with my fishing string, I pushed with Dooha through the goat- and cowherds that with the first rays of light were trampling down Bab Salah Street. Armed with short brooms black-robed Bedouin women kept after them, scooping up the droppings, hoping to buy bread for their children with the few sous a basketful of dung would get for them from some farmer.

As we passed the old pump, Reuben's and Palmidi's stones were already stuck among the cactus thorns. Coming out of the prickly-pear path, we saw a sea so calm it looked as if the Lord had poured a giant can of olive oil over the waters—a marvelous day for catching cuttlefish! Crouching together on a rock Palmidi's carrot head and Reuben's black one were bent over the crevices into whose shallow rivulets fish will swim in search of a breeding place. Scanning holes hidden by seaweed, cracks covered with moss, four pairs of eyes were straining to find a female cuttlefish. Be it ever so small, the moment we could lay hands on one it would then do the work for us, luring the big males we were after into its many-armed embrace.

"Here . . . I see one!" In his excitement Reuben forgot to keep his voice down. Rocketing in the direction of a hole the cuttlefish stopped for a second to spurt out a cloud of ink, backtracking a little before trying another flit to safety. The blurring tactics were in vain. We knew its tricks. Out it came, short arms helplessly dangling through the net, ball-like eyes blinded by daylight, plain and brown, its beautiful colors snuffed out at the first contact with the air. In no time we had the cuttlefish hooked to a string and back in the glimmering flow, walking it through shallow channels like a dog on a leash. At last, sensing romance, it flashed its dazzling color signals, its back turning from yellow with purple stripes to pink and blue, then red and green, finally pink again.

Attracted by the belle's fireworks, a big male had come into view. He opened his eight little arms, she stretched out hers. When they were well interlaced we flung the pair out of the water. After one more catch, we let the female fish paddle to freedom, Tony paying us two francs for the males which, translated into sunflower seeds and peanuts, was a fortune.

Swept onto Nabeul's shores by summer seas, the flat, oval bone of the cuttlefish, used by goldsmiths to mold fine jewelry, was another source of our income. There was not much of anything we had not learned to trade—even a bottle full of hailstones I once sold to a grocer, telling him they were a first-class remedy for burns. After a storm we would walk the shore for miles, eyes fixed on the sand, searching for jetsam and flotsam, a ring, a spoon or knife, but mostly coins that winds had shifted on top of little sand drifts.

Generally, ordinary coins—some of them were thick, green ones, circled by characters nobody could read—were not negotiable. They were similar to those bearing the flimsily clad likenesses of goddesses my grandfather used to find in the myrtle valley, dating from the time of the Phoenicians or their conquerors, the Romans, who had given our town its name, Neapolis. From my grandfather Rafael I must have inherited the gift to unearth coins where others came up with rusty bottle-caps, a flair that later helped me through the first years on the meager but ancient soil of Israel.

For all of the twenty years I worked as gardener in the Galilee I never met with one of the demons that people Nabeul's underground. Israel's sacred soil, on the other hand, abounds in skeletons, coins, seals and pottery. Since I never came upon artifacts in the sands of Nabeul, it must be true what the old fishermen were saying, namely that Neapolis was swallowed by the sea and Nabeul was rebuilt farther inland in its place. They also said that on calm days one could see deep down under the water the ruins of a town: hewn stones that must weigh many tons and a huge gate covered with studs.

Constantly the sea threw up new marvels. Brownish pebbles—shaped like eyes and with a hole for the pupil—were considered lucky; the tail fins and vertebrae of big fish were used to ward off evil spirits. Coral and a rare, diminutive white shell were the surest bet for prosperity. The most sought-after harbingers of good fortune, however, were the square, widely traveled copper nails used in shipbuilding.

Who could resist paying a franc or two for a lucky boat's nail? Whenever my friends and I were in urgent need of cash we would wander northward where, in a shallow bay, lay the skeletal remains of a ship. We would work for hours to pry some such nail from an oaken beam. Three of these were strung in a row over my parents' bed, revered because they bore witness to the greatness of the Almighty's creation hidden in the deep.

New Adventures

My First Train Trip

On a fine Saturday in late summer my father gave me one of his not-too-frequent smiles:

"Tomorrow you and I are going on a trip to Tunis. You're big enough to be of some use; you can help me carry merchandise. Huani will be only too glad to be rid of you for a while."

Too excited to fall asleep, I turned for hours on my sheepskin. In all my thirteen years I had never been to the capital, I had never been out of Nabeul but for the pilgrimage to the grave of Rabbi Fraji from Testour.

Palmidi, the only one of my friends who had been to Tunis, had come back with such incredible stories that we were sure he had made them up. So there I lay trying to conjure up a capital, turning and twisting in the dark, painting unknown views before my open eyes until they finally fell shut.

"Up, up—trains do not wait," my father's voice reawakened me almost immediately. "We still have to go to morning prayers." Having kissed the mezuzah on the doorpost, we recited the prayer for voyagers, then were on our way, toting an assortment of empty baskets to be filled with bales of cloth we hoped to get on credit.

How I used to envy the fortunate allowed onto the wagons drawn by the puffing monster engine. Now, at last, I was on one of them. I sat glued to the glass pane in the window, letting Nabeul glide out of sight and the whole world race by. Where on earth did all those goats and camels come from? There seemed no end to waving shepherds nor to the coastline we were following as it took the train three and a half hours to cover a distance of thirty-five miles. Mightily whistling and trailing smoke, the train stopped at one small town after another where the houses, bare of Nabeul's red pepper strings, looked naked in their blueness.

The last station was Tunis. The platform was bustling with more farmers and their cattle than in our Friday market. Unloading a batch of bicycles from the freight car, grandly uniformed officials were overrun by sheep; their loudly swearing fallah owners tried hard to push into the same car, all to the cackle of a hundred hens jerking their little heads out of a mound of baskets. Views such as women in short dresses freely conversing with men in suits, excessively white collars and ties, were less familiar. I could not help gaping at Moslem beauties under silken kerchiefs, painted black eyes smiling over equally black lace veils. How much prettier they looked than the women of Nabeul who would not cross the street unless wrapped up from head to toe in plain brown, or, if they were Jewesses, in white fabric.

Still more than by the elegant ladies of Tunis, I was impressed by the size of the roof spanning the railway station—an iron sky sheltering tracks and trains, milling crowds and panting engines flexing their muscles for the next race. Out in the street I was prepared for the height of the buildings but not for their colorful fronts, the cleanliness of the sidewalks or the smell of Lysol and chlorine hanging in the hot air. It was so hot that I was afraid my sandals might get stuck in the melting asphalt so I ran most of the way.

I do not remember the names of the relatives that gave us food and shelter on this occasion, nor can I recall any of their faces. I was completely absorbed by the view from their window, opening on a thoroughfare straight above the wires of the tramway. Fascinated, I waited for the sparks flying from its hissing tail as it screeched around the corner. This was my first acquaintance with electricity. Another novelty to me was the row of shop windows across the street, one of which in particular attracted my attention. Two men and two women were grouped inside that window, but hard as I stared from my lookout they never changed positions nor would they move a limb. Why were those four standing so stock-still and shut up behind glass for everyone to see? Was it some kind of French punishment, for French is what these people looked like. My father told me they were only manikins but even after we had gone down into the street where I could inspect the quiet company from close up I still suspected something fishy.

We were approaching the port where my father's supplier had his warehouse.

"Who is that?" I asked in amazement. Brandishing a myrtle wreath at the heat-blurred sky, a huge green woman stood towering over the square, and as if that itself were not strange enough she was half naked into the bargain.

"Watch out where you are going!" said my father angrily as I tripped over his feet. "Don't you remember what the Holy Scriptures say about idols?" He dragged me along, but now a church came into view, the most beautiful building I had ever seen. Ignoring my father's nervous tugging I stopped to look at the cross-topped steeple, taller than anything I had imagined. Yet rather than this formidable and forbidden sight, it was the pigeons that made me gasp in astonishment, swarming all over the square, pecking their way among the rows of beggars clogging the entrance to the heathen sanctuary. Suddenly my eardrums fluttered, the air whirred with wings. At the thump of a crutch the whole flock soared up as one, spinning like a flag around the belfry.

"Why have I been given a son more stubborn than my donkey?" Exasperated, my father prodded my ribs with a still empty basket, violently pulling at my hand. He kept grumbling as I followed with my head turned backward, trying to catch a last glimpse of the birds.

In Nabeul pigeons were precious, kept either in cotes or cages. Out in the streets they would not last five minutes. How was it possible, I mused, that the beggars had not eaten these for dinner long ago?

I was still pondering this question when we arrived at the cloth-merchant's warehouse, stacked to the ceiling with bales of muslin, satin and brocade—all imported from France. The beauty of the many-colored silks and velvets took my breath away. For a moment I felt sorry that I had wanted to become a shoemaker. Since he special-ized in village weddings, my father chose only the brightest satins and the coarsest lace.

Pink being the hue preferred for the dowries and wedding dresses of dark-skinned fallahs' daughters, pink it was to be. One bale after another was spread out before us. Pink with blue bouquets and yellow bows. Pink strewn with lilac wreaths and the greenest of green leaves. Flesh color dotted with big golden dandelions and shell pink scattered with dainty silver sprigs. Peachy pink with white. And rosy pink with cream. They all went into our baskets. For the more adventurous among the brides-to-be we added some lengths of shiny orange, ruby-red, grass-green and violet. After tiny cups of coffee had been passed around to close the deal, we were back in the street.

Slowed down by the heavy load, I was relieved to see the sun setting, the asphalt under my tired feet feeling like solid ground again.

"Father," I probed cautiously, "is that sidi cloth-merchant a Jew?"

"Of course he is. Couldn't you see so for yourself? There was a mezuzah on his door. He is a Gorni, one of those who came over the sea from Italy hundreds of years ago. They never settled in Nabeul, but here in Tunis they are the richest and most powerful among the Jews. To do business with them we are good enough. To let us marry into their families . . . never!"

"But, father," I was coming to the point, "drinking his coffee bareheaded . . . how can he be a Jew?" Granted, his fabrics were beautiful enough to bewitch any woman, his coffee strong and sweet, but was this sufficient reason for my father dealing with a renegade? "Father," I began again, "why do you buy from a Gorni, then, a Jew who does not cover his head?" At last I had him trapped.

"He is a grown man and I am not his keeper," explained my father with unusual tolerance. "One day he will have to account for his actions to someone higher up than me. . . . Besides he is the only one who gives me credit."

On our way back to say evening prayers with our relatives my hopes to catch another glimpse of the pigeons, the church or the green lady were not to be. My dutiful father, tired as he was, took a detour where I only saw a brown bronze general seated on a horse.

A Shopping Spree on Doomsday

The day after, once more watching Huani's offspring, I had to answer so many questions about the capital that I was hoarse by the time I left work. Reuben, whose circumstances would not permit him to stick his nose beyond the outskirts of Nabeul, met me to get a firsthand account of the big city. He had the perfect remedy for my sore throat, he said, but to get at it we had to pass through Madame Guillaume's garden. Seeing no connection between my throat and the flower garden of the recently deceased headmistress of a French girls' school, I nevertheless was sure that resourceful Reuben knew what he was doing.

A dog growled, the maid of the departed eyed us through the window.

"My teacher, Maître Mauricet asks if you could perhaps spare some roses. It's his wife's birthday . . ." Reuben addressed her without hesitation.

"Well, go ahead, cut a few sprigs, but don't touch the yellow ones. They used to be her favorites. . . ." The Arab servant wiped away a tear. To take the girl's attention off the garden and because I was truly hoarse and thirsty I asked her politely for a drink of water. Slowly sipping, I leaned against the door with one eye surveying

Reuben opening his penknife to cut a length of garden hose, with the other eye admiring the deceased Madame Guillaume's salon, especially a glass case full of books standing at attention. It was hard to believe that the imposing headmistress, her hats flowing with violets and veils, should have disappeared forever from the streets of Nabeul. The French poodle, which used to pull her along on her outings, sat now in front of the bookcase, snarling. Called to order by the maid, it rested its head on its front paws with a sigh of resignation, rolling two mournful, slightly bloodshot eyes toward a bottle on the upper shelf. Watched over by a pair of glazed camels, topped by a cross and inscribed with golden letters, I had never before encountered such an important-looking bottle.

"What's that?" I asked the girl who stood waiting for my cup.

"Why, that is Madame Guillaume, of course. They burned her." The girl was barely able to conceal her contempt at my ignorance. "Can't you read French?"

Retreating backward into a bed of pansies, I think that I forgot to thank her for the water. In any case, revealing my astonishing discovery to Reuben, we both agreed that if this was what they did with dead Christians we were lucky we had been born Jews.

The gruesome image I had tried to hide from myself for the past year once more invaded my mind in its stark horror: the charred body of Mario, the blacksmith, lying in the gutter. I could still smell the burned flesh. The Moslems had said Mario had cursed their Prophet Mohammed, so they had poured a whole can of gasoline over the big, friendly Italian, then set him on fire with a flaming rag. My friend tried to cheer me up:

"Come on, Fallu, let's drink our wine now. Didn't I promise you something for your sore throat? What do you think I cut that piece of hose for?" In the alley behind Haham's wine shop we joined the rubber hose to an end of lead pipe and then forced open the rotten shutter to the storeroom window. Only an iron grille separated us from a row of barrels lying prone on their fat sides, taps facing upward. Easing out the nearest stopper with a wire sling, the rest was child's play. The pipe slid into the tap, the hose on the other end alternately into Reuben's mouth and mine.

If the wine did not cure my throat, at least it flushed the burned bodies out of my thoughts and put Reuben into an enterprising mood. He decided to go shopping. It being Friday it was high time to think of his family's Sabbath meal. Spotting Ahmed's cart in front of Kikki's grocery, he jumped to help with the unloading, hoisting a sack onto the coachman's broad back.

"Yah, Allah, what a tear here in the bottom!" Reuben exclaimed, puncturing the sack with his pocketknife. "The rice is running out like water. . . ." Covering the hole with his beret as it to stem the leak he let it fill with rice instead. Next he needed sugar so he pushed and pulled hundred pound sacks over the storeroom floor until a hole was pierced in one of them. My neat friend swept the white trail into his shopping bag. Sugar and rice in hand, Reuben tried for vegetables. Burdened down with provisions, shoppers thronging the Friday market were always glad to find a husky porter. Relieving a happy housewife of her load, he dragged not only two overflowing baskets after her, but also his feet as he stopped here and there to throw some ballast overboard. A large eggplant, half a pumpkin, and a lettuce head came flying in my direction. Less voluminous produce such as carrots, peppers and potatoes were stuffed under his shirt and into his pockets. The fee for his services, three sous, was only a fraction of the money needed to buy a calf's foot or an oxtail for his mother's stew: a paltry detail for a provider of Reuben's mettle!

We were passing shoemakers' row when my friend furtively picked up something fallen from a workbench and a lonely leather slipper went to join the sugar, rice and vegetables in his bag. Even Reuben's mother, who could conjure up meals from thin air for her orphans, would not be able to cook this one into meat, I thought, afraid to look stupid if I asked too many questions. Pointing at the slipper's abandoned partner on the bench, Reuben cleared his throat,

"Isn't that weird, Fallu . . . do you remember the one-eyed Arab we saw half an hour ago, trying to sell a single slipper the spitting image of this one?"

"What are you talking about . . . what single slipper? Am I crazy to sell single slippers? It's a pair!" muttered the shoemaker, turning his booth upside down to trace the missing shoe. He understood that he had been robbed. "Where . . . where did you see the Arab?" he shouted, ready to run after the thief.

"Oh . . . a long way from here," Reuben dragged out the words. "He was sitting in front of the tiled wall outside Abu Samir's bakery. . . ."

"How much does he ask for it?"

"Ten sous," said Reuben, estimating that the pair of slippers, reunited, would be worth four francs. The man counted ten sous into my friend's palm:

"Three more sous for you, son, when I hold that slipper in my hand!"

Having paid the monkeys a leisurely visit, talked to the snake-charmer's parrot, and enjoyed the Booshadia's somersaults, we returned to shoemakers' row with Reuben brandishing the slipper from afar, panting as if he had run for miles. Richer by thirteen sous and still in my company he now directed his steps toward the kosher butcher shop. He kept staring at me, I kept staring at him. Why was he changing color like a cuttlefish? His black hair was turning purple, his blue shirt to brown. Not only my friend's countenance was flushed; houses from white turned pink, then orange, then the sky seemed to come down on us in one solid red mass. A great gust of wind snuffed out the last pinpoint flame of sun. Shoppers, fleeing through the sudden gloom, were bumping into each other's bags and baskets, into fretting camels, sheep and donkeys as everybody rushed for shelter.

Amid panicked neighings and bleatings, frantic cries of mothers for their children they were barely able to see in the thick red darkness, Reuben and I were running side by side. Arms raised in a vain effort to shield our eyes from biting grains of sand, we tried to reach his mother's place close by.

"Sodom and Gomorrah . . . Shma Yisrael . . . repent, repent. . . ." I had come up against old Rabbi Bishlino, his bournous blowing high above billowing pantaloons, loudly reciting the Shma Yisrael as he was trying to recapture his galloping tarboosh. Though frightened to death, I could not help laughing at the sight of him with a red beard—but not for long because instantly my mouth filled with sand. That ashen taste of dust more than the darkness and the lashing wind was a reminder; what if this was the end of the world and I had just been up to my ears in thievery? Reuben at my side remained dauntless.

"Here we are," he muttered through sand-clotted teeth as we began to smell the market latrines situated in the same courtyard as his family's living quarters. Struggling against the storm, we managed to open the door to the stinking hole Reuben called home. I do not recall when I have ever been so happy to arrive anywhere. His mother gave thanks. His brothers and sisters, undeterred by the thick red dust covering both of us from head to foot, clung to him. His little mongrel dog, on the other hand, after a few happy jumps and sandy licks, retreated into a corner, whimpering.

We were lucky there was no window, for though every crack in the door, rattling like the devil, had been plugged with rags, still sand was whistling in. At the flickering light of an oil lamp, Reuben's mother prepared coffee. As the sand and sugar came pouring out of the shopping bag, she began to tell about the red storm she had witnessed as a child. It had not been the end of the world then, she said, stroking some sand from my hair, and she did not think it would be now either. People had run into the mosques and synagogues confessing long lists of transgressions, the sky clearing even before they had been able to get through them all. The storm had only been a sign. A sign that He had taken notice of the four fresh graves in Nabeul's Jewish cemetery: the blood of Rabbi Yomtov and his three sons killed by Arab robbers had been marked by the red.

"Today it's not a warning to the Arabs. It's those fine, French ladies with their flimsy skirts and spiky brassieres . . . saw one walk the streets in short pants, too. . . ."

As we huddled with the others on a worn-out mat sipping coffee, the little dog snuggled up against us. I felt reassured. It was quite cozy in their midst once you got used to the smell. Howling in a stream of sand, a blast of wind extinguished the light. Reuben jumped up to replug the door with rags.

"A golden son," murmured his mother, pouring the rice into one of a row of rusty cans. "Look here: sugar, rice, barley, groats, beans, couscous, lentils . . . Everybody loves my boy and gives him presents. . . . What would have become of us without my golden boy?" She hugged Reuben, probably knowing in her heart where it all came from. As her golden boy got up to unplug a rag and peek outside, she made me feel the fine material of her black widow's skirt. "A gift from Madame Carrera," she whispered. "As good as new."

She knew as well as I that her skirt had never seen the rippling, rustling wardrobe of Madame Carrera, richest Jewish lady in town. Reuben, of course, had pinched it from the first clothesline.

"It's still blowing red, but much lighter," said Reuben from the door. His mother was right. The storm had only been a warning. After the winds had blown the red dust together with themselves out into the sea, our town reemerged under its old blue sky.

As I ran home to Bab Salah Street to welcome the Sabbath, I could see the first three stars rising, too late for Jews to sweep the dust out of their homes. We settled down to a rust-colored weekend, every mouthful of couscous and hameen grating between my teeth— a reminder of His mercy.

XIX

The Reckless Years

For a while I had become afraid to accompany Reuben on his shopping sprees. Anyhow I was busy taking the first steps in my craft. Having looked after Huani's children for a full year and to everybody's satisfaction, the second stage of my apprenticeship had started: I was learning how to make shoes—how to oil the sewing machine and to use my hands and feet together. I pedaled back and forth for days, threaded and unthreaded the needle until my eyes were popping out. The day came when I could at last begin to sew, following the lines, circles and zigzags Huani had traced for me. After miles of meandering over leftover leather, I arrived at molding and cutting and, having mastered this more intricate art, was allowed to make shoes.

My comrades were well on their way to becoming craftsmen in their own right. Together, feeling the need to affirm our manliness, we would drink wine whenever we could lay hands on a bottle, tapping the barrels in Haham's storeroom when we saw no way to supply ourselves by more honest means. Once a week, knotting blue scarves around our necks, we went to meet with the young man from Tunis who had come all the way by train to speak to us about our ancient homeland, Eretz Israel. Seated around him at the synagogue we listened to tales of the young braves of Betar, afraid of nothing in the world, including Arabs, who were waiting for us in Palestine to help them rebuild the land of our fathers.

Looking at the illustrated newspapers our instructor used to bring with him, I liked to fancy myself among the heroes facing me so straightforwardly from its pages, riding horses or plowing the ground, each with a rifle slung over a shoulder. Curiously enough most of the photographs were those of girls—laughing girls wearing boots, and, to our amazement, trousers, sometimes even short pants. Some were planting trees, some were laying tiles and the prettiest one of all was standing in the middle of a chicken coop waving a flag graced with the Star of David.

Even though I took exception to the trousers, those photographs and stories of a country of my own made me feel prouder to be a Jew than all the lessons taught to me by the rabbis. My whole outlook was changing. I was beginning to see that there was more than just water on the other side of the horizon. A big, mysterious world was waiting to be discovered! The yellow, green and lilac of Monsieur Mauricet's maps were real countries, not just images in books.

They said America, shining with mountains of gold and silver, was the richest of them all. Huge Russia was made up of ice and snow, transparent like the ice blocks a van was bringing lately from Tunis for our butcher shops and restaurants. France, our protector, was a grassy place filled with officers and gendarmes, the Eiffel Tower rising in the center. Our own Africa was a reservoir of blacks with tattoos, earrings, and rings stuck through their noses—tall and frightening as the Senegalese soldiers I had always tried to avoid.

Slowly I was also grasping that not every custom and belief I had taken for granted was necessarily Torah from Mount Sinai. Things I had resented in silence I was now openly rebelling against. It went so far that I dared to refuse kissing my father's hand. In respect to girls I became completely mixed up.

The days when I had forced candy on them were long past. Quite the opposite was happening. Clumsy hearts inscribed with "Rafael, *je t'aime*" or "Rafael, *mon amour*" appearing on the walls of our courtyard put me beside myself with rage against fat Lajla's daughter. As soon as I had finished scratching over one, a bigger and blacker one would spring up overnight so that my mother, to whom writing was but scribble, would gently scold me:

"What has come over you, Fallu? Look what a mess you are making of the walls. Haven't I enough trouble with your brother Fraji?" For nothing in the world would I have told her what was written there.

One midmorning in early summer the heat in Huani's small workshop was unbearable. Beads of perspiration were stinging my eyes. They blurred my vision and my sticky fingers left dark spots on the leather.

"I must drink something," I said, jumping from the sewing machine without waiting for an answer.

Outside it was, if possible, even hotter; my sweat instantly dried up in the searing wind sprung from some desert caldron. Having gulped down a lemonade, my steps were turning to the sea all by themselves. Passing Palmidi's carpenter shop, I found my big friend panting over his saw, groaning that, burning up inside and out, he felt ready to welcome death by drowning. One bottle to a man was but a drop in his sea of thirst, he said, gathering up our emergency stores: four bottles of red wine drawn from Haham's barrels for a rainy day. Then Palmidi closed the shop. His sister, Habiba, who was sweet on me, pushed a can of sardines and a chunk of bread into my pocket, and Palmidi and I made straight for the bay with the wrecked fishing boat.

What is more delightful than to cool off in the salty sea when the air burns like hot pepper? Nothing, on the other hand, makes one thirstier. After a short swim we sprawled out in the shade of the decaying sloop, making trips into the future in between gulps of wine. Palmidi spat a sardine tail into the brackish water at the bottom of the hull.

"I shall have a chain saw with a motor, mark my words . . . maybe even a compressor. Like butter I will cut the wood, carve out all kinds of flowers and animals and glue them to my doors: deer, birds, lions—all in pairs. Every Arab on Cape Bon will want a door with birds, every Jew one with lions. My prices will rise sky-high. . . ." We were both lying on our backs. Lazily shifting my head, I could see a freckled nose turned up to the sky, one pale eye framed by carrot fringes staring dreamily into the blue.

If doors were on Palmidi's mind, shoes failed to fire my imagination.

"I shall sail a trawler with a cabin," I said, swallowing the last of my wine. "I will catch sardines in the Delta of the Nile, mullets in Lake Bizerte, and sea turtles in the Straits of Gibraltar. Then I will sail to see America and Russia, Jerusalem, and Eretz Israel . . . " Rolling with the movement of the surf, an empty bottle was sleepily bumping against the rotting boards, back and forth—back and forth. The last thing I remember was the sky over Russia, one huge, brilliant block of ice.

When I woke up the sun was setting in a yellow haze and I felt very cold. Everything was in a haze. It was a strain to make out Palmidi calling me from the beach. The skin was hurting all over my body, but worst of all was my head, throbbing as if a hammer banged inside, burning hot while I was shivering with cold. Staggering over the boulders, I crouched down beside purplish Palmidi, who was kneeling and vomiting into the sand, his baby face puffed up like honey cake baked in hot olive oil.

"That damned sun had to turn on us . . ." he retched. "We have slept for eight hours. . ." He was lucky to live nearby, while I had to drag myself through the whole length of the prickly-pear path vomiting my heart out, squeezing my head between my hands to keep it in one piece.

I must have looked truly frightening, for I do not remember being scolded when I arrived home at last. In fact, I cannot remember much of anything that followed. It seems I fell terribly sick, so sick that first Hafzeah and then the rabbi advised my father to call the doctor—the same doctor who, having brought a whole hatful of tricks from the University of Paris, had used Uncle Goliath's blood to save the dying effendi. He did not tamper with my blood though. Seeing that I was burning up, that clever young physician had my head packed in crushed ice from the restaurant instead.

Palmidi, who had been sleeping on the lee side of the hull, only came down with a bad case of sunburn, whereas I blacked out for many days, delirious with fever. I dreamed strange dreams then. One I remember very clearly. Three men were walking toward me, stocky and dressed in white cloaks, three pairs of black eyes fixing me in silence. The oldest had a white beard, the second a black one and the third was red-haired. As they came near and pulled my arm I tried to scream,

"Go away, don't take me, please. Who are you anyway?" I

meant to shout but only a few pitiful croaks came out. Nevertheless I got an answer.

"We are Abraham, Isaac, and Jacob." The one with the white beard waved his hand at the others as if I were nearsighted.

"But I thought you were dead . . ." I said, very surprised and without my voice.

"We are on leave," smiled Abraham. "Came down here just to help you. . . ." And softly at first, then stronger and stronger my three ancestors started massaging my back, shoulders, arms and legs, six powerful hands stroking and kneading me until I awoke in the arms of my mother. I was covered with sweat and too weak to lift a finger. To this day I am convinced that without the massage of the Patriarchs no ice pack in the world could have kept me alive.

"To whom were you talking all the time, what Araram . . . and who is Abob?" my mother asked over and over. I simply said I had forgotten. At ease with white-robed Prophets and long-dead rabbis, I knew from then on that something wonderful was about to happen every time they would visit. Abraham, Isaac and Jacob I have not seen in over forty years, but then, I have never again been so near the edge either!

So long as I was thin and weak I thought a great deal about my visitors, trying to figure out why of all the hardworking, thrice-a-day praying boys of Nabeul they had bothered to come to the rescue of a rascal like me. For whatever extraordinary purpose they might have wanted to save me, until my mother's thick broths and stuffed pigeons had put the flesh back on my bones I was regularly going to synagogue, trying to live up to my destiny. Thoughts of inescapable piety were, however, reburied in a rarely opened drawer of my mind as soon as I went back to Huani's shoes, to my friends and the beach.

There followed a chain of uneventful summers and winters, linked by the Jewish holidays and beaded with seashore ramblings and fishing parties. Like a pack of young dogs, my friends and I were playing and gamboling through those carefree years—my animal years is what I call them in my heart. How often my father would scold me in his exasperation at seeing me squander precious time on fish, birds and lizards, time which I should have spent studying the Torah. He shouted that one day I myself would turn into an animal. It was sheer luck he did not know how near the truth he was!

My playmates' appetites had become as insatiable as mine so we spent all our resources on food and drink. What we liked most was a concoction of oxtails, calves' feet and chick-peas that we threw together in large oil cans. This mixture along with many spices was left to stew and sputter all night through in our donkey shed. Next day we would transport the treasure can to the beach, embalming the prickly-pear path with the vapors of garlic, cumin and turmeric. To keep Palmidi, panting after us with a big ring of barley bread, from dipping up the sauce before we reached our destination, we had to run most of the way.

Still, it was not so much limitless gluttony or the voracity with which we fell on any kind of nourishment that makes me look upon this period of my life as my animal years. Animals are more discriminating. I think instead of the crass ways in which we tried to satisfy our growing curiosity about women.

Of Arab girls I would not even dream. They might as well never have existed. Huani had given me sound advice on how to deal with female Moslem clients whose feet I had to fit:

"So long as you have to do it for a living it is no transgression. Think firmly of a wooden pole and do not look above the ankles."

With Jewish girls, on the other hand, things were less simple. Plain or pretty, I was not supposed to let my eyes linger on any of them, notwithstanding the prospect of having to choose one of them for a wife in the not-too-distant future. And what was I to do when my opposite did not mind the rules, like for instance, fat Lajla's almost full-grown daughter, embarrassing me so with her scribbles and swoonings in front of my friends that I could have choked her. She was not the only one. One of my cousins would more and more frequently drop in to help my mother with a household chore. By six years my elder and very plain, she would start stroking and kissing me the moment we were left alone. She was stronger than I, so no sullen faces, grimaces or even kicks would shake her off. Only when I threatened to tell my mother that she pulled me on her lap did she finally stop bothering me.

French women with their forward manners were another matter altogether. Walking trimmed poodles in front of the Hôtel de France in tight skirts cut off at the knee and on spindly heels, they seemed to have stalked out of the showcases of the capital, mere curios to be gaped at. And gape at them I did.

The wives of gendarmes, officers and postmasters kept servants and had plenty of time to kill. In the dunes not far from Ramoo's restaurant these ladies had their bath huts where they could undress before dipping into the sea and then lay themselves out for their sunbath. Having for some reason taken it into their frizzy heads that it was desirable for their skin to be like that of a Bedouin woman forced to work in the fields, they would baste each other with oil as so many roasts, suffer sunburn and itching until they became an ugly brown. Some of them who came without a girlfriend would ask us to rub the oil onto their back—a task astonishingly entertaining even though most of the women were old enough to be our mothers.

It was Reuben's idea to dig a tunnel under one of the bath huts.

Lying flat on our backs in a sand hole, we discovered fascinating vistas through the loosely joined floorboards of a cabin belonging to the customs clerk.

We decided to do some more boring on the following day, a Thursday, when we found the jetty full of anglers, mostly Jews, trying for some sizable Sabbath fish. In no particular hurry to reach the huts, I sat down with the others, my feet dangling from the pier, waiting for the line to twitch between my fingers. Shaded by an old straw hat with two holes through which my father, on hot days, used to pass the donkey's ears, I was lazily gazing at the little white crests riding crisscross on the choppy waves. The sea was gleaming with the sharp blue-green that always made me feel lighthearted; luminous lilac shadows brushed over Tony's sail. Chasing each other in the direction of our coast, finely combed clouds were streaking in from where Sicily and Pantelleria were said to be—forerunners of the rains soon to blow in from those distant waters. The light breeze tempering the September heat would in October swell into lashing winds. The surf would darken with shoals of gray mullet, and bands of dolphins would play along our stormy shores.

For now, sniffing the summer tang of fish and tar still clinging to the jetty, I watched crates glittering with sardines and mackerels being hoisted onto a donkey cart. Nearby, Arab merchants from the Island of Jerba were tying up their large, flat boat piled high with pottery for the Friday market. Not only were their boats dumpy, but everything about the Jerbans was—their broad faces, their tarbooshes, their coarse bowls and jugs; amplest of all were the behinds of their women. Moslems and Jewesses alike got that way guzzling couscous while squatting on the ground.

More interesting, a giant, pinkish-red manani fish had caught my eye. Tall as a man, it was being hauled on top of the sardines. What a catch! It must have weighed near to a hundred pounds. And where was I? Although it was unquestionably a day for big fish and my lucky Thursday into the bargain, not even the smallest fish had swallowed my hook. At the other end of the pier Shishi, the dwarf, seemed more fortunate.

"Help, help, I must have caught a whale!" he screamed, staggering to his feet and reeling backward in a supreme effort to hold on to his fishing rod. "Rabbi Shimon, Rabbi Meir . . . please, help me," he begged, but apparently those two saints were too far away. Not even two Arabs folding nets nearby could get to him before the fish had toppled Shishi from the pier, his yapping little dog diving in after its master. So far, so good. We pulled out the dog and we pulled out the dwarf, soaking wet and weeping because the fish had got away. What was worse, it had got away with Shishi's fishing rod.

A bachelor in his forties, the tiny man lived in very modest circumstances with his widowed mother and two sisters on Bab Salah
Street. Too proud to accept assistance from the comité, the family
depended for its livelihood on the proceeds of Shishi's fishing rod—if
one did not take into account small presents the sisters received from
an occasional male visitor. Poor Shishi could not get over his loss. So
disconsolate did he look, huddled there with his dog, both of them
dripping on the pier and on each other, that my comrades and I
decided to try giving fate a push. Reuben and Palmidi collected
money at Ramoo's restaurant, Dooha and I appealed to onlookers on
the jetty; the sum we were able to push into Shishi's wet pockets was
sufficient to dry up his tears if not his clothes.

In his dry state the dwarf was an astute salesman, counting the
elite of our community, like Madame Carrera and Sidi Tarbulsi,
among his clients.

"But, Shishi," they would say sometimes, trying a feeble protest
against his methods: "Why do you throw those small fish on the
scales? I want only the big one. . . ."

"They are a mother and her daughters, Madame Carrera. I
know, I pulled them out of the water. You would not want to separate a mother from her children, would you?" Being so short, Shishi
liked to pass for a child himself whenever it was to his advantage. On
Purim, for example, he would stand in line for one of Sidi David
Tarbulsi's toys.

"You are not one of us, you got a mustache," the boys behind
him would grumble.

"Is it my fault if I was born that way?" Nobody could contest
such an argument.

Seeing half-dry Shishi roll a cigarette and satisfied that he could
be left to his own devices, my friends and I went on our way. The day
seemed to hold muddled fortunes for fishermen but for running and
jumping it was perfect. Romping among the bath huts, we holed into
the cool sand underneath the floorboards of one of the cabins where
we soon dozed off.

I don't know how long we had lain there, our ears filled with the
pounding of the surf, when a woman's voice purled through the
droning; French words, cajoling, dropped into my drowsiness.

"Qu'est-ce qu'il-y-a, mon petit chéri . . . il a mouillé ses petites pattes?
Viens, Fifi, viens chez ta memère . . ." The words were followed by the
sound of a dog shaking out its fur. Very quietly the four of us drew
our heads together, concentrating on a knothole in the floor. Groaning and creaking, the boards came bending down, almost touching
our noses. Bare legs planted themselves on top of us, a bathing suit
dropped down. The prospect was overwhelming. One eye glued to

the knothole, I lay breathless, oblivious to the water dripping down or to a long-haired little dog sniffing in our direction.

"What is the matter, pet, do you smell a mousie?" Still naked, the woman bent down to stroke Fifi, who was whining and scratching the board over Reuben's head.

Long, hairy ears swept the ground, tickling my forehead. "Arrrh," snarled Fifi viciously, trying to push his nose through the knothole. Luckily, he had the shortest nose I ever saw on a dog. Out of a small brown face, pancakelike as if flattened by some fist, two enormous brown eyes glared into my own. I should have suspected it was not solely to calm her restless pet that his mistress crouched down beside him; I was caught by surprise when her piss streamed down. Flushed out of our hiding place, we tumbled over each other in a mad scramble for the sea with fiercely yapping Fifi on our heels. Only on the farthest rock jutting from the waves would he stop. For years I had to make a detour everytime I saw him from afar.

XX
Innocent Evenings

The following summer I became independent. Huani, having taught me all he knew, helped me set up my own shop. My old patron, Baruch Tarbulsi of the comité, let me have one of his booths at low rent while my father, reluctantly plunging into his meager savings, came up with enough money to buy a secondhand sewing machine. Selling my shoes at half price to attract clients, I had after a while more orders coming in than I was able to fill at my pace of work. Since it was not my nature to tie up money in a sock, I would ride my sewing machine until noon or at the most one o'clock when I would close shop to take the old prickly-pear path straight down to the sea.

At home, where I spent very little of my time, I was now contributing my share to the upkeep of the household: a little money, a chicken here, an oxtail there. My mother was as loving as ever, my sister pleasant to look at in the black apron of the girls studying at French school. But it had become clear that my brother Fraji, beginning to cause serious trouble, was retarded. The synagogue saw me mainly on weekends and sometimes on Wednesday evenings in the company of my father. Wearing the blue scarf of Betar, tied around my broadening neck, I would then go to hear more about the feats that our people were accomplishing in Eretz Israel and about the men who had led them there: Theodor Herzl and Ze'ev Jabotinsky.

When Baruch Tarbulsi returned from a business trip to the Holy Land, the souvenirs he had brought back went on display in every Jewish place of worship in our town. Eventually, it was Rabbi Hai synagogue's turn to show the exhibit. Standing in line, the congregation pressed around a table where three small objects were laid out on an embroidered cloth. The largest among them was an *etrog* box carved from olive wood. The lid, adorned with embossed copper, showed Jews praying at the Temple wall. Next to it, barely visible among the silver lions of the tablecloth, lay a coin with a round hole in its middle, worth two mill, said Rabbi Ghez, encouraging us to pick it up for a close look at the mint. Had I not seen with my own eyes Hebrew characters beside the Arabic I would not have believed that Jews could have their own currency.

The greatest wonder, though, was the seemingly simple penholder Rabbi Ghez was now holding up to the light of an oil lamp:

"This is a very special occasion," he solemnly addressed our congregation. "Everyone have a good look at this precious pen . . . take your time . . . I want you to treasure this image in your hearts for years to come. . . ."

Apart from being manufactured in Jerusalem and being made of silver I could not see anything extraordinary about that pen until it was my turn to hold it. It had a window at its bottom. Peeping in with one eye, a miracle took place. There, inside a tiny piece of glass, stood the tomb of our mother Rachel in the sunshine, complete with its round dome, a door and windows, on one side shaded by a big green tree. Jews in prayer shawls stood in front, Arabs were riding by on camels and in the background rolled the brown hills of Judea.

Compared to this marvel, the snapshot of a Jewish policeman I had cut out of the Betar newspaper and pasted on a wall sank into nothingness. I was not even angry later when my brother Fraji tore it up.

To know portions of the Bible by heart is one thing, to understand Hebrew is something else again. Our Betar leader, the one who came from Tunis once a week, would teach us Hebrew songs which for me could as well have been Chinese, so little did I understand the words. Nevertheless I sang them with much fervor. Having been blessed with a parrot's blind memory for sounds, those songs remained in some corner of my head until many years later when, after coming to live in Israel, I could at last learn their meaning.

They were beautiful songs, I then found out—a pity that I did not understand them when the land of my fathers was still only a dream. They were about wild anemones and ears of corn swaying in the wind, of raindrops quenching the desert and hills dancing as young goats. The Prophet Elijah was walking on the shores of the Sea of Galilee and one very sad song told the story of Joseph Trumpeldor, a great hero fallen in a battle with the Arabs.

Hebrew songs, tales of Herzl and Jabotinsky took care of my Wednesdays. Friday nights, of course, were spent home with my family. Every remaining evening of the week, however, I would meet with my comrades at Majloo's café. A far cry from the chic of Café Sportez with its black-jacketed, white-shirted waiters, Majloo's cafe was much cheaper, much louder and also much gayer. Instead of transactions with several zeros signed on Sportez's tables, Majloo's clientele closed their deals with a handshake, noisily haggling over a sack of sugar or three pairs of shoes. More comfortable installed on the floor, they ate black, briny olives and spicy beans with their fingers to whet their thirst for Majloo's wine and an occasional glass of arrack. At the light of two kerosene lamps the café's arched pillars were hiding peeling plaster in their long, trembling shadows, giving the haunt an air of grandeur that was completely lacking in broad daylight.

With most of the place too dark for cards or dominos, we would pass the time singing. Rabbi Haim Shushan, the slaughterer, my old acquaintance, always to be found among one of the groups chatting on the floor, was ready to shoulder his fiddle for the asking. Earning extra money with his homemade violin and beautiful warm voice at wedding parties and bar mitzvahs, he made music at Majloo's café only for pleasure. I had long since forgiven him for killing my rooster.

"Give us the song of Fatma, Rabbi Haim . . . of Fatma, the unfortunate, whose liver got consumed with passion." I begged for my favorite love song, having lost much of my shyness in things pertaining to women. None were present anyhow as no Jewess or Moslem in her right mind would have exposed herself to the scrutiny of all those male eyes in a coffeehouse.

Most of the Arab songs were sad and long: loose girls fast coming to a bad end, decent ones—like poor Fatma—slowly dying through interminable verses of unrequited love.

"No, no . . . not Fatma," protested Palmidi. "I've had a hard day. Give us something happy!"

Lifting his bearded head, Rabbi Haim stared into the shadows, then scratched some sounds out of his fiddle that soon grew into sobs. He began to sing:

Dearest ship, tell me, where are you sailing
for my sweetheart is on board...
My waking hours I dream of him
at night I find no rest.
His spirit has sneaked into my body,
I cannot get it out...
Please, ship, tell me, what port will he get off
so I can write to him and find some peace...
Or shall I ask the bird to take me on its wings,
carry me to him.
Under the thorn-apple tree we will be reunited,
joining all three in a happy song.

Helping Rabbi Haim with the singing as best we could, Majloo in the meantime shuffled among the groups, busily refilling glasses.

"Yah, Shishi," we greeted our tiny neighbor, entering with a fisherman's cap drawn over one side of his large dwarf's face, his short arms cockily stemmed on his hips. The ring he claimed to have twisted from the finger of an Obeita, the demon beauty, was flashing on his pudgy little finger.

"Where is your fishing rod?" we teased Shishi, well recovered from his misadventure. "Do you know why Rabbi Shimon and Rabbi Meir did not help you? They saw you smoke on the Sabbath, Shishi . . . and so did the big fish . . . it still has got your rod; next time it will hook you. . . ." Furious, the dwarf ran out again. Only with promises of olives and wine could we persuade him to come back. We seated him beside mad Basha who, having produced a pencil stump from a greasy pocket, was covering a sheet of paper with rows of fugures and additions, neat in spite of the dim light.

"How is business, Basha?"

"Excellent, excellent. I just finalized a big deal. Bought the whole length of the street that runs from the station to the municipality. Some of my ships have also come in. Ten of them, each carrying a load of one thousand sacks of rice and sugar at twenty francs apiece. Ten thousand times twenty is two hundred thousand. Do you want a loan?" and without waiting for an answer Basha wrote out One Million on another piece of paper, signed it and gave it to me, gratefully accepting a handful of beans in return.

One or two of Nabeul's lunatics were always at Majloo's to entertain us. Sometimes it was Filla praising the virtues of his wife (he believed he was married to his goat); she ate little, never needed new clothes, gave him milk and rarely talked back. On other evenings well-mannered Gagu Ashkenazi, an elderly bachelor in shiny shoes and an equally shiny but spotless European suit, would honor our circle with his presence. Gravely sipping our wine, he would leaf through the folder he was carrying, filled with the records of Nabeul's Jewish widows. He was extremely well informed.

"Let's see now . . . Sshhh, Rabbi Haim, forgive me, but this is more important than your fiddling. Let's see . . . day before yesterday was the third anniversary of the demise of Pinhas Cohen, the charcoal hawker (Gagu Ashkenazi never missed a funeral), second husband of Rivka, daughter of Abraham Mammu, from which marriage issued five children, now orphaned, one son and four daughters—poo, poo, poo, not on our heads. Five weeks ago on a Tuesday the said widow Rivka remarried the widower Aaron, tanner from Mamoora . . ." Here we had heard enough. Showing no respect, we drowned the names and diverse fortunes of the widow Rivka's many children in another Arab love song.

It was past eleven when we went out into the moonlit street, drowsily wandering home after a full day of work and play. After some beachcombing and bathing we wound up the evening with wine and song. A slow, unearthly melody was floating through the still air, music more beautiful than anything we had been singing with Rabbi Haim Shushan in Majloo's café. The music was coming from the enclosure of the great mosque of Sidi Abdel Kader. How could I have forgotten that it was Thursday, the spirits' Sabbath, when Nabeul's pious Moslems were starting out on their weekly midnight procession to keep in check the ghosts and jinn of our town?

Embroidered banners, higher than the houses, were coolly glittering among the stars as flutists and drummers turned around the corner. With measured step and in single file, some fifty Arabs were slowly advancing on us, chanting pleas for protection from their saints. Reuben and Dooha had gone home, the singing was dying down, the drumbeat dulling as Palmidi and I were still lingering on in the green, murky shadows under Mama Hafzeah's balcony. In the last flicker of an oil lamp over at Mahfar's café a Bedouin was wiping the glass containers of the water pipes, then swept the pumpkin seed shells out onto the street and left.

"Look!" Palmidi breathed heavily into my ear and nudged my face in the direction of a small pool of moonlight in front of the closed café. "That is the spot! That's where I saw the blood before they tried to wash it off. . . ."

I felt a shudder running down my spine, not a wholly disagreeable sensation. Brawls were common in Mahfar's café, but the one that had taken place there several months earlier had been an exception. Two fallahs had come to fists over the right to an olive tree dividing their land. This was nothing out of the ordinary except that this time one of the contestants, having been subdued, had staggered after his victorious neighbor and knifed him to death in the exact spot we were now looking at.

A year had not yet passed since the murder. Since it was past midnight there was every chance that an Obeita might rise out of the blood-soaked ground. I hoped the demon was going to take on the appearance of the perfumed enchantress in white muslin I had heard so much about rather than the more ordinary one of a donkey or goat. With the example of mad Basha before me as a warning, I was going to outsmart any apparition. As normal as the next man, up to the time of his fateful encounter, the poor fellow—unable to resist the charms of an Obeita—had been tickled out of his mind in the process. Well, whoever entered the arms of a white-clad beauty after midnight had only himself to blame. I was reflecting on this when Palmidi broke the silence:

"I was not going to mention it, Fallu," he whispered; "maybe you will go home if I tell you . . . something happened here a month ago. You know my eldest sister's husband—the one they had to bring for her from Jerba where they like their women big? He had been at Majloo's until closing time. Passing here under the balcony he hears a voice behind him, 'Bah-bah,' the prettiest little white goat is leaping up at him licking his hand. Until he comes up with a piece of string from his pocket, there is no more goat to tie; in its place a donkey stands staring at him through white lashes.

" 'So far, so good,' he says to himself, being from Jerba where they don't have Obeitas. 'My wife's parents will like a donkey even better than a goat. . . .'

"What shall I tell you," Palmidi went on. "The instant my brother-in-law swings himself onto the back of that donkey he understands that something is wrong. He feels himself go up into the air, higher and higher. In a few seconds his nose is brushing the herbs Mama Hafzeah is cultivating on her balcony. He tries to hold on to the iron railing but the beast grows so fast that, at the very last moment, he can barely throw himself on the old woman's roof and shout for help. You know how Hafzeah is getting deafer every day? Don't ask what she did to him when she found his feet dangling over her window in the morning! He was blue and yellow for a week!" As Obeitas go he was lucky to get off so lighly, I said sleepily and, disappointed that no apparition would show up that night, I went home.

Why could I never catch sight of a single jinni in the heathen country of my birth as so many of my friends did at the time? Here in Israel spirits and ghosts are nonexistent. Not the smallest jinni is hiding under the floor of my flat, and I can drop heavy shoes at night without apology. Sheltering the bones of those who will rise on Judgment Day to go up before His throne above Jerusalem, the ground here is clean of evil spirits.

XXI
The Faces of Romance

Instead of meetings with apparitions I had other, more palpable encounters. I was in my sixteenth or seventeenth summer when I had a strange adventure with an Arab girl. No love affair, God forbid, although I held her naked body in my arms. It was the most beautiful body I have ever seen.

It happened one morning soon after Palmidi and I had thrown our lines into the water. We sat on the mossy rocks to wait for fish dumb and greedy enough to sink their tiny teeth into our bait when a feeble echo of screams drifted over the water. Drawn out of one of my daydreams that, despite occasional visits under the bath huts, still centered on fish rather than women, I looked up and down the beach. Far behind the rocks, where Arab girls used to bathe and no man dared to tread, there seemed to be a terrible commotion. It was one of those occasions when one runs first and thinks later.

"Woah-woah-woah . . ." As we closed in on the forbidden stretch of beach, the screams were coming ever sharper. The nearer we drew, the harder we ran, our feet hitting the wet sand so fast that for once Palmidi seemed weightless. Scattered over the rocks, I could make out a group of females beating their breasts. Nobody was in the water. Then I saw a pair of hands reaching out of the waves for an instant, disappear, and come up one more time. Someone must have skidded into an eddy.

I was well built and Palmidi had a lot of muscle under the fat, still, entering a whirlpool is no child's play. We approached from two sides. Groping through the dark rush, Palmidi caught a foot, I grabbed an arm and some long hair, trying to keep the girl's head above water. She was not struggling anymore, but though her body was extremely difficult to hold on to, limp and slippery as a dead fish, we managed to pull her over to the shore. Laying her face down we pressed her belly on a rock until the girl at last started to gasp for breath, gargling out more water than any camel could drink.

"*Binti-binti-binti-binti* . . ." Above the screams of the other females running like scared hens aimlessly from rock to rock, one
woman had been screeching louder than the others until, at last, she
understood that her daughter was still alive. Stopping to beat her
heart with both fists she covered the retching girl with kisses and
pieces of clothing.

"Allah be praised who gave me back my only child," she sobbed.
"May you grow old in health and happiness, the richest men in
Nabeul!" She turned to us, showering us with blessings, inquiring
after our names and places of work. Then a fallah with a horse and
cart was summoned from the fields to carry the resuscitated victim
home while Palmidi and I, careful not to mention the accident to
anybody, went back to town. If the rabbis found out that we had seen
a naked woman we could count on severe punishment. The girl's
family, on the other hand, was even keener to hush things up, for
who was going to marry a Moslem maiden whose body had been
seen by two Jews?

A few days later in the dead of night the girl's father brought a
full donkeyload of presents to Palmidi's shop and mine: chicken,
oranges and mandarins, goat cheese and butter—in short, the cream
of his produce.

"People whisper," he said. "Something came to the ears of my
daughter's betrothed but I was able to convince his parents that the
two of you, being the most pious Jews in all of Nabeul, were keeping
your eyes shut fast throughout the rescue. . . ." Next, it was my
father's turn. Some kind soul at the synagogue or at the steam bath
must have told him.

"Such ugly rumors are going around about my son. I cannot
believe my ears. Did you truly pull a naked heathen female from the
water, Fallu? Where were you on Wednesday morning?"

"Where should I have been on Wednesday morning? At my
shop, sweating over shoes! Am I crazy enough to have my eyes
scratched out at the women's beach? That's all I need now, jumping
into the water after Arab girls!" With that the matter seemed closed
save that the girl's grateful father came one more time to my workshop. Without haggling over the price, he ordered all the footwear for
his daughter's dowry, then from Palmidi all the doors and windows
for her house. With every nail my friend drove into the furnishings
destined for the young couple, his big chest would heave a sigh and
his water-blue eyes would grow murky:

"It's not fair. Why must she be an Arab? By right she should be
mine, for without me she would now be wherever Moslems go after
they are dead—where only worms would still enjoy her loveliness.
Do you remember her eyes? Two black suns. My God, her breasts are
rounder than her father's melons, and her legs . . . her legs are honey

jars. . . ." I kept quiet at the depth of my friend's romantic outburst though I could lay just as much claim to our find as he. But what was the use anyhow? Shortly after, the girl was married.

Some knowledge of the drowning affair was also reflected in the secret glances with which the girls of our own faith had started sizing us up as we passed on our Saturday-morning strolls. None of them would do so openly, of course, bashfully lowering their eyes or shielding them with one hand as we paraded by, taking a good look at them as they stood in their doorways. The moment we turned our backs, the roles were reversed:

"You wait and see. Black eyes with the leather belt is for me." someone was giggling behind me.

"You can have him. I prefer the redhead. A bit on the heavy side but much taller than yours."

The whole street smelled of Sabbath on those long-past Saturday mornings. The delicious aroma of hameen and stewed okra would greet us as we emerged from synagogue in our white sandals, freshly washed white shirts and white caps. On every threshold sat old men wrapped in the traditional jebbas, gravely cracking sunflower seeds in the company of their grandchildren; marriageable maidens wearing transparent stockings and modern dresses, barely reaching over their calves, were clustered behind. Stopping here and there as if to scratch a leg, we would try to get a better view of the pretty ones, quickly bouncing back as Rabbi Ghez approached. His head was bent so low that only part of his head stuck out of the hood of his bournous. He would trip past with rapid little steps, taking no notice of his surroundings.

"*Mevorah, mevorah,*" we welcomed him, snatching his right hand for a kiss on the wrist. Display of devotion was part of the Sabbath. Nevertheless, it did not prevent us from stealing away in the direction of the Hôtel de France for a forbidden game of pool at very low stakes. Upon arriving on the main street opposite the church, we would put outposts on either side of the hotel and slip in when no other Jew was visible on the horizon.

In the late afternoon we would join the big Sabbath exodus to the seashore. Resembling from afar a long envelope brightened up with postage stamps the "Jewish" beach was scattered with blankets, tiny red-white-and-black-robed figures crawling in between or grouped around their picnic baskets. This was another golden opportunity to examine and compare members of the opposite sex even though they would not enter the water before nightfall and then fully clothed. In public, plain girls would be seated beside beauties, whenever possible, in the hope that a little of the latters' radiance might enhance poor, colorless faces.

In her day, Fortuna's mother used to make some money on the side with that practice. Now she is shriveled up—her face all crumpled. What can you expect from an old woman with a dozen great-grandchildren? Yet in her youth she was a renowned beauty, hired to adorn the wedding of every ugly bride in town. Even there on the beach she was still shining over other matrons. Surrounded by her daughters in the pretty Sabbath dresses they had sewn for themselves, she sat there—a big bloom stuck in the middle of six blossoms.

The day was not too far off when I would pick one, but as yet I was far too happy in my roving ways and in the company of my friends to think seriously of marriage. And who wanted to get mixed up with six sisters? I was looking at girls strictly for the fun of it . . . at best for future reference. Nevertheless I nearly became entrapped that fall.

I was now seventeen years old, easygoing, well built and well fed, with the ruddy complexion and shiny eyes that plenty of sea breeze and red wine lend to a healthy youth. At the same time that I was flowering into manhood, my old sewing machine was fading fast. Always famished for grease, it croaked and rattled, jumped stitches and lost screws. After a last effort at finishing the shoes ordered by Moslem clients for Mohammed's birthday, it gave out for good. On that all-important holiday every Arab must wear new shoes. Why, I don't know, as everybody takes them off again upon entering the mosque. In any event the Prophet's birthday business provided me with money to shop around for another secondhand sewing machine.

On a clear November morning I climbed on the train to go in search of a bargain. After the long ride to Sousse, two Jews at the station advised me to go on to Sfax where they said a used machine was for sale. If there was one I surely did not find it. Instead the Jews of Sfax told me to try my luck in Gafsa where a shoemaker had recently closed his business. I arrived in the early afternoon to find a large hamlet with low, mud-plastered houses. I was baffled to find the Jews there indistinguishable from their fallah neighbors. I also found the retired shoemaker among them and in his cowshed a beautiful, fairly new sewing machine of recent make. Haggling over the price took time so that when we finally shook hands on the bargain, the last train back to Sfax had left. I was forced to accept an invitation for an overnight stay in this desolate, landlocked place where, except for an occasional chicken wandering through the room to pick at something on the earthen floor, I was all alone with my host. He pinned me down with questions.

"Are you married?" Cautiously he poured me a cup of coffee. "Does shoemaking feed a man in Nabeul? Could it feed a family?"

Every now and then during our negotiations I had seen the ripple of a curtain at the top of the stairs. It seemed to me an eye was peeping through a tear to one side of the frayed fabric. But when I looked up again the red-and-black Bedouin weave hung motionless, the hole was dark and empty. Instead, loud clapping of clogs captured my attention. The noisy shoes belonged to a very pretty girl my age clattering down the stairs and fussing about in the courtyard, sweeping left, sweeping right, one moment bending down to shoo away the cat, then raising herself on her clogs to rummage in the dovecote. If she wanted to show off her suppleness she had made her point. Still, I could not put my finger on it, but something was wrong with her.

Meanwhile my interrogation was continuing. How old was I? What was my father's business? Which rabbis had taught me? To what synagogue did I belong? After the girl had clattered off again and darkness had fallen, my host lent me his prayer book to recite Maariv, of which task I absolved myself to his visible satisfaction. His wife, in the meantime, deposited a big bowl of couscous and two bottles of wine on the threshold. We proceeded to take our meal under the renewed stare of the mysterious eye. To impress it and my host still further, I put all the devotion I could muster into grace—so much so that now the retired shoemaker came out with a proposition:

"I liked you from the start, my son," he said, looking me full in the face. "The way you recite your prayers has convinced me that you must be a good Jew and will make a good husband." Here he patted me on the back. "The finest girl in Gafsa—what am I saying—the finest girl in all of Tunisia, and rich into the bargain, can be yours for the asking. . . ." At this point the curtain opened to let through an imposing woman, her amply cut, striped garb weighed down with massive necklaces and bracelets. It was the girl's mother. Smilingly descending the stairs, her golden anklets clanking with every step, she graciously extended her husband's invitation to join him for a cup of tea.

I was taken aback by the brightness of the upstairs room carpeted like a mosque and shining with hanging brass lamps. Apparently the shoemaker, tenant of his well-to-do neighbors, was intent on earning a matchmaker's fee. But what I could not understand was why on earth the girl's parents would want another shoemaker in the family and as the husband for their only child? Were eligible bachelors in such short supply in Gafsa's small Jewish community? Perhaps more learned sons-in-law were unable to make ends meet, relying on others to feed their family. A healthy young man with a trade like myself might seem a good catch. I was given to understand that the girl's father was the owner of a soap-manufacturing business employing seven workers. An only daughter would be well provided for.

I had had an opportunity to observe her gracefulness busying herself about the yard. Only now, as she was bringing in sesame cookies, did I fully realize her loveliness. Her face was clear, finely shaped as a bird's egg, her long neck heavy with curls, blue-black bunches of grapes. And her eyes . . . I recognized that lively, liquid look. It was she who had peered at me from behind the curtain.

Had I ever considered opening a modern shoe shop in a small town? her father was asking as she came back to take away our empty cups. Mumbling something about lack of funds, I was sending a sidelong glance at the hillocks in her spring green garden dress, my eyes wandering all the way down a flowery and seemingly interminable path until they arrived at the carpet. I sat up with a start. Where were the legs? Now I knew what had been bothering me all along; the extreme modesty of the girl's hemline. Only the very Orthodox would still wear it that long.

While I was politely replying to a host of questions, troubling images kept flashing through my mind. I was glad when I could at last go down to the shoemaker's room, stretch out on a blanket and wonder whether I had been stupid to refuse the money. Nobody had ever offered me so many bills before; a whole wad of them my would-be father-in-law had wanted to give as a pledge for his good faith. My fingers itched to take his offer. Don't touch, Fallu, an inner voice ordered while my lips were promising marriage the moment my parents agreed to the match.

Had I eaten too much couscous, drunk too much wine? As I lay turning in the dark, the disturbing images were coming back in full force. I saw myself, walking along a never-ending mud-brick wall, always two steps behind the broad back of a man who kept dropping bills with his left hand. Tryng to catch them, I was forever shuttling between a shoe shop and a synagogue, searching in vain for a familiar face, a strip of blue on the dusty horizon. Now I sat on a beautiful carpet in the upstairs quarters flanked by two tall featureless figures except that one of them had an eye swimming in the middle of its naked egg-shaped face. That figure, bundled up in a long stiff gown, fed me my favorite food, liver, and after every mouthful I would plant a kiss on the hand of the other figure which seemed to be a man's.

As I was at last drifting into a fitful sleep, the figures dissolved to make room for two girls linking arms. One was combing her thick black curls; the other, who had the same sandy-colored hair as my cousin Miriam, was cooing for her pigeons. Just then, when I was finally slipping into the dream that I like even better than my dreams of dead rabbis—the one where I become a bird among fellow birds—I was awakened by a curious, clucking sound. Lifting myself on one elbow I was staring into the eyes of the same brown hen that had been wandering through the room the day before. It brought back to me all those strange dreams, the brilliant but uncomfortable marriage offer of the previous evening. No, I resolved, not the loveliest bird, the richest girl in the world, would trap me into entering her baited cage. The bird catcher had always been me, and it was going to stay that way. Even though, I had just decided to remain a bachelor, at least for the time being, I nevertheless renewed my promise to inform my parents of the marriage offer the moment I was back home. The train carrying me and my new sewing machine had not yet rolled into Nabeul's station when I had put the Gafsa girl out of my mind.

To this day I regret that I did not have the courage to tell the girl's parents the truth: "No, thank you"—and have it over with. On that morning where were the fibs and excuses that ordinarily flowed so effortlessly from my lips? I could have said my mother might object to a girl I had met on a Monday, having proclaimed Thursday to be my lucky day . . . that my father would probably not like his oldest son to marry so far away from home. Anything to spare their feelings would have done. However, tickled at being a sought-after bride-groom, I wanted to play that unaccustomed part a little longer. My cheap conduct was to cost me dearly. Later on it would change not only the course of my life, but also that of my cousin Miriam, the sandy-haired girl I had just seen in my dreams.

Standing on the threshold of the happiest year of my life and unaware that my star had already begun to totter, things were look-ing rosy enough. Freedom had an even sweeter taste than before. The new machine made work easy. I was surrounded by friends, the sea was full of fish and Majloo's café was well stocked with wine. I did not breathe a word to my parents about my escape from a brilliant match. My mother would have cried and torn her hair while my father twirled his mustache in a rage at the loss of such an opportu-nity. Another reason I would not bring up the Gafsa girl was a fact her black curls had brought home to me, namely that I was in love with my fair-haired cousin Miriam. Blind to this simple truth up to the time of my trip, I had always taken her for granted. Who would have said my soft-voiced, soft-faced cousin in her unobtrusive ways had the power slowly to push much more striking girls clear out of my mind? Nevertheless this was exactly what was happening.

One of the many children of my mother's eldest brother, I had known Miriam all my life. As a quiet, friendly toddler she would rely on me to protect her from her bullying brothers. Later on, every time my father banished my mother from our home, we had gone for extended visits to my uncle's house. There, as we would compare copybooks full of dried treasure, I sometimes let her have bugs or butterflies for her pressed flowers that were worth much less. At the time of my bar mitzvah the friendly relations between our two families had suddenly cooled down to a bitter frost. My father, having had the rotten luck to see all his savings drowned by a wet season when he had speculated on a dry one, had also lost some of my uncle's money in the process, and the two men had quarreled. Notwithstanding, I still went regularly to visit my sickly grandmother who lived under the same roof with her son, unaware that it was really the company of my cousin I was seeking. At thirteen, when she had menstruated for the first time and her mother had prepared a feast in her daughter's honor as custom required, I had been more interested in the menu than in her red palms, painted with henna to bless her path into womanhood. Miriam had changed after that. She had become a little plumper and much more reserved. Still she would not flinch when I touched her hand or arm as others did. Smiling at me out of calm, gray eyes, she now began to cook up little dishes for me at each of my visits: an omelet, a fried fish. I should have guessed then what she had been thinking all along—that we were fated to become husband and wife one day.

At first I fretted at being in love. Since I had to marry somebody it could be only her. That was self-evident. But why must I be tied down so soon? Then slowly I began to worry. My gentle cousin was so appealing that some brighter prospect than myself might snatch her from under my nose regardless of whether her father gave her a dowry. True, neither her father nor her brothers could force her into marriage against her will. On the other hand, I knew that she was too obedient a daughter to dare stand up to them. The thought of seeing my cousin married to another was so unpalatable that I resigned myself, took my mother into my confidence and then went to ask Miriam to become my wife. She accepted without the slightest fuss. After some haggling between my parents and hers the match was agreed to. The bride was allowed to accept my presents: linen for sheets and a golden bracelet.

Never having quite forgiven my father for the loss he had once caused him, my uncle was not overjoyed. On top of the old rancor, he was well aware that his nephew and future son-in-law spent as much time on the beach as at work and prayer. Yet, after all, if I was not the hardest working shoemaker in town I was healthy and handy, and my mother was his sister. Most important of all, my uncle had three more daughters left to marry off.

A few days after my betrothal, while sitting on the floor of Majloo's café, a hand slapped me on the shoulder. Pooga, the van driver, was standing over me. To my astonishment he asked Majloo to pour me a glass of wine. Grinning he winked at me, reminding me that the route of his delivery service included Gafsa. He did not beat around the bush.

"What's the good news, Fallu? I take it that your parents grabbed with both hands at the Gafsa match?" Twinkling with his other eye he pulled a small bundle from his belt, playfully unfolding five crisp one-hundred-franc notes. "Hurry, boy, the girl's father is impatient to draw up the marriage contract."

Choking on my chick-peas in embarrassment, I mumbled that my father had been out of town, but that I would speak to him as soon as possible, then left without finishing the wine. I did not touch the money.

The year that followed was the happiest of my life and I dare say the same for poor Miriam. We had no forebodings. Palmidi's sister, Habiba, on the other hand, was crushed by the news of my betrothal. My friend was upset at first—he had so hoped we would become brothers-in-law. How could I tell him that his kind, blue-eyed sister was too heavy? Had Miriam never been born I still would not have wed Habiba. I had been weary of fat women since my earliest childhood—since the day when, peeping through the lattice window, I had seen monstrous Lajla crawl on all fours to get at her food. They smell, need double lengths of fabric for their clothes and gorge themselves on their husbands' hard-earned money. From Miriam I had nothing to fear. With the kind of trim little figure that could still squeeze into her wedding dress after half a dozen births and twenty years of marriage, she smelled of soap only, with a whiff of cinnamon and dried orange peel from her father's spice shop. As the tiny shop had a large family to support, my ailing grandmother included, nobody could pretend that I was marrying for money. But I was not going to be at the beck and call of rich in-laws either. So everything was running a smooth course save for one snag: I was supposed to work with greater zest from now on, dropping the best part of my earnings into the slit of an earthenware kitty, cornerstone of my future household. With my aunt obligingly looking the other way, Miriam had given it to me with a first shy kiss on the cheek. Placid and dreamy-eyed, my bride was waiting for the day when the box was chockful of coins and bills: we would break open its pink-clay belly, rent a room, order a woolen mattress and fix the wedding date.

What is the big hurry? I thought to myself. Why work my fingers to the bone and rush headlong under the huppa when wedlock could hardly be more pleasant than my present state? With the addition of a happy courtship, leisure's taste was sweeter than ever. So even though I had lately been turning out a slightly higher number of shoes than in the past, my money was rolling in the direction of Majloo's coffeehouse and Haham's wine shop rather than squeezing through into the slit of my kitty.

How luminous were the Sabbath afternoons I spent on the seashore with my betrothed. Forty years of grayer days could never dull their glow. Chaperoned by one of Miriam's younger sisters, we would stroll hand in hand in the breeze, jumping apart every time a head—Dooha's or Palmidi's as a rule—would crop up from behind a dune. Walking fiancées of their own, my friends watched over their every step as if afraid the robust girls in their bright Sabbath dresses might be blown away any moment. To leave our charges unattended was out of the question. One of us had to stay behind every time we went for a swim or to get peanuts, cake and lemonade from Ramoo's beach café—on credit, of course, as the Sabbath was with us.

The future brides would savor every minute, every bottle of orange soda to the last drop, knowing full well that, once married, they were going to be left at home waiting for babies. A young woman who failed to become pregnant right away was not to be envied. Coming at first with pointed inquiries, her mother-in-law would soon start nagging:

"I don't know what is the matter with the young women of today. Six weeks after my wedding I was under way with twins. Why can't my son's wife carry at least one?" If the wretched girl remained childless over the years, then her husband's family would treat her as an outcast:

"Look at you . . . an empty, useless belly and still primping. What is wrong with you anyhow, don't you like babies?" A woman who felt disgust at the sight and smell of dirty diapers was not granted children, people believed; in any event, a wife barren after ten years of marriage could be divorced without further ado.

The first among my friends to get married was Reuben. I have already mentioned that besides having no father to look after him, he was born under a cursed star. Always hoodwinking him in the wrong direction it steered him straight into the smooth arms of a hussy. But getting him under the huppa was less easy. Eager to get a flighty daughter off his hands, the girl's father made the groom so drunk he would have wed a prune-faced she-devil, the more so a pretty, little loose fish. Wedded bliss was of short duration. Since she was with child right away we did not see much of his wife while Reuben himself, taking more and more to the bottle, spent all his free time with his friends. What happened next was so unheard of that the shame of it would cling to Reuben until the day when, remarried and gone blind, he took his own life in a bathtub in Tiberias: his young wife took off with an Arab painter. Having to beg for bread in the streets of Nabeul, being caught red-handed and branded as a thief—anything would have been better than to have one's wife run away with a Moslem. Left with a baby daughter on his hands into the bargain, who could blame my friend for trying to drown his bitterness in wine?

Mahmood, Kasham and Abdel Kader—the companions of my childhood—I saw only seldom now since they had all married and moved out of our neighborhood. We kept to polite greetings on the rare occasions when we met in the street. Long ago, around the age of eleven, they had forked off in different directions. All their resources and energy had from then on been concentrated on making enough money to buy plots of land and stock up stones so that each of the three of them could build himself a house. They had to get ready for marriage, for as soon as each one turned sixteen their mothers began to shop around for a suitable bride.

Our family had been invited to assist at all three of the ensuing weddings—festivities that lasted each time for a week. The erection of a wooden stage in the yards of both bride and groom would start the celebrations. There the groom was feted in his father's house in the sole company of male kin at the same time that his bride was being prepared for her nuptials in her own home by female relatives and friends. Days for singing and days for blessings, days to dress up and days to show off the girl's dowry would on the sixth morning culminate in a visit to the steam bath. Prettiest of all was the ceremony of henna painting. Young wives in embroidered gold-and-silver crowns would be seated on the dais, lending radiance to the bride throning in their midst while nine- and ten-year-old girls decorated her soles and palms with the propitious red. The seventh day was the day of the actual wedding. A cow and several sheep were slaughtered, then a big trough full of couscous would be put outside in a sheltered spot where the poor could come to eat unobserved. On that day also we would bring our gifts: jasmine or orange blossom perfume for the bride, some money for the groom. Climbing on the dais, my father would spit on a coin and glue it to the prospective husband's forehead.

"Long live Hamus Uzan who gave a present of five francs." Holding up the coin for everyone to see, the bridegroom's best man shouted his appreciation over the furious beating of the drums.

The bride's presence was not required for the wedding ceremony which took place later in the day. The imam drew up the marriage contract, the men of both families signed, and after nightfall the great moment finally arrived: tambourines, drums, the high-pitched sing-song of the women's escort was approaching. Seated atop a mule carrying the dowry, the young wife made her entrance. Still hidden in white veils, she was led to the bridal chamber and her waiting husband. There the two, who had never met before, were left alone as family and guests sat down to a night of music, feasting and merrymaking, all without the help of alcohol which is forbidden by the Koran.

When at last the sun rose over hoarse, overgorged singers and a tired-out orchestra, it was time for the two mothers to enter the young couple's room and check whether everything was as it should be. As a rule they would reemerge warbling jubilantly, having found proof of the bride's lost virginity. Yet, sometimes it happened that the two women came out screaming insults at each other and a terrible brawl between the families ensued. A midwife was called in, and compensation money offered to the groom. In such cases, more often than not, the bride minus her dowry was sent home much less ceremoniously than when she was brought in. Poor thing. Some time after the bride's disgraceful homecoming she might die in mysterious circumstances, rumor having it that her own father had been forced to strangle her to restore the family's honor.

Jewish weddings, usually lasting less than a day, were much more modest. The old custom of throwing whole fried chickens from a balcony to the poor waiting below had already been abandoned. Occasionally the festivities took an unexpected turn, as when a penniless and lonely youth from our neighborhood made up his mind to wed. Living from hand to mouth, buying eggs from fallahs and re-selling them to Jews, he could not aim high, yet had his sight on the comeliest of a cousin's numerous daughters. One bottle of wine and a thin silver ring was all he had to offer her to get betrothed. Nevertheless he was accepted, both parties formally agreeing as to what each of them had to contribute to their future union.

For four weeks, from dawn till night, the young man hawked his eggs with a vengeance, saving every sou he had to meet his obligations. On the appointed day he was ready for the wedding. He arrived for the ceremony with two pairs of shoes for the bride, three sheets and a set of bowls and cups as arranged, proudly inspecting the veiled girl and her dowry—a big mattress propped up against the wall.

"Where is the prayer shawl . . . you promised me a prayer shawl. . . ." The young man held onto his basket with both hands, while his eyes went over the assembled guests to the rabbi waiting with the huppa.

"There was no money left after I paid for the mattress . . ." the father of the bride apologized. "God willing I shall buy you one for the first brit milah." The groom was deeply offended. Tears burning in his eyes he turned on his heels to walk out of his own wedding. Rabbi Ghez ran after him into the street when he was called back.

"Rabbi, Rabbi, the bride has fainted!" And, "Water, water . . ." cried the women, removing the girl's veil to let her breathe more freely. Moved by the pretty young thing's plight, huddled there unveiled and sobbing, one of the guests, a Jewish soldier from Algiers, whispered something into the rabbi's ear. He, in turn, drew the rejected bride's father into a corner, talked to the flustered mother holding her daughter and then sat down to set up a new marriage contract as fast as he could write. Agreeing to take the bride with nothing but her wedding dress and mattress, the soldier pledged two thousand francs' worth of jewelry as soon as he could make it to his father's house in Algiers. He promised five thousand francs in case of a divorce.

Hurriedly the girl was rehidden under the veil, her brothers and cousins grabbed the four posts of the huppa and the wedding took place after all, the sole difference being that the groom wore a French soldier's uniform and the ring had to be borrowed.

Sahrutas, songs, and blessings . . . the first youth was forgotten. His ears ringing with the joyous echoes of a wedding that should have been his own, he sat bitterly weeping on a stone outside, still clutching his basket with the shoes and sheets. God is great and poor parents in search of husbands for their virgin daughters are many. The young man was not left weeping for long. When Rabbi Ghez, having performed his duty, came out carrying the folded huppa, he was at once whisked away to marry another couple a few houses farther down the street: the egg vendor—his eyes still red from weeping—and the fourth of our grocer's raven-haired daughters. Running as fast as his legs would carry him to buy the groom his prayer shawl, her father had even given the young pair a table and two chairs on top of the mattress.

The grocer's daughter married poor and stayed poor as was to be expected, while the girl who went to Algiers had drawn the big prize of the year. That her soldier was well educated and handsome could be seen with half an eye; that he was the son of very wealthy parents became plain only later when his young wife came back to visit, a great lady with beautiful babies.

So everybody was getting married except me.

"How much longer?" Miriam kept sighing as I played with the tiny golden earrings in her rosy lobes, promising her big ones for the wedding. How was she to know that my kitty was still only half full?

Slowly my bride's light, soft loveliness had become so unbearable that I was afraid longing would get the better of me every time her mother left us alone in a room. And just now, when I was truly eager to save money this commodity was harder and harder to come by. As yet only dolphins and an occasional trawler were disturbing the placid skyline of our waters. On the other side of the Mediterranean, however, cannons had begun to rumble. Germany, which I vaguely remembered as a yellow blot in the middle of Monsieur Mauricet's map of Europe, had gone to war against her neighbors. One of those was France, our protector. Since her ships were in danger of being sunk at every crossing, raw materials were getting scarce and

more and more expensive. Especially the price of leather had shot up
to such heights that I could not afford to cut new shoes. Anyhow
most people nowadays made do with wooden clogs or simply went
barefoot.

The young Betar leader from Tunis did not come anymore. In his
place our Rabbis were speaking of persecutions that our brothers in
Europe were suffering at the hands of the Germans. A week earlier,
in synagogues as full as on the High Holidays, we had all prayed and
fasted from morning till night for our people's safety.

Stretched out at Miriam's feet with my head resting in her lap, I
tried to explain why I could not yet fix the wedding date.

"How can I make shoes without either leather or nails? Even
thread is only to be found on the black market. Do you know where
the red slippers I gave you for Purim came from? Chopped up wire
beaten into nails, one piece of an old tire for the thread, another for
the rubber soles. Would you have guessed the crimson tops were
once my father's Sabbath tarboosh? To this day he thinks he lost it."

"You see," Miriam's clear gray eyes were smiling down on me,
"everything will be fine. Those slippers are the prettiest and most
comfortable I have ever worn. If you make more of them people will
snap them up. We will have plenty of money and a beautiful wedding."

"Please, try to understand, Miriam," I said, turning my head a
little to let her massage the muscles of my neck. "It is not only shoes.
Now think, who is the greatest enemy our people ever knew?"

"Why, Amalek, of course, may their name and memory be
erased!" she answered promptly.

"Right," I mumbled, my face buried in the spicy warmth of the
apron. "Well, they have risen once again, Amalek, this time in Germany. Rabbi Ghez says they are terribly powerful. They break the
shops of all the Jews over there and throw them into prison. . . ." I
had to lift my head, "They hate us, Miriam, they are killers!"

"Shhh, Fallu, don't worry, they will never come here. How could
they? Shhh, don't move now. I think I saw a louse. . ." It was her
way of making me forget my troubles, parting my hair and caressing
my head, pretending she was only after lice. I used to promise her a
franc if ever she came up with one of the tiny tormentors, but she
never got lucky. When she was through with her hunt then it was my
turn. Opening the smooth, light brown tresses I would let them
ripple all over me, wind some locks around her throbbing throat and
feel her cheeks, hot and downy as nestlings. Then we would kiss and
sigh—she with longing, I with regret that I had not saved more while
the saving was still good.

Ordinarily my nose is very sharp, especially when it comes to
sniffing trouble. In everything bearing upon my cousin it smelled

nothing but cinnamon and roses, as if fate wanted to play a trick on me. Enveloped in a happy haze, deaf and blind, I had let myself be carried from one day into the next, from the beach to Miriam, from Miriam to Majloo's café, unaware that my star, blinking uneasily right from the start of my betrothal, was fast slipping behind a cloud. When that black cloud burst all of a sudden it seemed to me lightning had struck out of the blue.

Coming home from the beach one day I saw my brother Fraji, now a seven-year-old, standing at the gate. This in itself was nothing unusual. He was always standing there on his short, sturdy legs, gaping empty-eyed at passersby, at donkeys, goats and camels. He was fidgeting with his arms and muttering, acting as if he wanted to warn me of something. Inside I found my mother, my sister and Aunt Kooka crouched around a bundle on the floor and weeping.

"What is the matter with you three?" I asked. No one answered. My mother only cried harder while Aunt Kooka, her face averted, kept pointing to the handkerchief. Annoyed at so much fuss about a bundle, I tore open the knot, then recoiled as if stung by a snake. The golden bracelets, the sheets, the beautiful white satin for Miriam's wedding dress, even the comb and an apron—each and every present I had given my betrothed—came tumbling on the floor.

"Believe me, Fallu, I did everything I could," sobbed my good aunt. "They had to force me to bring it back. What did I not tell them . . . that you were their own flesh and blood . . . sure to straighten out once you were married. They would not even listen to me. I don't know what got into my brother and his sons. They were so angry. . . .They said people saw you drunk and singing in Majloo's café, drunk and fishing at the beach. . . ." 'My daughter for that good-for-nothing loafer? Let him marry a fish!' your uncle kept shouting."

Sobs choked the rest, but I had heard enough. Kicking the presents in every direction and shoving poor Fraji out of my way, I ran back out into the street. With smarting eyes and furious strides I walked and walked I don't know for how long, until I finally found myself huddled in my workshop, my face pressed to the cool wheel of the sewing machine. Though there was little leather left, its smell still clung to the place, reminding me to behave like a man.

"Pull yourself together!" I heard my voice ringing. "Other fathers will kiss your hand to have you take their daughters—richer ones, prettier ones . . ." It was no use, I have never felt so wronged and shamed in all my life. Sure of Miriam's love for me, it was not so much tears of grief rolling down my cheeks as it was the insult that was burning deep inside. What had I done to them? What was wrong with taking a last fling before becoming trapped in wedlock? Lighting the oil lamp, I looked at the lonely wine bottle that used to brighten up my working hours. So they dared call me a drunkard, a beachboy! Why not also a thief while they were at it? But I would show them. I would make them sorry! The best husband in Nabeul I would be, but to another. Taking the bottle by the neck, I waved it menacingly at the crooked shadow of my sewing machine.

"You will be sorry!" I shouted as the bottle came crashing down on my left hand. Dooha said that, entering my shop, he found me staring at my lacerated palm and a widening pool of red at my feet, a mixture of blood and wine. I recall the large crowd all around me later at the pharmacy, the sharp odor of iodine bringing me back to my senses. My huge white bandage was impossible to hide. People had something to talk about for a while.

"He had it coming to him," said my loving relatives, making Miriam swear she would never see me again.

Several months passed before I got my first chance to talk to her. Suddenly she stood before me drawing water from the pump by the prickly-pear path, the same old well through whose rusty gutter we had so often fished for coins when we were children. As in one of those dreams where one gropes vainly for some dear one who has left us, she drew out of my reach when I tried to touch her. Afraid we might be seen together, she did not even let me help her with the water pails.

"Miriam," I begged, "listen to me. All is ready and planned for. Night after night I have been thinking it over. Come to Tunis with me. I promise you we shall get married the same day. If only you will come with me I shall work like a slave. You will see. . . ." Her gray eyes looked into mine with a long, sad look.

"You know my brothers, Fallu, they will beat us to death if they catch us. They will cut off my hair. . . ." Slowly retreating with her buckets she turned her head back once. "Don't forget me," she said.

It took years before I learned who had stirred up all that unhappiness. Pooga, the van driver, had long since ceased to bother me with the Gafsa match. The Gafsa girl had completely slipped my mind. I had not noticed that lately Pooga had ceased to greet me. Furious to have been led by the nose and convinced I had cheated him out of a nice, round matchmaker's fee, he had vowed to take revenge. Cleverly spreading half-truths about me where they would hurt most, namely with Miriam's family, the whole bunch of slander was easily swallowed by her parents and brothers.

For five more years we would keep waiting for each other, Miriam and I. But finally we both ended up married to someone else. The blow was harder to bear for her. Thirty-five years have passed since the day my presents were returned to me. I fear those years made her shed thirty-five buckets of tears over her fate. As I had kicked those presents out of my sight, so I managed with time to keep at bay the memories. But not so for Miriam. Her brothers claimed I was not good enough for her. And what happened? They married my gentle cousin to a brute, this one truly a drunkard. It took me a long time to understand that the Almighty might have had a hand in our separation. Miriam and I are first cousins; my brother Fraji is retarded, Gaga deaf and dumb. Who knows whether the strange chain of chance events that forced us apart were not simply His design to spare our children? At the time I was unaware that marriage between cousins could hold danger, and long after my hand had healed, the taste of humiliation was still bitter in my mouth. Nevertheless, I would continue to clutch at her parting words, "Don't forget me."

XXII

German Tanks and Arab Justice

I did sometimes forget Miriam during the year that followed, and more than once did I thank God that we did not marry. The war was drawing nearer all the time. Gray blots were sprouting from the pure skyline; more and more planes were droning above the sea as English bombers strafed Italian warships. Sometimes the echo of explosions was carried over the water. One of the blots would shoot up in flames and black smoke would linger on for days. In the sands of Cyrenaika, Tobruk, El Alamein, Benghazi and Darna, we were told, great battles were raging. Tanks pitted against tanks, planes against armor, trying to destroy each other. Airplanes, zooming through the sky like nasty flies, were no longer a novelty to me. But I had no knowledge of tanks. Soon enough I was to know.

Beware of buying anything labeled MADE IN GERMANY the rabbis would enjoin their congregation every Saturday, as if boycotting German products could shield us from the approaching enemy—the implacable new Amalek named Adolf Hitler. Rabbi Ghez need not worry about German products. With my poor mother unable to make ends meet, there was not even enough money in the house for our food rations. Things were no better in the capital where I went hitch-hiking to look for work.

At least one member of our household was happier than before though: our donkey was taking it easy. Instead of staggering under the old bales of fabric, it was now fairly dancing through Bab Salah Street with nothing heavier to carry than ribbons, hairpins, lace and chewing resin. Even its master had grown lighter. Then, for a little while, we were less hungry. It was after my bedridden grandmother let my mother have the treasure she had for months worn hidden in her bosom: a few dozen bobbins of thread which my father sold for a good price on the black market. Since all those taking part in this new field of trade were thriving, I eagerly grabbed my slice of the cake when Sidi Haim Pardu asked whether I wanted to make some money. All I had to do, said this respected wholesale merchant, was to accompany a truckload of goods to a certain place in Tunis where he would be waiting for me.

The next morning after prayers, the truck driver also being Jew-ish, we both set out for the capital. Our cargo looked ordinary enough: crates of oranges, lemons and carobs. The twelve sacks of high-quality leather Sidi Haim intended to sell in Tunis were safely hidden in the back. After we had traveled for two or three hours and were passing through Mégrine, the last town before reaching the capital, the driver braked so suddenly that I was bolted off the oranges to come down on the lemons.

"Stop, stop!" Two wildly waving men in the uniform of the French police were barring our way, "What have you got in there?" They turned to me, the driver standing back as if the whole thing was none of his business.

"Oranges and lemons," I said. "See for yourselves."

"*Fisha, fisha,*—get them out!"

Slowly I started unloading, sweating more profusely with every crate that brought me nearer to the leather. The policemen were in no hurry, patiently they waited until the last of the sacks was exposed.

"And what is that?"

"Leather," I said as if it was self-evident that leather and carobs have to travel together.

"And for what fruit market are these twelve sacks, if I may ask?" grinned one of the policemen.

"That's leather," I repeated. "It's mine." I pulled out my shoe-maker's license. "I bought it from some Arabs in the cobblers' market back in Nabeul. . . . Want to take it to tanners' row in Tunis to have it all dyed black. . . ." As they slowly and thoroughly checked the con-tents of every sack it appeared to my luck and great surprise that all the leather was either light brown, yellow, red or tan. Now they examined my license.

"Well, well, Raful . . . Rafael Uzan. . . . What extraordinary co-incidence! We were just waiting for someone by that name. A little bird has told us that he has been smuggling leather from Nabeul to Tunis for months." (Later I learned that the "bird" was an Arab, Sidi Haim Pardu's former driver, who was angry because his lucrative smuggling job had gone to cheaper Jewish competition.)

In short, the truck with its load of fruit was allowed to go on to Tunis but the leather was confiscated and I myself put in jail.

After a night spent on the dingy stone floor of a cave, I was transferred to the capital where I was to pass another twenty-four hours in a horribly stinking cell among thieves, drug dealers and drunks. I related my misadventure to the one prisoner who was clean and friendly, that is to say, I repeated over and over the same lies I had just told the police. I had no idea that my sympathetic listener had been put there to sound me out. Having nothing else to do, I invented so many reasons about why I needed my leather black, took such airs of hurt innocence, that besides convincing my interrogator I myself began to believe the story I had made up on the spur of the moment. My luck had not completely deserted me. The police spy happened to be Jewish. Wanting to help a fellow Jew in distress my new friend set out for Tunis's suburb of La Goulette to search for one of my uncles who came promptly to bail me out. I was allowed to return home and there await my trial.

Immediately informed about our fiasco by his driver, Sidi Haim Pardu had not breathed word of the affair and my arrest to my parents. When, on my return, my irate father ran to square accounts, worthy Sidi Haim had conveniently lost his memory. He had no recollection whatsoever of any truck transporting leather nor had he ever talked to me. . . .

Right then events were taking such a turn that for some time I thought little about either the leather, my impending trial or even my cousin Miriam for that matter. The Germans were coming.

One morning as I sat sewing shoes from felt and rubber, a rumble louder than that that of my empty belly made me prick up my ears. Three motorcycles were approaching, thundering past my shop. Before settling in Upper Galilee, where they are common, I had never seen a brush fire. In Nabeul, where the fallahs used to keep their fields and orchards neater than their living quarters and even toddlers would crawl about weeding, nothing that could catch fire was left in the ground. But the day the tanks screeched up from the south the news leaped before them like tongues of flame:

"The Germans are coming! The Germans are coming!" Like everybody else I ran after the motorcycles, khaki-colored wonders with machine guns mounted on their sidecars. They came to a stop at the Arab barber's on Place Sportez. Three helmeted soldiers jumped from the saddles, three dashed out of the cars—all with heavy chains hanging from their necks: the vanguard of the German army.

As Jews stood looking on in silence, the Arabs were taking to the Germans like fish to the water, shouting with joy, using hands and feet to convey their delight at the unexpected visit. For years the Arabs of Tunisia had been trying to get rid of their French masters. Their liberation movement, the Neo-Destour, was powerful and widespread; whether in the towns or in the countryside, wherever one scratched the surface, revolt was smoldering. As usual, the Jews were caught in the middle. On one hand, they had to go out of their way to demonstrate what loyal subjects they were to their French protectors; on the other they had to contribute money secretly to the cause of the Arab nationalists or have their businesses smashed up.

"Close shop or prepare yourself for a beating. . ." The Neo-Destour passed around word to go on strike.

"Open up the shutters or you will get fined. . ." countered the authorities. I could not even smoke in peace without retiring to the toilet as the Arabs, who were my best clients, had put the Gauloises on their boycott list.

"Come to our meeting, Raful, six o'clock at Mahfar's café. . . . Tunisia is your homeland as well as ours!" I would always try to wriggle out.

"I simply must finish these shoes first, they are for a wedding, but believe me, I will do my best. . ."

French or Arab, be that as it may, just now we were on the threshold of six months of German rule, and I was racing with the others to catch a glimpse of the wild warriors of the north.

"Long live the pilgrims back from Mecca!" clapped and shouted an enthusiastic crowd as the first jeeps drove up between the two date palms in the middle of the square.

An old Jew looking through his window averted his face from the red, white and black swastika pennants. "The mark of Amalek . . . poo, poo, poo," he said softly and closed the shutters.

Motorcycles and jeeps were child's play compared to the queer contraptions that followed—huge chariots topped with guns and cannon. I could not tear my eyes from them. Not until the teeth of those slow steel giants, the tanks, were biting into the ground of our Friday market did it dawn on me: a mighty monster manned with smiling, hard-voiced soldiers had just rolled over the Nabeul of my childhood. Its chains creaked through potters' row and the alley where I had bought my first pair of canaries, chewed up the dust in which the Booshadia used to squeal and grunt, then clanked to a sudden halt under the gray tree of the gray monkey men from Algiers.

Clouds were coming in from the sea, blotting out one white house after the other with dark shadows, taking the red out of the drying pepper strings. I shivered in what was left of a pale November sun. Behind one of the tanks a donkey belonging to Kikki, the grocer, brayed with heartrending sadness—nothing would ever be the same again.

The sahrutas of the Arab women were still echoing from the rooftops as the occupiers had already dug in, doing so with a speed and orderliness that left both Jews and Moslems baffled. The officers took up lodgings in the abandoned houses of French officials and nationals who, leaving everything behind, had fled to Algiers or the countryside. The armored corps set up two camps: one right behind the corn market, the other between the railway station and the prickly-pear path, near the old well where I had seen Miriam for the last time.

Freshly escaped from a desert hell where they had seen many of their comrades maimed and dying and in sharp contrast with their Italian counterparts arriving after them, I never heard one word of complaint coming out of a German mouth. In Nabeul all that soldiery had a good time. They were wined and dined in the houses of our Moslem fellow citizens who had first taken care to hide their grown-up daughters in some shed or back room. Their camps, on the other hand, were well stocked with food, soap and wine requisitioned from the Jews. Processions of twelve- and thirteen-year-old Moslem girls carrying fruit and flowers did homage to the officers. But none, neither Arab nor Jew, could be seen in the street for the duration of the occupation.

I did not know what to think anymore. The Sabbath sermon at Rabbi Hai synagogue had been longer than any I had ever heard before, delivered before an unusually large, disquietingly silent crowd. Warning us to obey the Germans, the rabbi had said that they were exceedingly powerful, yet not stronger than little children in the eyes of the Lord of the Universe.

"Help each other, give to the poor, and if we all follow His commands to the letter this scourge will surely pass." Then we read psalms for hours.

If these Germans truly were Satan incarnate then I must say the devil's face did not seem all that terrible. Many of the soldiers had laughing, light-blue eyes—not unlike Palmidi's—and did not look older than myself, some maybe even younger. Together my old friend and I went to survey the tanks and cannon lined up in the sands behind the market, admiringly turning among the armored cars parked under the arcades. I can still recall how I envied the whistling men brushing and greasing at their equipment. Little did I dream that soon I would be cleaning more tanks than I could imagine.

Crossing Place Sportez on my way back home, I had second thoughts about the smiling Germans: those I now saw were not only

smiling, they were bending over with laughter, lowering sacks from
Baruch Tarbulsi's balcony and throwing them into a big heap on the
square below. There went the stocks of the president of our comité:
all the rice, sugar and barley, the noodles and the canned food, much
of it surely kept to help hungry Jews in an emergency. How far away
seemed the days when Sidi Baruch's wife would call me from that
balcony to come up and taste her cooking.

Too much was happening to wax nostalgic. At the Arab coffeehouse across the street there was also something going on. Waving
the flag of the Tunisian nationalists, a group of men streamed out into
the street.

"Bourguiba is free, Bourguiba is free!" they shouted as they
marched toward the Abdel Kader mosque, the whole Arab population running after them. Their great leader, Bourguiba, put behind
bars by the French, had been let out of prison by the Germans.
With Jews nowhere to be seen amid the tumultuous celebrations, I
was walking as fast as possible to reach Bab Salah Street when a
familiar figure caught my eye. I recognized the waddling gait of my
brother Fraji trying to keep up with a flag-waving band of Arabs in
front of us.

"Bourguiba, Bourguiba," he shouted with the rest. Fraji, who
was unable to pronounce one whole word at home, startled me.
Proudly he held up a big chunk of fresh meat for me to admire,
beautiful red meat tied to a string.

"Bourguiba," he said. Pulling him home after me, I gave him a
good box over the ears once inside—the only way to teach him a
lesson.

"Bourguiba, Bourguiba!" he wailed stubbornly. My mother
could not believe her eyes. That much meat she had not seen for a
long time.

"Who gave it to you?" she kept asking. But by now my brother
had retired into sullen silence. From time to time Fraji would come
home with a frayed shirt or a pair of trousers, some ears of corn or a
few oranges, for who would not take pity on a retarded child? If only
we could have got out of him where that chunk of meat had come
from.

"It must be the Arab butcher who gave it to him. He must have
gone crazy with joy over Bourguiba. . . . Any Jew would have
wrapped it in newspaper," speculated my mother and heaved a deep
sigh as she threw it to the cats.

The streets were still resounding with noisy celebrations when it
was rumored from one Jewish house to the next that most of our men
would be led away in a matter of days. As if that were not enough I
was home on borrowed time, out on bail, with the approaching
leather trial weighing leaden on my neck. Having spent two days and

two nights in prison, I would much rather do forced labor for the Germans than be shut up in a stinking cell, I reflected on the train that brought my father and me to Tunis for the trial. The moment the going became rough I could always count on his surly help, as now when, bitterly reproaching himself for having fathered me, he had scratched together the last of his money to pay for a lawyer. Putting the precious bills into the deep pocket of his Sabbath bournous, he had torn me from my weeping mother's arms, steering me through the armed German patrols at the station and onto that train. In the capital we were joined by the Moslem lawyer.

"Remember," he said to me as we were arriving at the court-house, "*yah nakr, yah rebah*," and pointed to the fat, black Arab char-acters on the marble cornice high above our heads. *Yah nakr, yah rebah*—Deny and win: a fair enough warning to wrongdoers, but a rather odd inscription over the entrance to a tribunal, I thought. Looking up again I was sorry that, although I spoke nothing but Arabic, I could not read one word of it. The rabbis, afraid we might get to know the Koran, had strictly forbidden the study of that lan-guage. Would the lawyer who had just pocketed the last of my father's money make fun of us? As for me I gladly took his word for it: *Yah nakr, yah rebah*—Deny and win suited me fine. I was ready to lie the sun out of the sky if it could help to keep me from rotting in prison. Had it been a mistake to try and make a little money on the black market? Maybe so. It seemed to me that my real shortcoming, however, had been to lack the hundred-franc note necessary to bribe the two policemen who had arrested me in the first place.

Apprehensively, I glanced at the two massive court ushers lead-ing away a dejected little man—no doubt to prison. An awe-inspiring pair they were, clad in immense pleated breeches, splendid turquoise tunics with gold buttons, red tarbooshes, and mustaches as stiff as if they had been twirled up with black boot polish. I sniffed their mar-tial smell of snuff.

"Rafael Uzan!" Now they came for me.

"Here." I took a deep breath as I was ushered into the courtroom and into some kind of wooden cage from where I faced the judge like a chicken in a coop.

"Guilty or not guilty?" his voice barely audible, the judge lifted his weary eyes from my file.

"*Yah nakr, yah rebah . . .*" my lawyer whispered through the bars, and, "Not guilty, Your Honor," I could hear myself say loud and clear. At that, the tired judge sank back into his chair, letting the prosecution and defense take over. They immediately entered into the liveliest argument about my character.

"Can't you recognize an honest face when you see one?" The

defense made a sweeping gesture toward my enclosure. "Frankness is written all over him. . . . The very hands of a craftsman. Here is the youth's shoemaker's license. . . ."

"Shoemaker indeed." The prosecution drowned him out. "The fellow is much smarter than he looks, Your Honor. . . . Must have got thousands stashed away in his mattress. . . . And, by Allah, not one franc of it from shoemaking!" To my horror I saw the Arab truck driver, the same one who had denounced me in the first place, take the stand. Although he had informed only against me, his true target had been Sidi Pardu who, by hiring a cheaper driver, had deprived the man of his profitable smuggling job. Not once mentioning Haim Pardu's name during the inquiry, but instead stubbornly incriminating myself as the sole owner of the leather, I had sorely disappointed the Arab. Who was now going to believe him that the twelve sacks belonged to someone else? Having come all the way from Nabeul to testify and have his revenge, he took his frustration out on me. He hardly knew me, yet stated that, as an inveterate trafficker, I had made the same trip many times, even swore on the Koran that all the leather had been destined for the black market—that I had told him so.

The prosecutor had a heyday. Twenty times or more I must have made the jaunt, he shouted. Twenty times twelve made two hundred and forty sacks of illegal leather. At only three hundred francs per sack, he pointed an accusing finger at me, I had pocketed seventy-two thousand francs at his very lowest estimate.

Having not yet said one word, the tired judge adjusted his smoked glasses to get a better look at the gifted young moneymaker. He did not seem impressed at what he saw. "Now tell me the truth, son," he said not unkindly. "How many times did you do it?" Once more I repeated that this had been the first time ever I had brought leather to the capital, intending to have it all dyed black.

"But what on earth can you want with twelve sacks of black leather?" interrupted the judge, apparently aware that Jews, who loathe the color, wear black shoes only on the most solemn occasions, like funerals, and Arabs not at all. "Are the Jews of Nabeul dying out?"

"Your Honor," I said very seriously, "it's true, lately many of our families have been in mourning." Now the prosecutor, bombarding me with questions, made an all-out effort to catch me at a lie, but could not, while my lawyer, trying to prove that the Arab's statement was false, could not either. Truth is that everybody was lying.

Was it because of the old baby-bag filled with black beads and blessings I wore over my heart or my father's most powerful talisman, the tiny shell I fingered in my pocket? Was it because it was a

Thursday or was it simply the fairness of the judge? I was fined one franc and set free for lack of proof. It was not yet the end of the story. The Arab lawyer turned out to be worth every one of my father's last twenty francs.

"What about the confiscated leather?" he insisted. "All the young man's savings went into it, a year's toil . . . his family's livelihood." My father, with his naturally dour and worried features, looked perfect for the part, while I, unable to hide my relief, simply hung my head, promising that I would take the leather straight to tanners' row.

"All right then," the judge finally said. "For once I will make an exception. Here, have it your way. Have your leather black!" With that he handed me a note on whose presentation at a certain warehouse the twelve sacks would be returned. We thanked the judge, thanked my lawyer and went on our way: my father to see whether the Gorni would yet one more time let him have some fabric on credit, I to find the customs' warehouse in the port.

It was too good to be true, but I was given all the sacks untouched and sealed. Twelve sacks stuffed with beautiful, light-colored leather: every single one worth five hundred francs on the black market any day. Never in all my life had I been that rich. Who cared that the whole port area was crawling with German uniforms, I was walking on air behind an old Arab carter pulling my fortune over the cobblestones. Now they would let me marry Miriam! I could almost see her on tiptoes, passing me my lunch over a mountain of shoes, when a bicycle intruded upon my lovely daydream. This one was for real, riding at a distance behind me. To get my leather home as fast as possible I had been on the lookout for a truck going to Nabeul but now I smelled a rat. I told the Arab to rest for a minute. Looking back I saw that the bicycle rider had also stopped short; he was puttering about one wheel, but as we crossed into a side street he was once more behind us.

"Take the shortest way to tanners' row!" I changed my orders. What was I going to do? What was the use of twelve sacks of black leather? I had no choice but to tell the tanner to dye all my leather in this unlucky color, asking, however, to wait until I would be back with a ten-franc deposit.

"Young man, someone is after you," he warned when I returned with my uncle. "You had barely turned your back when a plain-clothes man showed up here. . . . Kept asking questions about your leather. I told him that crazy as it seemed, you had insisted to have it all dyed black. . . ." To keep him quiet my uncle gave the tanner fifty francs and, in turn, he gave back the leather. Two sacks we sold on the spot. The rest we brought home to Nabeul the same night. My father snored on the sacks all the way back, but I sat open-eyed in the dark, singing to the happy hum of the engine: "Six thousand francs—six thousand francs." The whole truck rumbled my song as it rolled homeward over bumpy roads.

My mother was still waiting up for us, her eyes red from weeping. Returning a free man, I had expected a jollier welcome.

"Eat this and go to sleep, Fallu, my dear son," she said in a choked voice. "You will have to get up early. . ." and out it came with sobs and sighs. Rabbi Tsion had made the rounds all day long, going from one Jewish home to the other with lists of those who have to report for work in the morning. Nobody knew where the Germans were going to take us.

The Camp at Menzel-Temime

I had not slept one wink when my father told me to get dressed, then escorted me to Place Sportez where four gray trucks stood waiting in the dawn.

"Remember what the rabbi said," were his last words as I joined the ranks of Jews with pickaxes and spades. "Obey and say your prayers. . . ." Distributing bread, jam, oranges and sardines, my old patron Baruch Tarbulsi from the comité told everybody that we would be back in Nabeul in a fortnight, promising that the other half of our Jews were then going to take over.

"*Vorwärts, marsch!*" shouted the armed guards. Roji Mamu, son of the richest banker in town, having once lived in Paris where he was a student, shouldered his pickax with dash. He tried to give us courage by marching in front as if it were the most natural thing for a young man of means to do.

By now the square was clogged with townspeople and fallahs gleefully clapping their hands or gaping openmouthed at the unheard of sight: Jews carrying picks and shovels, tools they had always taken for granted to be purely Arab. They pointed at the armlets with the printed Star of David that we were forced to wear.

"Welcome, welcome, pilgrims home from Mecca!" they shouted

as they had done for the Germans, only for us they were jeering and hooting. At the small airfield near the village of Menzel-Temime where we were driven, I came for the first time face-to-face with airplanes. They were fighter planes and we were ordered to build walls of earth and stone around each of them. What they were to be protected from we were soon to learn.

My outdoor habits, which at home had earned me vociferous disapproval at best, now served me well. Working with pick and shovel was not the novelty for me that it was for most of my companions: merchants, clerks, bookkeepers, tailors and goldsmiths. Their smooth-skinned palms had never before grabbed the handle of a spade. By evening many of them were smarting with open blisters. I was too tired to get down even half of the bread and jam provided by the comité; I threw myself on the smelly straw of the empty cowshed we had been given for quarters and at once fell asleep. I awoke scratching in the middle of the night, my head, my back, my groin, my whole body was itching like hell. They were all around me, the thick of night coming alive with bloodthirsty vermin, bugs, fleas, lice—and scratching is what we were doing from now on when we were not shoveling, carrying basketsful of earth or lifting stones. If we could have at least washed! Nobody except for the kitchen crew was allowed onto the nearby shore however, and drinking water was brought to the camp by truck. Anyway, what was the use of trying to get clean in the cold December sea if a few hours later we had to go back to sleep in the same dirty straw?

On the whole though, things were not too bad, not much worse than I had expected. The overseer of my team was a heavyset, easy-going German in his forties, who would not budge from his comfortable seat on the earth wall, but readily accepted any oranges we could spare from our comité rations. He enriched my German (already consisting of "Heil Hitler," the soldiers' heathen greeting, and *"vorwärts, marsch!"*) with three new words, *"langsam aber sicher"* (slowly but surely), which he kept repeating to refresh our spirits during the long hours of shoveling. After about a week of *"langsam aber sicher,"* we at last saw something to relieve the boredom of digging. Having emptied the umptieth basketful of earth, I was chasing after a particular nasty flea inside my trouser leg (nowhere have I ever seen fleas as fat as those of Menzel-Temime), when a low zoom made me look up at the sky. Tiny crosses were circling in the clear blue sky above our heads.

"Tommies, Tommies!" the Germans were shouting, crews running to the beach to man their four-pronged guns.

"Pack, pack, pack." Balls of pink and gray cotton-wool were puffing up among the cruising toy planes, a charming spectacle. How was I to know that these "Tommies" belonged to the Royal Air Force and had come to photograph the airfield?

Curious to see the "pack, pack" guns from closer up, I volunteered after lunch for the kitchen crew that had to pull its cart with dirty caldrons to the beach for cleaning. Shining aluminum pots to high gleam with sand and rags, I was slowly drawing near to one of the slim, fascinating cannons and the soldier watching it. I stammered French and stroked the cool steel until I got my heart's desire. After the young gunner let me try out his high swivel seat, I went happily back to more shoveling.

The evening, I remember, was dark and peaceful. Tired Jews, talking longingly about their wives' cooking and the pleasures of the steam bath, stood rubbing their itching backs against the walls of the cowshed; others were still praying Maariv. The sky was deep and starry, as it is only on moonless winter nights, when I took leave from my old comrade Dooha to bed down in my own shed and my own stinking straw.

Having become so used to the incessant itching that vermin could no longer disturb my sleep, it was now burst upon burst of "pack, pack" which made me sit up instead. It had to be hours before sunrise, yet the shed was flooded with light streaming in through the cracked mud walls. Rushing out with everybody else, I was awed to see the black winter night turning white. Eight blazing stars were slowly descending from the heavens, and one of them, an immense parachute of brightness, was floating straight down upon us. I did not know then that these stars were flares; blinded like an owl, with airplanes menacingly droning overhead, the strings of "pack, pack" did not seem so amusing to me anymore.

"Hooo-o-o-o-rrum-m-m . . ." A screeching howl ended in a hollow, earsplitting explosion. The earth shook as the first bombs fell. Everyone was either running or crouching low, praying Shmah Yisrael, but I stood petrified, staring at people, trees and stones outlined more sharply than in broad daylight. And then I saw my own shadow. More frightening than any bomb, it kept calmly growing into a monstrous black shaft stretching out far into the orchard. No way to get rid of it. Hitched to the monstrosity, I was now running in the direction of the trees when some of them crackled into flaming torches, and two men passed me in a mad sprint.

"Mama mia . . . misericordia Madonna . . ." They were the first Italian soldiers I had set eyes on. Racing for their lives, they did not see the open irrigation well before them. The one in front fell in, the other tumbled after him head over heels, still pleading for heavenly mercy. Even if I had wanted to, I could not have helped them. Bombs were crashing louder than thunder. Fires started all around me. A terrible conflagration lifted me up, then threw me to the ground.

With Joseph (a fellow from my work team) following hard on my heels, I tried to run toward a round structure at the end of the orchard. Desperately throwing kisses at the sky, Joseph kept calling for help from Rabbi Meir, Rabbi Shimon Bar Yohai, and the Almighty as he pushed into the little mud-walled dome behind me. It was an oven for baking Arab bread.

"Hide me, Fallu, hide me!" He plunged head forward into the still-warm ashes, sobbing that he would rather have his legs cut off by bombs than lose his head. I wondered why his hands were full of blood when he did not appear to be seriously wounded. Still huddled head down in the ashes and with his naked feet in my face he was little by little regaining enough composure to tell me what had happened.

Running, he had stumbled over an Arab lying in the orchard. Shouting "Up, up, Mohammed!" he had wanted to assist him until the warm wetness on his hands made him understand that he was trying to haul a dead man to his feet.

I don't know for how long we had crouched in the soothing warmth of the ashes when the explosions became more isolated, the "pack, pack" more spaced out. Finally they ceased altogether, as did the muffled cries of those two miserable Italian devils that had resounded from the bottom of the well. The harsh noise of low-flying planes was ebbing off into soft humming. In their place, German voices were grating orders in the distance.

As we crawled out into the smoky night air, a fiery fringe skirting the airfield showed us the way back to camp. Steps in the dark should not bother one whom the Angel of Death had let go free. Yet a whisper from behind made me feel uneasy. Must be fallahs, I thought. They knew we were unarmed, must be fancying that we had money in our pockets. I mustered what little pluck was left after the trying night.

"Away with you or else!" I brusquely turned half circle. Two husky Arabs stopped dead in their tracks. It was baffling.

"Have pity on us, Sidi Jews, please, let us walk behind you . . ." they begged. "You have nothing to fear from us. Don't you know that the Bey of Tunis himself has written a letter to our *mukhtar*? He gave orders not to harm a single Jew staying at our village. . . . We would not hurt a hair on your head, not lift one piece of your clothes from our cowsheds. . . ." The murmur became more insistent: "Won't you let us stay with you? The planes will be back any minute now. . . . The English never let a bomb drop on a Jew's head. They make you out by your black caps. . . ."

"All right," I whispered back with a straight face. "But on one condition . . . off with your tarbooshes!" The two were so thankful, they would have kissed our hands if we had let them. Hiding the offensive red felt hats under their armpits, they kept close to us for the rest of the walk. Too weary to crack a single joke at the crazy pair, I learned later in the morning that their village had suffered heavy casualties in the bombardment. So had the Germans at the airfield. Only our cowsheds had remained unscathed. As if by a miracle none of our people had been hurt. One by one, the Jews were slinking back into their filthy stables—green in the face and very quiet, but without a scratch.

With sunrise it was back to shoveling. The orchards by the way-side offered a sad sight. A group of ghostly candlesticks stood stiffly erect where date palms, swaying in the breeze, had fanned a swarm of wild pigeons the evening before. Lush lime and orange trees had turned into smoldering skeletons. Old olive trees truncated, their crowns neatly chopped off by the ax of war, kept rustling with their white-charred leaves. The ground nearby was wet with blood, but the airfield itself seemed to be hit the worst. Turned inside out by the upheaval, it stank of molten metal and burned flesh. The platforms and earth walls we had worked so hard to build were in ruins. Many planes had been destroyed; their slick silver bellies were ripped wide open, their wings torn into blackened shreds.

Just as black was the mood of the Germans. Standing among the lamentable wrecks, they lashed out at us with their orders as with whips. All of a sudden we had become *verfluchte Saujuden,* to be cursed and kicked around. Most of the men in my outfit were detailed to dig bunkers while I stayed with my old team, building walls from scratch. No more *"Langsam aber sicher."* Now it was *"Dalli, dalli, faules Judenpack!"* (Faster, faster, lazy Jews!) as our once friendly overseer kept at us with his boots and his rifle butt.

Was it our fault that his comrades had been killed? So many of the planes destroyed? I was getting angry. Around noon tiny Tom-mies were once more circling overhead. Again the slender guns of the Germans dotted the sky with colored cotton-wool. Now wiser than on the previous day to the pretty performance, I was worried.

In the evening I took Joseph, Dooha and one other neighbor from Bab Salah Street aside, and we made up our mind to escape that same night. We would try to pass for fallahs. I appropriated one of those shapeless, loose peasant shirts from a clothesline. Dooha found a tarboosh someone must have lost in the heat of the bombardment. We all trussed up our trousers to resemble poor folk who have to economize on fabric. Then we regretfully abandoned shoes and socks in the tangle of a young palm tree. We must have looked genuine enough by now, none of us having washed for a week. However, afraid to take chances, we added a last touch, smearing our faces, feet and clothes with mud.

We changed our names to Ali, Ahmed, Abdallah and Mo-hammed. Sneaking through an orchard about two miles from the camp, we saw that last night's awesome spectacle was going to repeat itself. It started with the same harsh drone, the "pack, pack," the white flares and the tracer bullets. Searchlights were groping for the English planes. And again came the bursts and thuds and blazes and red-hot scraps of shrapnel slithering over the road behind us as we sped on our way. Avoiding the highway with its cars and questions, we kept to the fields, taking an oath that whoever happened to be captured would not give away any of the others.

The danger seemed to lessen once we were clear of Menzel-Temime and the night turned to night again, dark and quiet. Only the sharp angle of a goatskin tent disrupted the flatness of the fields. Here and there glowed a charcoal fire in the distance—a fallah stood brewing himself a cup of tea to relieve his loneliness. But except for some peasants on watch in their vegetable plots, we did not come upon a living soul. The night was crisp. Warmed by a fast pace and the thought that every barefoot step was bringing us nearer to home, we were happy when the bridge of Maamoura rose before us. Only six more miles to Nabeul.

"Stop!" someone shouted in German, flashing a light into my face. Shielding my eyes I could make out German uniforms, soldiers guarding the bridge. One of them was an Arab.

"Jews?" he asked.

"In the name of Allah, we are sons of the Prophet," Dooha answered for us, trying to suppress his Jewish accent.

"And where are you going at this time of night?"

"Why, home to Nabeul . . . want to be early for the market. . . ."

Slowly and suspiciously the Arab moved his flashlight from our faces to our clothes, let it linger on the trussed-up trousers and eight unspeakably dirty feet. I kept scratching my head, Joseph his back. The Arab was not yet convinced.

"Ashhadu . . ." he started.

"The spirit of the Lord Mohammed rose to Allah. . . ." We completed the Moslem statement of belief without the slightest hesitation.

"Arabs," the soldier said to his German comrades and we were allowed to pass the bridge. It was still dark when I arrived home. No neighbor saw me enter. What a relief to get out of my flea-infested clothes and have my mother clean my head. Three days I spent happy and well nourished in the donkey shed, sleeping at night on my own sheepskin in my parents' room. Then they found me. I was feeding my quail early on the morning of the fourth day when I was interrupted by a succession of knocks on the door. The sound sent me flying under my parents' bed, landing among the salted fish and our last beans and rice. The knocks grew into banging.

"Open up, it's only me . . . Rabbi Tsion. . . ." My poor mother knew what that meant. With shaking hand she put planks over my refuge, then went to open the door.

"Where is Fallu?" I heard Rabbi Tsion's voice.

"I wish I knew," my mother said. "From the day they took him away to work I have not set eyes on him. . . ." The two soldiers who came with Rabbi Tsion did not lose any time. Dragging me out of my hiding place they shoved me into the street with a few good pushes of their rifle butts. Rabbi Tsion, of course, was unarmed. One of two go-betweens for the Germans, and clinging with zeal to this unenviable position, he had to comply with their growing demand for Jewish labor. One of our lesser rabbis, he had started to instruct first- and second-graders at Talmud-Torah school after my old teacher, Rabbi Parienti, had finally been called into the next world. Since Rabbi Tsion, stepping out of the school gate, was murdered by two Arabs shortly after the war, there is no need to blacken the name of one who has met with such an end. In contrast to him, the other members of the comité did what little was still left in their power to help their brothers.

With Menzel-Temime turned into hell by the Royal Air Force's nearly nightly bombings, more and more Jews forced to work at the airfield were escaping. Smarter than I had been, they would not return to Nabeul and get caught.

"Three men missing!" the Germans would shout to their shovelers in the morning. "Five men short!" Angrily they would count and recount the shrinking teams.

"Killed by bombs . . ." the Jewish foreman kept repeating. "Come and see for yourself, sir, we are just going to bury them. . . ." The Germans never checked. They had enough to worry about their own casualties, on top of which the Arab village had been decimated. Why, of all people, should the Jews fare better? Nevertheless they did. Bugs and the continuous bombardments drove them almost out of their minds, but throughout more than five months of forced labor not one Jew was killed at Menzel-Temime.

When the president of the comité, Baruch Tarbulsi, and his staff drove up to the airfield to look into the complaints of the workers, they were taken prisoner by their charges. Surrounding the visiting dignitaries in a tight circle, the workers aired their grievances with the help of their fists before forcing the comité into one of the cowsheds. Only after three days of scratching and three nights of bombing were the prisoners finally able to persuade their captors that with the entire comité pent up in a stable at Menzel-Temime nobody could provide for their pay and rations. That little push had perhaps been needed for the Jews of Nabeul to turn their pockets inside out and come up with the last of their provisions. It did not help the workers against bugs and bombs. It must be said, though, that never before and never afterward have our people helped each other as during the six months of German occupation.

To the secret satisfaction of the unlucky ones still at Menzel-Temime, no amount of digging and shoveling could keep up with the pace of destruction wrought by the English planes. Spending their days filling in holes ripped up during the night, they would find bigger ones the next morning, making the runways useless.

Passover came around with the Jews still slaves to the German Pharaoh; unlike what is promised in the Haggadah, Jews were also the victims of the plagues that by right should have been visited on their oppressors: fleas, lice, worms, boils, lack of clean water and constant fear of being slain. At every Seder table in our town the word "Egypt," recurring time after time in the Haggadah, was read Menzel-Temime instead.

"This year we are slaves to the Pharaoh in Menzel-Temime. Next year free men in Nabeul . . ." the Jews were reciting, pleading with the Almighty to let His people go—which He did, one month later. As for me, I was never to go back to Menzel-Temime after that first week.

XXIV

The German Occupation

Now I will tell what happened the day of my capture by Rabbi Tsion and the soldiers.

Shoving me out into the street, one soldier had struck my head so hard with his rifle that despite my efforts not to cry I felt tears rolling down my cheeks. The fear and pity in the eyes of our Jewish neighbors made me more keenly aware of my plight. I was not yet dressed when they came for me. Barefoot, bareheaded, half-naked in my undershirt and drawers, I was walking in front of my captors. In place of my cap, lost in the scuffle, my hair was covered with dried couscous and the fish brine I had upset when they pulled me from under the bed. And in that state I had to cross most of the town to be taken to the *Kommandantur* near the railroad station. It was the most mortifying half hour of my life.

Arabs were running from all over to get a look at me. At first they only laughed, here and there hissing "Jew dog." But when we arrived at the market, they formed a line to send me off. Clapping and shouting, my townsmen fell into a tune:

"They caught up with Fallu . . . Fallu, they got you . . ." And when I had to pass the cobblers' row, the singsong had swollen to a scream. My Arab colleagues hammered out the beat on the round shoemakers' tables before them. There was not one among them with whom I had not traded, joked, cracked melon seeds or shared peanuts. Why did they now all hate me? What had I done to them?

Sometimes, when I feel hot anger welling up inside me because of what Jew does to Jew in his own country, that wall of sneering faces comes back to me. I hear the cobblers' hammers: "Fallu, they got you . . ." I stop my ears, thankful that I am here with my own people for better or for worse.

I thought we would never arrive at the French hotel that served the German staff. At last I was pushed into a room where someone kicked my legs sideways, teaching me how to click my naked heels together when standing at attention before a commanding officer. But what were Joseph and Dooha doing here? No more need now for the story about how I had escaped without taking anyone into my confidence; only one of us had not been caught.

The officer's French was better than ours, but he used it sparingly:

"Why did you run away?" was his first question.

"Because of the bombs," we answered.

"Into the water tank, all three of them!" was the sentence. A short trial and to the point I thought as we were led away. I had a pretty good idea where our prison was to be. As a boy I would often go to play by the big, round tank behind the railroad tracks, waiting for hours for an engine to back out of the station, puff to a screeching halt and take its fill of water. I was right. The guard led us to that same tank.

"*Dalli, dalli.*" Aiming his rifle at us he gestured at an iron ladder, made a movement as if to dive, and once more threatened us at gunpoint. Unpalatable as the prospect was, we did not seem to have much choice. We climbed up and, holding on to the pipes lining the tank's inner wall, let ourselves glide through an opening from above.

We surely would not die of thirst, I said to myself, looking down at the mass of water glimmering through the dimness. But where would food come from? I felt hungry already. When Rabbi Tsion had burst in on us, ruining my morning, my mother had only just lit a fire to cook breakfast. Though I had fed my quail, I myself had not yet eaten. Rabbi Tsion was the one who had led the soldiers to my friends' homes also, they told me now. But they at least had had time to get dressed. Shivering in my underwear, it was hunger rather than the cold that bothered me during the days that followed. Sleeping three nights half-naked under a December sky, I did not even catch a runny nose.

Through most of the first day my friends and I, balancing each on his pipe, were able to keep our stomachs in check dreaming up ways and means to get back at Rabbi Tsion. Having exhausted every possibility in that direction, however, pangs of hunger drove me up onto the roof. The moment I stuck out my head to survey the surroundings for something edible, the guard took aim at me. I was too famished to give up. After several more attempts I found out that the guard would make the rounds of the installations about every quarter of an hour, giving us time to speed down the ladder and grab a fistful of the *hubeiza* weeds growing along the tracks. Their small, lentil-like grains taste pleasantly enough, and cooked, as the fallahs used to eat them, do not harm anybody. Ripping them off their stems we munched them raw, however, which may take the sting out of one's hunger, but what comes afterward I do not wish my enemies. Time will take care of everything I consoled myself, trying not to think of the near future as I ran every quarter of an hour to stuff myself with grains. It did not take long before we all shit green and shit a lot. Steam engines came and went, the water level fell and rose and so did we, hurrying down the ladder to grab more hubeiza," climbing up even faster to relieve ourselves in the tank. As the Germans used the engines to pull wagons with ammunition, I hope the polluted water may have clogged the machinery so that our torments were not entirely in vain.

Toward the evening of the third day, lying prostrate on the flat metal roof to ease our aching bellies, we heard children's voices speaking our own Judeo-Arabic. Just as I had done when I was their age, two boys were coming to look at the engines. The guard, with his back turned, was pacing the far end of the track.

"Tsss . . . tsss . . ." We frightened the two out of their wits. "Run straight to the comité and tell Sidi Baruch that Joseph, Dooha and Fallu are in the water tank dying of hunger—run, run!" They did indeed transmit our message and our parents, worried to death by now, were informed of our whereabouts. Envisioning their sons swimming for three days and three nights in a water tank, they rushed to Sidi Baruch, pressuring him to try and save us at any cost.

After another nauseating night and no more taste for hubeiza for breakfast, we lay in a stupor atop the tank when I heard steps approaching. Someone was whispering in French. I rubbed my swollen lids. Was this the end? Was I going out of my senses? Outlined in the first light of dawn, a couple was embracing right under my nose. As if lovers embracing in the early morning behind the water tank were not a strange enough sight, one was the German officer who had tried us, the other a pretty Frenchwoman I knew "intimately" from my digging in under the bath huts.

"I hear voices . . . someone has seen us." She drew away from him.

"You know what you are afraid of? Three Jews in a water tank!" he laughed and pulled her closer. They kissed.

"What a waste," she sighed. "Three husky fellows idling in a tank. What kind of punishment is that? If I were you I would have found hard, healthy work for them, believe me." He gave her an admiring look and they trailed off, tenderly enlaced.

An hour had not yet passed when someone banged on the tank. "*Komm, komm. Dalli, dalli* . . ." The guard winked us down. Back in the room where we had received our punishment three days earlier, it seemed as if weeks had passed, weeks of living on raw hubeiza. When the officer entered, we jumped so fast to attention that the guard, for this once, came too late with his kicks.

"You three will be put to work," snapped the officer and consulted his watch. "In exactly two hours from now you will report back to this base. Here are your passes. Now mark my words. Whoever plays tricks again will long for that water tank. . . . *Raus!*"

Much later I was told that Baruch Tarbulsi had given the French woman a diamond ring as an inducement to work for our release. After the German army had been driven out by the Americans and the English, the poor girl could not show her face in town; people were shouting "traitor, whore . . ." and pelted her with stones. Then came others saying she had been a French spy working for the underground in Seillonville, so that she was left alone again. Whatever the truth, she did me a great service.

Some of the women I passed on my way back to Bab Salah Street lit matches or jingled coins to ward off the ghost. With a face as green as hubeiza, still in my underwear, I hurried home through back alleys, keeping close to the walls.

"Food, food . . . give me something to eat!" I cried already from the gate, before even a greeting. Sobbing harder than for my arrest, my mother ran to fetch anything edible in the house. A neighbor warned me to eat little at first or else I might have become even sicker to my stomach. Regretfully, following this advice, I went to report for work without stuffing myself.

Though I did not know it then, the worst for me was over. Handy I had always been; now I became a handyman doing odd jobs for the German army. Cleaning and greasing tanks, loading and unloading crates with ammunition, hoisting fifty-kilo sacks of potatoes on my back—wherever help was needed they would call me. Gladly I did everything I was told to do in order not to be sent back to Menzel-

Temime. Best of all, if I could say that, I liked to shine the aluminum caldrons from the officers' mess, big vessels to whose wide bottoms clung delicious leftovers—mashed potatoes with gravy, bean stew, green peas and meat. The first mouthful of nonkosher food stuck for a moment in my throat. The rest went down more smoothly. Nothing singular happened. I carefully kept the secret from my parents. Though there was little to eat at home, they would have been mortified to learn that their son was pilfering Amalek's unclean food. I thrived on it. Reluctant to throw into the sea what I was unable to eat myself, I saved the overflow for some of my less fortunate and half-starved cousins working at the other end of camp. I would not tell them where it came from and they would ask no questions. Balancing lidless cans full of noodles, boiled cabbage and goulash in the deep recesses of an old overcoat, I would stalk with measured steps to meet them behind the latrines, feeling fat gravy trickle down my legs. With every can of sauerkraut and sausage, the frayed worsted shone greasier. But with our German masters, shabby dress had its advantages. The more wretched you looked, the easier was the task they gave you. Only a fool would come to work dressed up in suit and tie. It would be the surest way to be assigned the hardest, dirtiest chore—like cleaning out the cesspool.

No two people could be more different than the Germans and their Italian allies who came a short time after them from Tripolis. Full of songs and jokes, the Italians were the most easygoing fellows in the world. Also they were the only ones to give a Jew a little business in these hard times. For a chicken, a dozen eggs, a few bottles of wine, they would let you have the boots from their feet, bring you coats stolen from their camp, even their pistols when they had nothing else left to barter. With one in particular, Palmidi and I had become very friendly. He taught us how to dismantle mines and get at the small cakes of dynamite neatly arranged in a round inside. Later on, when the armies had left for good, one after another—the Germans, the Italians, the English, the Americans, and the French Senegalese—Palmidi and I found plenty of those mines half buried on the beaches or abandoned in the empty camps. The fishermen liked to use explosives to increase their catches and until the French authorities got wind of the matter, we did a roaring business.

The Germans were different. They never set foot in a Jewish shop, never bartered anything with anybody. Looking down upon everybody, their Arab friends and Italian allies included, they worshiped one god only—their mighty, metallic war machine. For all its sanctity, the idol was not beneath feeding on the despised Jew: more oil, more sugar, rice, beans, peppers, macaroni—it was insatiable. Bled dry, our comité had to keep up with the ever-growing exigencies of the occupiers. From spices and wine to spare parts, soap, linen and hard liquor, Baruch Tarbulsi had to conjure up the Germans' every whim besides giving pay and rations to our men forced to work for the army.

Having never been so busy in my life, I found to my surprise that I liked odd jobs better than shoemaking. Also I must admit that I learned many useful tricks from my taskmasters—the kind neither my parents nor the rabbis had taught me. Amazed to see how much can be accomplished in a day when it was sliced up, every hour squeezed out as a lemon, I could almost put my finger on the minutes. The Germans did not only divide time, but also bread, meat, sausage, cheese and even cucumbers. With them, everything was cut up into neat, thin slices. Willingly or not, a little of their weird sense of cleanliness and order stuck to me. As I had been bred to try not to hurt my fellowman, to turn toward Jerusalem in my prayers, and to bend with the wind when the goyim got tough, so these Germans had sucked in skills together with their mothers' milk. How to repair an engine, fix a radio, clean a rifle, also all kinds of crazy little rules like using one piece of cloth for blowing one's nose, another for wiping one's mouth after eating. Their brains were stuffed with rules as were their duffel bags with socks and shirts, and not one of the latter wrinkled!

Kept busy all day long, seldom did I find time to sew a pair of shoes. The leather salvaged from my trial had not brought me the hoped-for riches. People have to take care of their bellies before they can think of their feet. Black market prices for essentials were so high that those able to buy shoes were the exception. In the end I had to sell one sack of leather after another if I did not want to see my family go hungry. I don't know who told Sidi Pardu about the outcome of the trial or that his twelve sacks had passed into my possession. In any event the knowledge brought back his memory. All of a sudden he recalled who I was and where I lived.

"You bum, you thief . . . robber. . . . Give me back my leather!" One fine evening he stood in our doorway, roaring his head off. Remaining stretched out on my sheepskin, I removed the cigarette from my mouth:

"Who are you, my dear man? What leather are you talking about?" I inquired politely, as he had done when I was in the lurch because of him. "Why don't you go to the police if you are so convinced I got something of yours?" Scum settled at the corners of his mouth and for a moment I was afraid a stroke would fell Sidi Pardu right in our doorway. However, he lived on for many more years and died of old age in Israel.

On my way home from camp, my sleeve marked with the Star of

David, I would often linger by the well, hoping Miriam might come along. These were no times for elopement and marriage so I would simply smooth her hair on the sly, look into her eyes, and if nobody was around she would sometimes let me carry her bucket.

We were into February already. It was the eve of Tu B'Shvat, the festival of the trees. Her apron was flapping in the wind.

"Happy holiday, Fallu." She smiled a sad smile, tightening the shawl around her shoulders. I gazed at the thorny hedge behind her.

"What happy holiday?" I asked with bitterness. Still bare of blossoms, my old prickly-pear hedge seemed to mock dates on the Jewish calendar or any festival of rebirth. Indifferent it was at best, and alien as most everything around me had become.

"After the war . . . I will go . . . to Eretz Israel. . . ." The wind had torn it from me. Startled at my own words, I took a step backward. Miriam put down her pail so heavily that half the water splashed over the sides. Why did she have to wear an apron printed with green bows? They looked so sour that it set my teeth on edge. Where were the faded pansies that smelled of her father's spice shop? Was it the unfamiliar apron, the manginess of the spiky cactus leaves that made me suddenly feel like an outcast—a stranger on my native soil? There at the well on the eve of the Tu B'Shvat I knew that I would have to leave with or without Miriam.

I did not tell her why I was so sore, what had happened to me in the morning. Nor would I burden my mother, I decided when I came home and she set a small plate with dates, figs and nuts before me. Already at the gate I had been greeted by the smells of Tu B'Shvat: roast fowl stuffed with liver, rice and turmeric. The last of my pigeons had to have its soft throat slit so that my mother could present her firstborn with the traditional dish. I should have asked my younger cousins to share in the feast as custom required, however, and without taking into account that there was scarcely enough for me and Fraji to eat, I was in no mood for feasting. I felt numb and the back of my head was aching.

That same morning I had been bending over a soldier's boot, shining it into a mirror when a blow on the neck had nearly knocked me over.

"Jew's wages," the soldier laughed, pulling the polished boot beside the other one, already finished. Then his fist, like a sledgehammer, came down once more. His comrades would pay me with half a bar of chocolate or a few cigarettes. Sometimes they would just walk away. Never before had they struck me. "Obey . . . they are very, very strong, yet only feeble children in the eyes of the Almighty. . . ." I had tried to hold on to the words of our rabbi, but the shame and hurt were too much for me. Huddled in the greasy overcoat, my throbbing head hung between my knees, I had sat there crying in sight of the whole camp, hot tears dripping on the black boot polish.

"*Qu'est-ce qu'il-y-a?*" It was the voice of an officer for whom I had run errands addressing me in French. "*Was ist los?*" he asked a group of soldiers when I remained silent. Of all their mutterings I had only understood the word *Jude*. I had heard the officer bark an order and boots thumping. Looking up, I saw several dozen soldiers standing three rows deep. The soldier who had hit me was in front of everybody else. Every last trace of a smile had disappeared from his face when the captain, finally through with him, turned to me:

"Get up, man. Tomorrow, seven o'clock sharp at my quarters. . . ." And with that I was promoted from handyman to officer's servant.

His little flat near the railway station looked tidier than any dwelling I had ever set foot in. Why he wanted it cleaned every day was beyond me. I did as I was told: made the bed, washed the floor, scoured the kitchen and beat the carpet until threads started loose at the edges. Next I dusted the books. But what about that horde of graven images? Was I supposed to wipe those too? I thought of my father. How lucky that he did not have to see me standing there, cleaning one after another of an astonishing number of mostly naked women made from dirty-looking, pockmarked green metal, chipped marble and worm-eaten wood.

I could not understand why the captain had grouped them all over his neat room: the bookcase, the desk, the shelf and even the windowsills were crammed full of these abominations. Any good Jew would have averted his eyes, either calling them "heathen's work," if he could not help mentioning these things, or "antiques" if he were more open-minded. He would not besmirch his tongue with the word "sculpture." Had someone then told me I myself would one day mold figures out of clay and dig for antiques in—of all places— the sacred soil of Eretz Israel, I would have called him a liar to his face.

I was still dusting the sculptures, looking them over to get used to them, when the captain came back. Walking straight over to his bed he was groping under the pillow.

"Where is my pistol?" he asked. "And the money?" His voice rose, he knelt down on the floor to search under the mattress.

"Obey . . ." the rabbi had said. But I had found out that to get on with the Germans it was no less important to appear half-witted. Wide-eyed and letting my mouth hang open, I had the captain search for a few more moments before pointing to the drawer in his desk. There lay his bills neatly folded with the pistol on top as I had put them coming upon the captain's valuables in the most unlikely locations. A German officer scattering money under his bed! Any child could see through his scheme. It must have been quite an effort for him to throw anything at all under the bed—a needless effort. Uninvited, I would not even taste the wine he had me bring for him from the comité.

The captain seemed to be more afraid of bedbugs than of bombs. During the three months that followed, I aired, sunned and shook out his bedclothes at least ninety times, scrubbed the floor with green soap, polished his desk until my face glared at me from the dark veneer as a pale blob. Thoroughly as I dusted the sculptures they still looked old and dirty, some of them without arms or legs, one headless in the bargain. Handling them every day I had become strangely attached to the bunch, to the woman with the gilded crown smiling down at a child wrapped in the folds of her decayed, wooden dress. Best of all, however, I liked the girl with long curls and no nose, gracefully shielding her white marble belly with both arms. Those sculptures left me with my only pleasant memories of the six months of German occupation.

Liberation

Throughout February and March the captain was in an excellent mood, now and then even offering me a glass of the comité wine. But in April he became absentminded. All day long he tuned in to his radio, poring over maps when he did not listen to the news. Coming in for work one morning in early May, I found him making his bed himself. He told me to run to the seashore on the double. A gang of some fifty Jewish laborers, many of them my friends and cousins, were already at work there unloading rocks as ordered by the Germans who wanted to extend the existing wooden pier farther out into the sea.

It was back to stone carrying and shoveling but here on my own beach, hopeful that a longer pier might help us to get rid of our oppressors, I did not mind the sweat. My head was as light as the stones were heavy. I dumped whole truckloads of rocks and sand into the water, pushed wheelbarrow after wheelbarrow to the end of the wharf. High up in the sky and invisible to the naked eye, Allied planes were humming—a constant reminder that deliverance was near. The Germans, meanwhile, kept gunning away at the seemingly calm waters: "Submarines," they said, not letting go of their field glasses for an instant. Working round the clock to get them their pier, the humming and booming was music to our ears. "Hamus is coming," we smiled at each other.

Hamus which means five—five fingers against the evil eye—was the nickname of good portent we had given the Allies. Incomprehensible to German ears, it allowed us to speak freely of our eagerly awaited friends.

Then, one night, my father woke me up pointing to the rosy crisscross in the lattice window.

"It's not the moon," he said softly so as not to disturb my mother. "It's the hand of the Almighty!" he exclaimed as we climbed up on the roof. Our faces shiny as oranges, we sat for a long while side by side, gazing at the blazing sea and a torpedoed Italian ammunition ship going up in fireworks. Had it truly been His hand guiding the missile? Who knows? Of one thing I am sure. It was not merely chance that made the torpedo miss me so narrowly the next morning. Even I can recognize a miracle when I see one. Afterward, I spent the whole evening at Rabbi Hai synagogue reading psalms.

Leaning against my wheelbarrow I had been catching my breath for a moment when I saw a straight white line racing toward me on the water. An earsplitting whistle made me jump aside and a huge cigar shrieked by, swallowed up by the sand behind me. The only torpedo to have reached our shore during the war, carrying half a ton of TNT, had just landed amid some fifty Jews (not counting the Germans) and failed to explode. Nothing but a small hole in the sand marked its passage. Having been snatched from the jaws of death, everybody responded in his own way: the Germans cursing and gunning, the Jews by blowing kisses to the humming heavens. The sky was now so thick with planes, the sea so crammed with submarines, that the Germans, apparently having abandoned hope at rescue from the sea, suddenly transferred us from the half-finished wharf into town to help them build rafts instead. They had been in a hurry to get their pier built; now our masters became frantic. The speed with which we had been working on the beach had been a snail's pace compared with the rush for the rafts. Still the Germans went on pretending. The haste was their way of getting things done. They said they were going to stay with us forever.

Welding empty petrol barrels to large metal frames, I could

hardly hide my joy. With every plank I screwed on the iron, I had to suppress a cheer. Having in this manner put together six rafts in five days and fitted each one with an engine, the Germans had us hoist them on large trucks. They then helped us haul the whole lot to the shore. And through all this I had to appear gullible enough to believe that the sole aim of the operation was a pleasure outing for the soldiers.

At sundown, after the last raft had been secured to the pier, the captain called me to his flat which looked as neat and trim as ever. It was plain to me that he wished to say good-bye, but how could he, poor man, when he was not supposed to leave in the first place and, moreover, a handshake with a Jew was out of the question? So he simply gave me one more order:

"Tomorrow morning very early you will come with a cart. . . . Take everything you see here in this room . . . understood?" If he pretended, so could I. Keeping my dumb face to the end, I nodded in silence, leaving with a last glance at the wooden Madonna, the marble girl and the captain, none of which I have ever seen again. Where had all those sculptures come from? Plundered palaces, bombed churches? Where did they end up I still sometimes ask myself. No Jew or Moslem would have had them. Did a looting Bedouin take them home to his tent for his children to play with? Might an Italian fisherman have taken the Madonna to ensure himself good catches? And the captain. Was he one of the few who made it to Pantelleria and Sicily? I wonder whether he got that far on those rafts. More likely he reached Kelibia, the small fishing port at the farthest point of Cape Bon which became the Tunisian Dunkirk. There the Americans advancing from the west and the English coming up from Tripolis drove the Germans into a blind corner, taking them prisoners by the thousands.

Moslems and Jews alike stayed home behind closed doors the night the Germans fled. Those Arabs who at dawn ventured out to loot the camps were the exception. If I still have two arms and legs I owe it to my father's strict order not to go near anything German for the next few days. Many who did were maimed by explosives attached to the doors of cars and tanks. Wherever one spat—on the beach, in the market, the fields with their ammunition dumps and of course, the railroad station and the camps—there were vehicles, weapons, every imaginable kind of equipment which had been left behind by their owners who, together with their rafts, had vanished into the night.

Unlike the morning a half year earlier when Hitler's soldiers had first rolled into our town, it was the Arabs who now peeked from behind closed shutters while the Jews expectantly strode up and

down the streets repeating as they walked: "Hamus, Hamus is coming. . . ."

As in a dream where some dismal event we thought long buried
in the past happens all over again, I felt the same sinking feeling
when the first Allied troops finally arrived. Once more soldiers in
khaki uniforms jumped smilingly off motorcycles by the barbershop.
Then two jeeps came to a standstill between the date palms in the
middle of the square in the exact spot where the Germans had
stopped six months earlier. Next came armored vehicles, guns and
tanks. Only when the crews began to shower us with chocolate and
chewing gum did I wake up to the sweetness of the hour. The joy was
indescribable. Blessings, tears, arrack mingled in our mouth as we
blew kisses to the sky, embraced in turn each other and our libera-
tors. I saw ordinarily tightfisted people like my father water the trees
with expensive liquor!

And then a song rose over Nabeul, an interminable song that did
not die down for three days and three nights. I let myself float with
the song:

> Allah elahna—Allah elahna,
> Hamus ekun maanah.
> The Lord is with us—God is with us
> And Hamus stays at our side.
> By day he takes photographs,
> Throughout the night drops bombs.
> Long live Hamus, long live Hamus
> Who has freed us from the pick and shovel.

Carrying the whole town away, the hymn went on and on. Every Jew
with a fast-running tongue added a verse or two. It even brought the
sulking Moslems up onto their roofs, staring with amazement at
some of their most dignified neighbors drunkenly dancing in the
street below.

Singing the praise of Hamus, we did not know that thanks to the
rapid advance of the English and American forces we had escaped
much worse than pick and shovel. Later we learned that the Germans
had already planned the construction of gas chambers destined to
take care of all the Jews now rejoicing in the streets of Tunisia.

Others besides our people were happy. The Italian unit, which
had stayed behind when their German allies had taken to the rafts,
were also in high spirits. For them the war was finished. As if they
were waiting to be taken prisoners, they were all over town, taking a
last fling at liberty. French officials too were very much in evidence,
covered with medals and cockades, their gala uniforms reeking of
mothballs. Pale-faced and red-eyed from a half year of hiding in clos-

ets, caves or whatnot, they blinked like rabbits venturing out of their holes to check whether the rain had stopped.

No less befuddled than anyone else on that first night of our deliverance, I can yet see the look of Rabbi Hai synagogue, overflowing with worshipers swaying unsteadily through psalms and prayers. I can still see the fat moon hanging in the skylight, the star-studded flag of the victors draped over the damp stains in Rabbi Hai's mirror. In his dusty room, the spirit of the red-maned kabbalist must have trembled with the cobwebs at the sounds coming from downstairs, where Rabbi Shushan was wresting blares from his ram's horn that were piercing enough to arouse the dead. A more palpable presence were our guests. American Jews in battle fatigues were occupying the coveted seats facing the Torah shrine, and halfway through the last prayer everybody scrambled for the honor to be host to them for the evening meal. Shooshoo, the shoemaker, and Sidi Hushhash nearly came to blows, each tearing at one arm of a lanky, bewildered-looking fellow in spattered uniform who seemed to want one thing only, a corner where he could lie down and sleep.

On the following morning we saw helmeted Englishmen armed with machine guns driving trucks full of captured Germans through our town.

"Amalek . . . Pharaoh . . . Satan!" The air over Bab Salah Street was charged with curses. Crammed into English command cars with their hands folded over their heads, the Germans seemed to have lost much of their arrogance. One could say that the hated host looked almost pitiable.

I am not proud of what came next, but since it happened I cannot simply skip over it. The whole wretched incident was started by a few old women. Learning that the people on the trucks were Germans they naturally spread out five fingers to ward off the evil eye, then screaming:

"Hitler . . . Hitler . . . poo . . . poo . . . poo . . ." They spat over their shoulders, in the end aiming their spittle straight at the haggard, unshaven faces of the prisoners. Since not even old women can spit forever, younger people had to take over as truck after truck rolled by. Soon they were at it with rotten tomatoes and any kind of refuse they could lay their hands on. They wound up splashing sewage from the rooftops. Hauling the stuff up from the cesspool by the barrelful, my friend Reuben entered into a frenzy of dirt splashing and I helped him. I did it too. First gorging ourselves on the frankfurters and kidney beans the soldiers were distributing to the hungry, we then used the empty cans for pouring. I intended the refuse to land on those prisoners who had pushed me with their rifle butts, the guard who had laughed aiming at my head, the sergeant who had

so liked to kick legs—all those Germans with the skull and cross-
bones. If I hit the captain or some of those nice Czechs who always
told us how they had been forced into the army against their will, I
am sorry.

Clustered around Café Sportez and the Hôtel de France, the
shovelers back from Menzel-Temime, ordinary Jews and Frenchmen
fresh out of hiding, were relating their adventures. Some were truly
hair-raising. I will tell the one that happened to Monsieur Grosjean,
the gendarme who, dead set against serving under the *Boches* as he
called the Germans, had decided to disappear. Thoroughly disliked
by the Arab townsfolk who would have been delighted to inform on
him, this was easier said than done. Monsieur Grosjean, however,
had hit upon a great idea.

Showing all the signs of overwhelming grief, his wife had informed friends and neighbors of her husband's sudden demise and
ordered an expensive coffin (later to be resold at a discount). His last
wish had been to be buried on the family's farm in the country, she
had told everybody when the casket with the "deceased" had been
heaved on the roof of the bus that was to take him to his resting place.
Having made sure her husband had been safely secured to the luggage rack, the "widow" took her seat inside the vehicle which started
on its journey. Stopping at every village the bus soon filled up, so that
one of the travelers, a fallah, had to accommodate himself on the
roof—as far away from the coffin as he could sit. The vehicle was
rattling on, the Arab nodding in his corner, when he suddenly stiffened—too horrified to make a sound. Slowly the coffin lid was
opening, a hand was groping. Finally managing one loud cry, the
panic-stricken voyager jumped off the roof. Until then unaware that
he had company, Monsieur Grosjean, hearing the shriek, had at once
reclosed the lid of his coffin. Hours later the body of the unfortunate
fallah was found lying in the road.

He, Monsieur Grosjean, had, of course, never been dead in the
first place, said the Frenchman as he told us his story, posing in his
gala uniform on the steps of the Hôtel de France. Hot inside his sticky
little prison, he had simply wanted to take a breath of fresh air!

Three days of celebrations the rabbis had allowed, three days of
pleasure, of wine and of arrack to drown six months of abuse. Roaming the streets every waking hour and for the best part of the night, I
lived off cans with orange-colored cheese and sweet milk so thick one
had to eat it with a spoon. There also were biscuits, chocolate and
chewing gum. For three days I fraternized with Allied tank crews and
tried to speak English. Then it was back to everyday life in a world
still very much at war, in a greatly impoverished community where a
Jew had to fend for himself amid his newly hostile Arab townsmen.

Thrown in a maze of foreign troops, I got on well with all of them—the Americans under Patton, the British under Montgomery, the French under General Giraud, not to forget the Senegalese. I eked out a living in a hundred different ways. My father and his donkey, however, had hit upon hard times. Same as before the war, the animal would bring my father home on Thursday afternoon, gaily braying when, turning the corner of Bab Salah Street, it caught a whiff of the females of the neighborhood. Its ears cocked through the holes of an old straw hat, it would at that point break into a trot despite the fact that its side boxes were still as full of wares as when the donkey and its master had set out on Sunday morning.

"Gold and silver lace, pure white muslin . . . grass-green satin . . . rosy silk for blushing brides. Rainbow ribbons, combs, clasps shinier than stars. . ." My father knew the words a fallah's wife could not resist; but nowadays they brought no echo from silent dirt roads broiling in the sun. Shutters remained closed. Only a sheep dog here and there barked a short welcome. My father, who had all his life been on cordial terms with the villagers, refused to accept the obvious which was that the fallahs would no longer buy from Jews. At the mosque the Imam had urged Friday worshipers to refrain from doing so. An old acquaintance and previously faithful client, this dignitary had squirmed like a fish when my father had cornered him.

"Now, now, Hamus, my friend, calm yourself. . . . Nobody here has a grudge against you. But what can I do? After all, I am a village Imam who gets orders from higher up. . . .

Here it must be said that many Arabs, having witnessed the humiliation of their Jewish neighbors at the hands of the Germans with wonder and a great deal of satisfaction, had become convinced that where there was smoke there must be fire. The Chosen People had brought it on themselves, they said. Something was rotten with the Jews. Also, with Arab hopes of independence from the French dashed by the defeat of their German friends, their hearts filled with consternation. On whom could they take out their disappointment if not on us?

For a while my father's business went from bad to worse, yet he would not give in. Stubbornly he kept lowering his prices until, little by little the fallahs started coming around. Why pay through the nose for striped cotton, even to one's own brother, when Hamus, the Jew, hidden under an olive tree, was selling rose-patterned satin for a song?

It was lucky I was there to help out during those months. My father had to admit it. The last of Sidi Pardu's hides was barely gone when I had come into another fortune. All the upholstery of the abandoned German trucks and command cars was there for the taking. Ripping out the leather, I soon had a new trade going—sewing shoulder holsters for Americans who liked to live close to their pistols and did not mind the price. Today I could hit myself to think of it, but at the time I had my doubts about those green narrow dollars—all printed with hatless old men in queer haircuts. If a client did not have any of our Tunisian camels or orange pickers I preferred to be paid in kind with coffee, tea, canned food and cigarettes.

After the upholstery had run out and the last Yankee had gone home, I found a way to make a living with the British, who were less affluent than their allies from the other side of the Atlantic. Since they seemed unable to resist oranges, I got myself a permit to hawk oranges in their camp by promising fixed prices. On the side I still found time for some trade in dismantled mines. Secretly I sold the explosive to my old friends, the Italian fishermen. I also once agreed to barter with French soldiers from Tahiti who, short on cash and fond of fishing, promised to pay me back in kind. In the evening they brought me a generous part of their catch which I had to keep cool overnight if I wanted to find buyers in the morning. Watching out for cats, I put the sackful of fish on the terrace, closing every door and window, blocking every access, stuffing up every hole and crack; then I went to bed down on my sheepskin. I had maybe slept for half an hour when the howling started. That night all the cats of Nabeul assembled on our roof. The neighbors would not speak to me for at least a week. Dead tired, the next morning I found my fish untouched and only slightly smelly. But from then on I avoided bartering with Tahitians.

For a short while I tried my hand at the pepper trade. Later, in partnership with Shooshoo, the shoemaker, I invested part of my earnings in a calf, walking it every day to pasture—rain or shine. It so thrived on the thistles by the seashore that after a few weeks of grazing, a butcher passing by made me an offer: a hundred and fifty francs instead of the hundred and thirty we had paid for it. Giving the good news to my partner, I proposed to split the profit in the middle. Shooshoo, however, would not hear of it.

"What middle?" he sneered. "I put a hundred and twenty-five francs into that calf for your five. Where do you see a middle? Take back your five francs and go in good health!"

"Oh, no," I said. "Have you forgotten how I slaved to fatten it? What do I get for all that grazing?" I then went straight to the calf to take possession of the pretty leather collar my partner had put around the animal's neck. In the end, we went to the rabbi. Besides my investment, I received five francs of the profit while Shooshoo got fifteen plus his collar. After that he did not want any more partnership with me.

When the French Senegalese arrived in town—tall, broad-necked blacks—women and girls could not tear their eyes from the sashes they wore wound around their waists. Such silky, bright red fabric they had not seen since the outbreak of the war. Generously cut, only two sashes were needed to make a dress. Before long every female in Nabeul boasted of either a gown, a skirt, a blouse or at least a pair of scarlet underpants. The whole town brightened up. Though I myself bought and resold quite a few of them, I have never understood from where these blacks got so many sashes. I also wondered why, as a boy, I had been so afraid of Senegalese soldiers that I would take long detours to avoid them. They were very friendly people once I got to know them. Cockily sporting one earring and always smiling with a broad mouthful of teeth, they would politely approach me in Bab Salah Street or anywhere else in town for that matter.

"*Où casser le coucou? Où casser le coucou?*" they kept asking. At first at a loss as to the meaning of their urgent-sounding request, I soon found out that all they wanted to know were the directions to Nabeul's one Arab brothel.

Even after the French authorities had traced the outbreak of red fashions to their source, the Senegalese continued to do business in our town. Before using the sashes, the women would simply dye them into less eye-catching colors. Since I wore mine underneath my father's kashabia, I left it in its original bright hue. It came in handy for the new profitable sideline I had just discovered: trafficking in pistols.

Fallahs and Bedouins had come upon large dumps in the countryside. Equipment from hammers and saws to electric drills and wrenches labeled MADE IN GERMANY were sold openly in the market. For years Jews and Moslems alike walked around in clothes cut out of khaki canvas. So long as trafficking was limited to tools, tents and uniforms and attracted less notice than red sashes, the French would rather look the other way. Having enough on their hands with the Tunisian liberation movement, with Bourguiba and his Neo-Destour, the authorities were mainly after enemy arms that fell to the Arabs.

Caught between embittered Moslems and fed-up French protectors, hampered at every step by the chronic lack of raw materials, how was a Jew to make an honest living? Worse still, life had become dull. After all the excitement of the past year, how was I supposed to sit in my shop day in, day out, making shoes out of car seats and tires? Also, since there seemed to be more shoemakers than shoe buyers, my Arab colleagues bore me a grudge for every pair of slippers I managed to sell.

"Good morning, Said," I would greet the cobbler next to my own shop, one of those who had been beside himself with mirth the day the Germans had driven me past his booth. Now outright sullen, he would not even lift his eyes from the leather stretched over an out-dated form:

"May Satan fly away with you, your good morning, and all Jew dogs . . ." I heard him mutter. Was it a wonder that I was disgruntled and saw more promise in the risks and glamour of the arms trade than in shoemaking?

Half a dozen pistols tucked away in the folds of my Senegalese sash, I took the train to Sfax, feeling very important. I must also have appeared suspiciously weighty with my father's kashabia thrown over my stocky and now pistol-belted middle because, alighting from the train, I promptly attracted the attention of a police spy. Seeing him behind me I realized that the dumbest thing I could possibly do was follow my impulse to run—and where to? Apart from the Jewish tailor expecting me at the other end of town I did not know a living soul in Sfax. Starting off in his direction, I found it so hard to slow down my feet that I turned cold with perspiration.

"Quick, I am being followed . . ." I said when I at last arrived at my destination. I unwound the red sash as fast as my clammy fingers could make it, and not a moment too soon either. A few seconds later my shadow threw open the door. By then the pistols were safely hidden. Smilingly, the tailor presented his cousin from Nabeul to *"monsieur l'agent,"* and I made a nice profit on the deal. However, since I was now under suspicion, my steps probably watched, it was back to cobblers' row again.

XXVI

After the War

My roving ways did nothing to endear me to Miriam's family, of course. More convinced than ever that they had been right to oppose our marriage, they were nevertheless beginning to worry—wondering why nobody else was asking for their daughter's hand. Soft and sandy-haired as ever, she would go to draw water in the afternoon. Yet even though I was lately coming less often to the well, no other youth would make a pass at her. As it was plain to see that my cousin and I were still waiting, hoping for our families to change their minds, nobody wished to spoil my chances.

"Miriam, look at me," I would plead as she stood there with one hand desperately pumping, the other clutching the handle of her bucket, afraid someone might tell her brothers I had helped her carry it.

"Last month it has been four years since we were promised to each other," I persisted. "And what have we got to show for it? Nothing. . . . Those years have run off like piss in the sand. . . . Your father still does not want to see mine, your brothers hardly talk to me . . . but they will, I promise you; everything will be all right if we get married."

Still no word out of her; only her lashes fluttered lightly, a tear was running by her nose. "Come with me now . . . with your bucket just as you are; I don't need you in a white dress. All we need are two witnesses and a ring to put on your finger. I say: " 'With this ring you are bound to me according to the law of Moses and of Israel' " and we are man and wife forever. Nobody can untie the knot against our will—not your father, not your brothers, not even the rabbi. . . ." She only sighed. How many years can one plead and beg, getting nothing but sighs for an answer?

I began taking strolls where people were more talkative, to the beach for instance. There I met, among others, my older cousin Jacqueline, chaperoning a white-clad belle. The girl's face was half hidden by dark locks blowing in the breeze; anyway it was her figure that intrigued me. The kind I liked: not too plump and not too skinny, not too tall and not too short, I observed while Cousin Jacqueline was inquiring about my mother's health and the price of a pair of shoes.

"For you four francs with prewar rubber," I remember saying as a gust of wind blew the girl's hair to one side, revealing a full-colored cheek, the mocking corner of a mouth and a straight nose. I thought I knew her—one of the six daughters of Camoona and Abraham, the greengrocer, if I was not mistaken. It was Fortuna, the one with the black apron and red buttons whom I used to pull by her pigtails on her way from school.

"Do you know my neighbor, Fortuna?" My cousin presented her companion who now stood restraining her hair with both hands and looking blank.

Where was that spark of admiration I had come to take for granted in the eyes of girls? Could she, after ten years, still resent me because of that paltry piece of licorice I once forced down her throat? I sharpened the crease in my trousers, pushed my cap over one ear, then let both hands underline the story of how the manani fish had pulled Shishi, the dwarf, into the water. At last the dark eyes lit up and when I came to the point where the fish had bolted with Shishi's tackle she threw her head back with laughter, showing me the full length of her throat. Well satisfied, I walked on to Ramoo's beach café to drink a glass of wine. I had completely forgotten about Fortuna, her white dress and soft throat when a few days later Cousin Jacqueline entered my shop to order the four-franc shoes.

"Don't you think it's about time a fine, healthy fellow like you finally got married?" she asked out of the blue. Bent in two to chalk the contour of her heel I did not answer. "If ever you make up your mind you will be welcome at my neighbor's. My feet itch to dance at your wedding. . . ." Her big toe played with the piece of chalk as she smiled down at me. Slowly straightening up, it was my turn to look down upon Jacqueline.

"I am not yet knocking on anybody's door, Cousin. Not before I am good and ready," I said. "Thank your neighbors for the kind invitation but such matters I decide on my own." There was no further mention of Fortuna when my cousin came to pay for her shoes.

Soon after this little incident I was forced to go and look for work in the capital since clients like Jacqueline had become rare birds indeed. I considered myself lucky when one of the many shoemakers in the big city consented to hire me.

Why is it always poor Jews who are the most generously blessed with daughters? For example, my cousin Heloo had nine girls and one son. His wife's face I cannot remember at all. Whether out of guilt or misery, standing or walking, her eyes were expecting bread for her hungry brood to sprout under her feet. Whenever my mother sent me to her with leftovers it took at most two minutes for any pot to be returned to me clean and shiny as the day it had come out of the potter's kiln.

Here I would like to mention that my cousin's one son, who became a tailor, went to France from where he sent for the whole family to join him and did not rest until he had found husbands for all of his nine sisters.

To the shoemaker who hired me, the Almighty had also given daughters with both hands. Seven of them. Once he had lodged me in his home it did not take long to understand why my cousin Heloo with his nine had become a heavy drinker. My boss, a kind man, was desperate to have me pick either his first- or second-born. No parents would consent to marry off their younger daughters as long as the older ones had not yet found a mate. Wages were good and the food even better, as the girls, under the expert guidance of their mother, spent most of their time in the kitchen preparing my favorite dishes. Then seven pairs of black eyes, silently pleading, would watch me eat—the oldest hoping to be taken off the hook, the younger ones wondering if their turn would ever come. After a couple of months in the shoemaker's house, I could not take it any longer. One more spoonful of lovingly stuffed squash and I would choke, I felt, running to take the train home.

My brother Fraji, as usual out on the doorstep watching passersby, was the first one to welcome me:

"Fuff—Fuff—Fallu . . ." he crowed happily, but my heart sank
when my parents came out to greet me. That my mother would shed
tears at our reunion was only to be expected. She had gotten thinner,
but the one who looked truly awful was my father. Heavily dragging
one foot he was pressing a chunk of honeycomb to a badly bruised
and swollen eye. Those parts of his face not covered by his beard
were disfigured by scratches. He had been worse when he first came
home, said my mother. Fallahs had attacked him in one of the
villages, robbed him of his merchandise and made off with the
donkey.

Lately the Arabs, from the learned Imam down to illiterate
farmers, were talking about nothing but "Falastina" as they called
Eretz Israel, where their Moslem brothers and the Jews were locked
in a great battle for the possession of the land. The day the radio in
the Arab coffeehouse announced an Arab victory their hearts would
burst with pride, the next with rage as the numbers of casualties were
revealed. It had been the same in the capital.

"*Klab—klab* . . . dog" rang in my ears wherever I went, muttered
under the breath of passengers in the streetcar or thrown at me together with an orange by a fruit vendor; "klab" whispered behind my
back or "klab" spit into my face. "Dogs, go to Falastina!" the mob had
been screaming, smashing shop windows near the great synagogue.
"Either die for our faith or live as free men. . . ." They kept chanting
Bourguiba's motto when the gendarmes arrived after the looting.
Bourguiba urged Jews and Moslems, both born on Tunisian soil, to
rise against the French as brothers, and I believe he meant what he
was saying. The problem, however, was that few Moslems wished to
have Jewish brothers and even fewer Jews—except for a handful of
young hotheads—wanted to get rid of their French protectors. Sons
of Nabeul's richest families needing a cause, anything at all to relieve
their boredom, were speeding along in their father's automobiles
spreading socialism, going to the secret meetings of the Neo-Destour.
Every time they were arrested their fathers had to come and bail them
out of jail.

"Better a mean French sparrow in one's hand than a beautiful
Arab Socialist Republic on the roof," they would admonish their met-
tlesome offspring, at the same time sending a contribution to Bourguiba's cause to be on the safe side.

On the other hand there were people like Hanina, son of poor
parents like myself, who had always been curious and enterprising.
While at Talmud-Torah school he had felt Rabbi Parienti's cane for
cutting up bugs during class to see what was inside and once during

French lessons had set fire to the cupboard in which Monsieur Mauricet had shut him up. He had come back from Tunis as an electrician,
the only one in town to ply such a strange trade. Besides copper wire,
china cones and glass bulbs he had brought a huge quantity of pam-
phlets to Nabeul, working harder on the distribution of the latter than
on his electricity.

Hanina was a communist, people said, lowering their voices.
Like the Neo-Destour, he never stopped talking of brotherhood; although with him it was the workers all over the world: white, black
and yellow . . . Jews, Moslems or Christians. If they were poor, he
would shout they were brothers and had but one enemy, the rich. So
far, so good. But when he started to speak up against the rabbis and
religion he was going beyond the mark.

"Communists marry their own sisters . . ." whispered horrified
Moslems to each other, while the Jews, sneering at the red pam-
phlets, wished they were printed on cabbage leaves rather than on
paper so they could at least be used for soup. They were only half
joking. My mother, for one, would have welcomed any addition to
her thin stews!

Limping back and forth between the battered drawer and the
window, my father was racking his brains trying to think of something salable, chiding me for having left my place of work in Tunis.
Still without another job I was sitting in the yard, shooing away
sparrows and starlings from the pumpkin seeds my mother had put
to dry in the sun when suddenly I heard a familiar braying. Who was
galloping toward me, trumpeting joyous "hee-haws" but my father's
donkey? The poor beast had lost weight, probably ill-treated by its
new master. It had run away, perhaps wandering for days to find its
way back home. Notwithstanding its faithfulness, my father was
forced to sell the animal once it had regained its strength so that he
could buy some new merchandise. From then on he became his own
donkey. He would himself carry the bales of fabric, ribbons, lace and
combs in two heavy baskets as he once more set out for the villages.

With the return of the donkey a modest share of luck had come to
me also. An Arab shoemaker hired me, though for very low wages. In
the afternoon I went to the well to share the good news with Miriam
whom I had not seen for three months. The last time we met was on
the day that I had gone to search for work in Tunis. Once more I
would ask her to marry me—the very last time I promised myself as I
saw her coming with her bucket. Sharp shadows underneath the eyes
made her look pale, older than the dove-eyed girl who had so softly
pushed herself between me and the shoemaker's seven daughters.
She had been sick with a fever she explained and, with no one
around, greeted me warmly.

"How well you look, Fallu, dear. I was worried. I thought they might let you go hungry in the city. . . ." She seemed a little thinner, maybe a little older, but the moment I felt her lips and heard her voice it was the same as it had always been. Bees were humming; the sweet scent of the prickly pears filled my heart with longing. In the shade of a big yellow flower, five young sparrows were perched on a cactus leaf as under an umbrella, clamoring for the fleshy scraps of fruit their parents were stuffing into their beaks.

"Look at them, Miriam . . . all my friends are married and have at least one baby. . . . We have lost five years already. . . ." Chasing a dragonfly out of her hair, I wound the strands around her throbbing throat. "It's true, Jacob waited fourteen years for Rachel, but that was a long time ago before all the wars—the Germans and the Arabs. I have to tell you, I am fed up with waiting—I am fed up with the word 'klab' . . . Marry me. Forget about everybody. We will start a new life in Eretz Israel."

She smiled. "We will," she said wistfully. "We will both go to Eretz Israel, just be patient some more. . . . When I lay sick with the fever I had a dream. One of those black dreams that are better forgotten. Don't ask me what it was. The moment I was on my feet again I went over to Tootoo's house to make sure it was a lie. But she took so long, Fallu, that I became afraid. She looked and looked into her water glass without a word. When she did say something in the end, it made me so happy that I gave her ten sous. . . . She saw both of us in that glass. You and me in Eretz Israel. . . ."

"Fine," I said, "we make it happen. Come along, I will dress the huppa in my father's courtyard right away. Tomorrow morning we'll apply for passports. . . ." Once more she spoiled it all, once too often. The sighs. The tears. Her brothers were going to kill her. I should wait just a little longer . . .

I meant what I had said. I was fed up. Too hurt to manage a good-bye, I turned on my heels and walked away. I was through with her. I did not go back to the well, and in all my life met Miriam only one more time, in Eretz Israel.

My new boss, the Arab, did not have much work. No money was left over for extras. If I wanted to eat, come evening, I searched the bottom of my pockets for the coin that would buy me a glass of wine or two at Majloo's café. Much as I tried to recapture the flavor of past pleasures, one after another they turned sour like spilt milk curdling in the summer heat. While I was rowing on a glittering stream of sunlight straight into the morning sky, all was peaceful and the fish were biting. Why did the Arab fishermen have to wink at each other and make snide remarks about the one miserable wall of our Temple still standing in Jerusalem? Why did they brag about thousands of "klabs" killed in "Falastina" as if we were not rowing side by side, old friends in the same boat. I knew better. We were winning. The Jews. The few against the many. But I kept silent, impatient to get back to shore and away from their sneering faces and baiting remarks.

Even the Friday market let me down. Inviting as ever it stretched out before me, the gay red carpet of tarbooshes and peppers woven through my childhood. Relishing the tickle in my nose, I plunged with a resounding *hatshum* into the waves of sneezers. Hatshum echoed in front of me and klab came from behind. Thinking I might feel easier among the animals, I pushed beyond fishmongers' row into the noise of hundreds of sheep, goats and cows herded into the cattle market. Their sounds joined the racket of hoarsely haggling Bedouins and fallahs. "Goa—goa—goa—" Snarling through foaming lips, an enraged camel was desperately trying to bite through the rope knotted around its nozzle. Forelegs and hind legs tied crosswise under its belly to keep it on its knees, the rabid beast had to be auctioned off for meat by its unhappy owner, so upset at the loss he seemed near tears.

"Ninety-five francs, ninety-five. . . . Who gives more will be blessed by Allah. . . . Ninety-seven over there. . . . Ninety-eight. It was the best camel on Cape Bon. . . . Like a lamb it went before the plow, drew more water than a pump. . . . Three hundred francs it was worth any day before Satan had to drive it mad."

Absorbed in the spectacle, I had paid no attention to the fact that mine was the only black beret in the crowd around me.

"Ninety-eight francs for the last time, who gives more? Since when do Jews eat camel meat?" The unlucky fallah's eyes had settled on my cap. "Would to Allah that Satan had entered a Jew-dog instead of my sweet camel . . . my lamb . . . my dove. . . ."

The strangest thing about it all was that I was beginning to feel truly guilty. Hot in the face, I backed away to seek comfort with someone who had never failed me—my beloved Booshadia. The market devil was fanning his feathers and rattling his boxes in the same spot where I had stood spellbound as a little boy, clutching my mother's hand. At the end of the war his act had been taken over by his eldest son, just as big, black and enjoyable as his father had once been. No more goose pimples on my arms, no more shudders running down my spine; still the old charm was working. His monstrous appearance, grunts and somersaults were enough to carry me back into my ancient world of jinn and fancies—free of Jew haters, unemployment and badly ending love affairs.

Rudely a fallah's voice returned me to the present:

"The seventh black cap to hit my eyes this morning. Surely an evil day ahead. . . ." A bony-faced fellow next to me pulled out of the ring of spectators.

"May Satan bring seven black years to the Jews in Falastina!" hissed another, spitting to the ground. That did it. I had had enough.

A Man Must Marry

It was Wednesday and important decisions should be made only on Thursdays, my mother always said. However, I could wait no longer. I went straight home to tell my parents that I wished to leave for Eretz Israel. My mother had seen it coming. Though the separation would surely break her heart she did her best to appear cheerful. My father, a deeply religious man who was surprisingly reasonable when it came to big undertakings, gave me his blessing. He made one condition: first, I must get married.

Letters had arrived from Israel, written by young Jews from Nabeul newly settled there. Some said they were fine, had plenty of work and did not need a thing. They urged their families to follow them to the land of their fathers as fast as they could. Others who had enlisted in the army the moment they set foot on firm ground told of heavy battles with the Arabs and complained of food rationing. On one point all of them agreed: one should not make the jump to the other end of the Mediterranean without a spouse. Married men served less time in the army and were given larger quarters. When it came to work, the more children they had, the better off they were—no matter whether boys or girls.

So here I was, finally forced to make a choice. Sitting in the shop of my Arab boss over forms and leather, I thought of all the maidens in Sabbath dresses I had seen standing on the doorsteps of their fathers' houses. Slightly blurred, their likenesses were passing back and forth before my mind, similar to the images on the badly stretched screen of the cinema—Nabeul's newest attraction. Girls with short hair and short skirts like those who used to stroll through the municipal gardens without a chaperone were not for me. Nor did I want the type who would wear dresses down to her ankles and would not dare to look at anyone in trousers. Since I had, not without great effort, managed to shut Miriam out of my mind, I was now left with a diminished line of skirts reaching to the middle of the calves, half a dozen trim waists and pleasant faces. Dark hair blowing in the wind, one of them kept cropping up more often than the others.

In the evening I played a guessing game with my mother.

"I have someone in mind," I said as she placed my bowl before me. In her excitement my mother ladled a spoonful of stew onto the rush mat.

"I am so glad to hear it, Fallu! May God grant me to see your children. . . . And who will be the wife of my darling son? Tell me . . ." My cheeks, burning like a boy's, my mouth full of rice and cabbage, I could only mumble.

"Let me guess now . . ." she smiled, squatting down beside me. "Does she live far from here?"

"Not too far."

"Perhaps right in Bab Salah Street . . . Hadad's daughter . . . the second one with the red fringe who helps her father sell the fish?"

"That one's got green eyes like a cat. Go farther to the left." My mother brought me another chunk of bread.

"Is it Smorda who lives with her widowed mother opposite Tibi's house—Mash'ood Tibi who trades in soap and stockings?"

"That one? That one I would not marry if she were the last Jewish girl in Nabeul! She's always scratching. No, no. Still farther."

"Oh, I have it!" My mother slapped her knee. "It must be between Hafzeah's herb shop and the prison. One of Amram's daughters. They are clean and pretty."

"Not either," I sighed, leaning back now with a full belly. "They are pretty but have the sharpest tongues in town." My mother frowned, a little puzzled.

"Who is it, then? Jacob, the watchmaker, who has a lean-to on the other side? He has one daughter left."

"I had completely forgotten that one. She never says a word. No. Go into Sheikh Munir Street." My mother thought hard.

"Who is there in Sheikh Munir Street but the rich girl over Bashu's grocery?" Her mention of the goldsmith's daughter reminded me of the girl in Gafsa and my ill-fated engagement to Miriam.

"Pass, pass . . . toward the corner, now you are getting there." Baffled she drew back.

"That's impossible, you cannot be seriously thinking of one of Tita's girls. They are mere children."

"Of course not," I laughed. "But, Mother, you are very close."

"Am I? Then it must have something to do with Cousin Jacqueline next door. One of her neighbors?" My mother was at the end of her tether.

"Can't you see?" I pointed in the general direction of Sheikh Munir Street. "It's Abraham's daughter, the third one. Fortuna!" My mother grasped her forehead.

"How stupid of me. How did I not guess sooner!" She hugged and kissed me. "Who else could it be but Fortuna! Such a lovely girl—clean and she can sew too. Every day her father went to synagogue when they were still living on Bab Salah Street. My dear son could not have made a better choice."

Coming home from the steam bath that evening, even my father seemed to approve. Less gruff than on ordinary days, he went so far as to pour both of us a big cupful of wine, announcing that on Saturday he would talk things over with Abraham.

To wait for three more days, from Wednesday to the Sabbath, was out of the question but I thanked my parents warmly.

"That's really not necessary. I am almost twenty-five years old . . . old enough to do my own asking." With that I shaved carefully, put on my white trousers and, whispering into my mother's ear, asked her to lend me some money. Steadied by a dozen more gulps from my father's bottle, I felt ready for my errand.

My mother's savings paid for three deep-fried egg and onion pastries, a few slices of cake and a bottle of wine—the whole offering barely covering the bottom of my basket. It had to suffice for a family of eight if I did not count Fortuna's two married sisters, my cousin Jacqueline and myself. My father's wine helped strengthen my resolve but not my legs which climbed the stairs to Jacqueline's flat somewhat reluctantly, independent of the rest of my body. My cousin took one look at me and one at my basket.

"Camoona!" she trumpeted in the direction of a downstairs window from where there came a loud, incessant rattling. "Camoona, do your best sahruta. Someone here wants to see your daughter . . ." and letting out a formidable, drawn-out whoop, she shoved me down the stairs into her neighbor's quarters, in front of two sewing machines and a roomful of wildly ululating women. There I stood on wobbly feet, sheepishly staring at my intended frozen halfway down a seam. The general warmth of the reception, however, put me quickly at ease. Not quite sober, not the hardest-working shoemaker in town—even if I had come completely empty-handed—in this house I would have felt welcome.

Happy for Fortuna and the fact that with her out of the way their own wedding dates had moved forward, her three younger sisters were cackling around me as excitedly as chicks on a hill of barley.

With little winks and a lot of giggling, they gave me to understand that in the exact spot where I sat sipping another cup of wine something lay hidden under the rush mat. It was the sisters' dowries, a thin parcel of chocolate-brown one-thousand-franc notes graced with caravans of pale-yellow camels—all the money they had saved through years of sewing. At night their mother slept on it. By day the girls would keep their hoard underneath the mat where they sat working. Now the time had come to open up the bundle. Ceremoniously, Camoona gave her daughter one of the four bills to do with as she pleased.

Fortuna did not seem to mind letting go of her caravan. Cheerfully she changed it into smaller bank notes: to rent a room, buy a few pieces of furniture and a mattress, sheets and towels, and the wine to which she treated me at every visit of our short courtship. With the last of her money she paid for her wedding dress, and by the time we made it to the huppa there were not even two francs left to carry us through our first day of married life.

During all the hard years that followed—first as penniless settlers in a new land, then bringing up our offspring on the salary of a gardener's helper, suffering through the death of one child and three more wars—Fortuna never once mentioned her "camels." Who can understand her? After the children had finally married, after we had paid off our flat and could breathe a little, just after I had bought her that useless wall clock she had wanted for so long, she suddenly remembers those brown bills. Since then she speaks of them with such regret and longing one might think it was part of herself she left behind under that mat in her father's house. Our fifty-shekel bills she stuffs into her purse without honoring Ben-Gurion with a single glance!

Despite his modest circumstances, Fortuna's father Abraham, a devout greengrocer, was highly respected by Jews and Moslems alike. Nobody, including his wife and probably himself as well, knew his income since he turned all his earnings over to the poor and to the synagogue. Over the years he must have given away quite a fortune, working for one purpose only, to secure himself a spot in the next world. He has been there for four years now, may he rest in peace.

Fruit and vegetables were but part of the picture. Abraham dealt in a profitable sideline. He served as honest broker for those in need of a favor from the Qaid who, mainly settling disputes over the ownership of land, had a higher standing than our Sheikh Tlatly from Bab Salah Street. Arriving at the dignitary's door with a basketful of spotless oranges and arm-long ears of corn, sometimes a freshly slaughtered sheep sent by a fallah with a difficult case in litigation, my father-in-law would be admitted to the Qaid's chamber of secrets.

Handing over his clients' gifts at the same time as explaining their requests, he would then inquire about the cost involved in bringing a lawsuit to its successful conclusion, haggling over the price into the bargain. All of his hard-earned broker's fee together with his commission on the fruit and vegetables which often came to forty or fifty francs, went to his charities.

Abraham's family, in the meantime, subsisted mainly on his six daughters' nimble fingers. As their mother's scissors swished through the fabric, they manned the sewing machines in crews of two for eighteen hours a day, turning out mounds of blouses and trousers for Arab peasant women. Sewing machines rattle when run. Accepting the unavoidable, neighbors showed understanding for the girls' long working hours. Heleefa, the landlord, however, did not see it that way. Occupying the whole upper story of the building, he was as mean as he was rich and he was a big landowner. To give you an idea of how rich Heleefa was I only need mention that, just to be driven up and down the streets of Nabeul, he kept a coachman on a full-time basis. In fairness, I must add that he sometimes had him drive his carriage to the surrounding Arab villages where most of his land was situated. From year to year his properties kept growing since Heleefa like my old patrons, the cousins Baruch and David Tarbulsi, was a moneylender.

Any fallah who had had a bad harvest could come to Heleefa for a loan. No money to buy seeds and fodder? Never mind, here are five hundred francs. At twenty-five percent interest, that's only six hundred and twenty-five francs to pay back after twelve months. If the next winter was a dry one, the farmer was forced to prolong the loan for another year. The added interest continued to climb. Before he knew it, his debt was growing faster than his crops. At the end of five years the fallah was trapped. If the fallah owed more than one thousand five hundred francs to Heleefa, part of his land would be impounded.

Up to this point Nabeul's moneylenders proceeded in exactly the same fashion. They differed greatly, however, in the use to which they put their earnings. Take for instance Baruch Tarbulsi, the president of the comité. A God-fearing Jew, he tried to keep his accounts with the Almighty balanced, doling out with his right hand interest-free loans to his brothers from the funds raked in by his left. Not so Heleefa whose hands, both left and right, served only one purpose: to grab. And if he opened them it was to discard rubbish, drop peanut shells and orange peels into the clean yard of Fortuna's family through the ironwork of his balcony. Because he was the landlord, he had the right to evict renters any time. They could not even protest too loudly, just sweep and sweep again, vainly begging him to have a heart. The more often the women had to clean up after him the better

Heleefa seemed to like it. Having little else to do but let himself be
driven around in his carriage, he would while away his days on the
balcony, munching anything with peel, pits or bones and preferably
wrapped in paper.

No trees are allowed to grow into the sky. Not long ago I met
Heleefa in Acre, of all places, a small fishing port on the northern
coast of Israel. From time to time in the summer I simply must get out
of the parched hills of Safed for a day, take a bus down to the shores
of the Mediterranean to fill my lungs with moisture and to gaze at the
open sea and colored fishing boats.

Leisurely walking toward the blue strip of water at the end of one
of Acre's avenues, I saw a little old man sitting on the curb, resting his
feet in the gutter. Just a street cleaner taking his lunch break I
thought, as he untied a plastic bag from the broomstick pinched
between his legs. Yet something about the wretch reminded me of
my youth, of Nabeul. The precision with which he spat the olive pits
into the sewer brought the days of my courtship back to me. I re-
mebered Fortuna's landlord flipping half-chewed olives at my bride
and me flirting in the yard.

"Heleefa!" I called out. Had it not been for the pits prompting me
I would not have recognized him—so stooped and thin he had become. The hair of his head was nearly all gone, his beard was the
color of a dirty dishcloth. Always three-cornered, his eyes were now
dropping outward as those of a much beaten dog, but the mean look
he gave me was Heleefa's all right. Losing little time to ask news of
my family, he lost himself in recriminations, taking me to task for the
shortcomings of the Israeli finance minister, the French, the Arabs
and our labor unions. Would I perhaps explain to him how his wife
was expected to make ends meet on a miserable half-time street
cleaner's salary? Of course not. Nobody could, he answered in my
stead, going over to the story of his downfall.

It had been very swift. Directly on coming into power, Bourguiba
had declared socialism, returning to Heleefa's debtors all the land it
had taken him so many years to seize. What little of his fortune he
had managed to smuggle out of Tunisia quickly dried up. Long gone
was his wife's jewelry—needed to marry off his daughters and to
help set up his sons. Not that he had gotten any thanks for it, he
added bitterly. They were too busy making money in the big cities to
look after their parents. Here most children had forgotten about the
Fifth Commandment, not like in Nabeul where the simplest Arab
would carry his old father and mother on his shoulders to the steam
bath at least once a month.

There was some truth in his grievances, most of all the last one.

Now both of us needed a glass of arrack to raise our spirits; however, afraid he might lose his job if the foreman spotted him in a coffee-house, Heleefa refused my invitation. So I said good-bye to him there on the curb, unable to feel any of the satisfaction I would have expected from such a meeting.

Leaving Heleefa to sweep the streets of Acre, I return to the Nabeul at the time of his prime and of my marriage, thirty years ago.

My father-in-law believed that if he laid down all his stakes for a corner in the next world the Almighty would take care of his family in this one. He knew my reputation. An easygoing man, he must have looked upon me as on a slightly straggly offshoot from a solid tree for, after all, was not an oil lamp engraved with my grandfather's name hanging in one row with that of Rabbi Hai before the Torah shrine of our synagogue? With four more daughters left to marry and a soft spot for jolly fellows of my kind, he agreed to have the wedding fixed at the earliest possible date. Naturally I did not want to spoil my chances by announcing that I was going to take my bride to the other end of the sea as soon as we were man and wife. Who needed complications? This time I was determined to bring the marriage off the ground and, by the way, I had already won out over an older, more serious suitor. Hoosha, the pious barber, the one who each Passover would immerse himself up to his shoulders in the sea to recite the song of Moses, also wanted Fortuna for his wife.

She loves to harp on that offer of marriage. Every time we quarrel she has to bring up Hoosha. Such a fine Jew, she sighs. His brother is a rabbi in Paris, custodian of a whole cemetery. Had she only accepted that barber then her flat would not now be filled with clay animals in place of furniture. He would not have passed his days painting childish pictures with the radio playing full blast.

I think it rankles her mind that she cannot make me jealous. It simply is not in my nature. Otherwise, just to have peace, I would gladly oblige her. The barber really was more dignified than I am. I don't know if I ever heard him laugh. Even so, it is doubtful whether she would have been better off with a husband who was run over and killed by a car in Ramla twenty years ago. His thoughts had always been wandering. I recall his barber's coat buttoned the wrong way, his bespectacled look in the mirror so absentminded it made me afraid for my ears. It is true that Fortuna's barber, unlike myself who was only too happy to close the holy books on the day of my bar mitzvah, had gone on to study Mishna and Gemara at a yeshiva. It is also true that I had nevertheless gathered some kind of more earthly knowledge from animals, from my birds, even from the fish and, of course, from people. I knew more about living things.

Fortuna might not have been aware of it, but she did not marry the barber for the simple reason that she had fallen in love with me. On the same Saturday I had met her on the beach telling the girls how the big fish had hooked Shishi, I had hooked her. I had known it the moment she threw her head back laughing. And after thirty years of marriage she still gets sick with worry every time I have to leave her for a day or two. None of her nagging, her pricks and her sighing for Hoosha can alter that nor the fact that from the first she was attracted to me because I was as different from her pious barber as chalk is from cheese. It was my ruddy looks she liked, my quick mind and my flashy way of dressing. Though she pretended to be horrified, she liked me even better for the pistol she discovered in my pocket as I was stealing a first kiss.

The gleam of Miriam's sandy hair was fading. Having at the start mainly settled on Fortuna in order to have a wife to take to Eretz Israel I was now fast falling in love with her. She was sweet, my brown-eyed new bride, teasing and supple as a cat. Just to see her move, fling her locks back as she was running toward me, was enough to put me into a happy mood. The day she surprised me with a fashionable haircut I almost came to tears. There is one other day of our courtship I don't care to remember. On that day I did cry, together with Fortuna.

She has never quite forgiven my father how he shamed her then and he, a great-grandfather of almost five, still stubbornly affirms that he was in the right on that occasion. Sitting at a respectable distance from each other on my parents' bed and in the presence of my mother, my bride and I were chatting with each other when my father came in. From the time he had been robbed and roughed up by the villagers, forced to sell his donkey and reduced to carrying his own baskets he had fallen into a sort of silent bitterness that sometimes made me miss his former loud eruptions into anger. Not now, however.

"Shamelessness," he thundered. "Impudence that cries to the high heavens!" There was but one kind of girl who would sit on the same bed with a man before he was her husband. Not under his roof though.

Many years later I was thumbing through a book when my eyes stuck to a picture: ADAM AND EVE EXPELLED FROM THE GARDEN OF EDEN read the caption. Their heads bent in shame, with nothing but their hands to try and shield their nakedness, two figures are chased by a huge, enraged-looking angel brandishing a Turkish sword. All of a sudden I was transported back to that mortifying afternoon—Fortuna and I running through Bab Salah Street in tears, fleeing the wrath of my father. Naked we had felt, in spite of being fully clothed.

Gradually calming down, we had talked things over, deciding that having done nothing wrong we would not let the nasty incident spoil the joy of our approaching wedding—only one week away. To sit brooding so close to the great day would have spelled disaster and so my friends kept hovering around me, trying to cheer me up with jokes and stories. Meanwhile, Fortuna, who had to be guarded against the evil eye of jealous spinsters, was watched over in her father's house. A continuous stream of females was fussing over her, her sisters, friends and cousins, dressing her up, making her smile at her pretty image in the mirror. In short, doing everything to have her enter wedlock in a mood of happy confidence.

A year and a half later, after the birth of our first son in Israel, Fortuna wanted to wash the mattress. Helping her to pull out the wool I cut my finger.

"And what is that supposed to be . . . a spell to hurt me?" Angrily I wielded a large piece of glass before her nose.

"Would I cast an evil spell on my dear husband? It's for your own good. A charmed mirror, it has been there right under your nose since our wedding night. Twenty-five sous I paid Tootoo for it. Please, Fallu, put it back and I will forever look to you as you saw me on that night. If we live to be a hundred . . ."

"Why then did you keep it secret?" I said, suspicious that there might be more to that piece of mirror than she cared to reveal. Crushing the thing under my heel I buried its fragments in the ground to the last scintillating splinter. Today, however, I sometimes wonder whether I should not have kept it.

Little feasting was going on either before, during and still less after our wedding. Fortuna's "camels" were all gone and my only contribution to the fare was the fish I got for free from my friends among the fishermen. Any money coming my way trickled through my fingers at Majloo's café where I spent my evenings drinking wine and playing dominos, taking a last fling before settling down.

Not only was I soon to be a husband, responsible for a family; I was going to live on the sacred soil of Eretz Israel, under the very eye of the Lord of the Universe.

The fifth day of my final week of freedom was the appointed day of henna, when the red dye which was to make Fortuna fertile and prosperous was carefully painted on her soles and palms. My share of all that prosperity was a red dot on the tip of my little finger. Everybody present at the ceremony had to taste the bride's couscous, first of all the girls who would thus more easily find husbands. Then, directly after the meal, began the long and arduous procedure of Fortuna's purification. With the help of small sticks dipped into hot, molten sugar, a woman hired for the light touch of her hand started to tear the down off my bride's cheeks, thinned out her brows until the soft, wide arcs looked like the twin strokes of a freshly sharpened pencil. As the operation from then on would proceed farther down, I was at this point asked to leave the premises.

On the next and last day before the wedding we made our way to the steam bath—separately, of course. The high-pitched ululations of the women echoing from one end to the other of Bab Salah Street, we were led along to the sound of drums and tambourines.

"Fortuna belongs to Fallu . . . Fallu is Fortuna's own," the procession chanted up to the entrance to the bath. Splashing in the pool inside I was then helped through my ablutions by the prayers of my father, my uncles, friends and cousins who then, hovering over me dry and dressed, sprinkled me with orange blossom scent.

Here again marriage preparations were more laborious for Fortuna, plucked as clean as a chicken on the previous evening. Left with only the hair on her head, her thinned-out brows and long, dark lashes she had nevertheless to undergo three complete immersions (face, hair and everything) before being allowed under the wedding tent. And so our huppa was dressed in the yard of Fortuna's home on a luminous autumn afternoon, under a sky as pure and spotless as my much-cleaned bride.

How extraordinary light and airy I felt inside the unaccustomed confines of a suit and tie. Who cared that it rained apple cores and orange peel upon the velvet canopy—Heleefa, the landlord, had not been invited. What did it matter that the pockets of my suit were empty except for a tiny golden ring as thin as thread and the one rusty key to our new home? A wedding present from my parents, it was my first suit ever—dark blue and made to measure.

A pen was pushed into my hand. I signed the marriage contract. In case it was I who asked for a divorce and did so on insufficient grounds I was to pay Fortuna a wholly imaginary sum. If, on the other hand, it was she who wanted a separation she was not entitled to anything. Nothing at all. Well, her father signed. We were ready for the rites. At last I slipped the ring on her finger. We shared the wine and I brought my foot down on the glass, crushing it hard under the heel of one of the black patent-leather shoes I had made myself for the occasion. We were married. Reminding the bridegroom in his moment of purest joy that the Temple in Jerusalem still lies in ruins, the breaking of the glass marked the end of the ceremony.

Blessings, kisses, earsplitting whoopings; as our guests intoned the latest Nabeul hit songs, we sat down to calves' feet and chickpeas, fresh, hot bread and wine—our last substantial meal for days to come. When it was time for us to be driven to our new home and Fortuna's father as well as mine flatly refused to pay for a carriage, it began to sink in. From now on I was on my own. What else could I do but take Fortuna by the hand and smile, offering snickering neighbors the spectacle of newlyweds in all their finery walking through mud and dirt, with loudly singing, ululating guests trailing unsteadily behind them.

Every time I have to search the shoe box with our documents for some receipt or address, I come upon the bleached-out little wedding snapshot of Fortuna and me holding hands. It always makes me laugh. Not at Fortuna, God forbid, lightly leaning on my shoulder with a shy smile. She looks as a bride should in that long white gown she had copied from a French journal. I cannot help laughing at my own image squeezed into that clumsily cut suit, that stringy tie that I thought was the height of fashion. With the flap of a felt hat hiding half my face, I seem to have come straight out of an old gangster movie. I remember my cousin Eli taking the photograph, counting to ten as I posed proudly in front of our first home, a drooping lean-to with little to crow about. We kissed the mezuzah, the key screeched in the lock, a last sahruta echoed in the distance as I opened the door to our room and to a long and fruitful marriage.

First Days in Israel

The windowless lean-to became a dovecote to a pair of roosting pigeons. Filled to overflowing with the bed, a dresser, a table and two chairs, we were convinced no home could be more elegant. And though the floor, of beaten earth, had been whitewashed in our honor, we steadfastly took our meals sitting on the chairs.

The presents we received for our wedding were few but pretty and added a touch of luxury. My good Aunt Kooka's pottery fish, meant to bring us prosperity, was hung over our bed. A good part of the table was taken up by the tray from Fortuna's five sisters. I am not too fond of most of them but I must admit that the tray was beautiful—a red-green-and-brown-glazed hen sitting in the center, surrounded by six yellow chicks. Since it would surely have been broken in the luggage, we had to sell it when we left for Israel and I still regret it. Forced to leave my own birds behind in my mother's care for lack of space, I had been unable to part with my plump, old quail. Clucking in its cage over the table, it sat peeking down at the food Fortuna served me in her brand-new earthen pots—if there was something to cook, that is.

Since my boss, the Arab shoemaker, had few orders coming in, I was lucky when I worked one day out of three. Too proud to accept food from my in-laws, I was gruffly refused help by my father who, glad to have at last married off his forever-famished elder son, would not even invite us for the Sabbath meal. From the day he had seen Fortuna and me sitting on the bed he displayed coolness toward her, and so my mother had to take to smuggling. Under the cover of darkness she would come to us, pulling little pots filled with hameen and fried fish out of the folds of her wrapper.

After three tender but hungry days in our pigeonhole, I had to inform my bride that we were about to look for greener pastures in the land of our fathers. From then on our honeymoon was watered down by tears. For three whole months, up to the day of our departure, she would not stop crying—from the hot tears she shed into her morning coffee to the sobs she stifled in her pillow when we went to sleep at night.

"You trapped me into it. You cheated me," she kept lamenting. "Oh, had I only known I would have never have married you. . . . Jerusalem is what he needs now, no more, no less. You only just got me and already you want Jerusalem! Well, Fallu, let me tell you: without my mother I will not go to any faraway place out of an old book!"

Who would have believed that once in Israel Fortuna was to become the most devout Jewess in our neighborhood, taking four different buses to travel from Safed in Upper Galilee to Bethlehem in Judea to measure the tomb of our mother Rachel with a blue thread?

But even my pious father-in-law did not want me to take his daughter to Israel.

"In a few years time we will all go there together, Fallu, the whole family," he tried to dissuade me. But I clung stubbornly to my decisior.. In the end we went to see the rabbi, he and I.

"To go live on the sacred soil of Eretz Israel is the greatest merit any Jew can acquire," said Rabbi Yitzhak who had officiated at our wedding. "It is greater than giving to the poor, greater than studying the Holy Scriptures. Let your daughter go with her husband and may they go in peace!"

That settled the matter. Requesting passports, I started selling everything poor Fortuna had just bought with her hard-earned "camels"—everything but the woolen mattress on which we were to sleep for twenty-five years. I had found an Arab willing to buy my sewing machine in exchange for my teaching him shoemaking in a nutshell. I now hammered together two wooden trunks in which to pack the rest of our belongings.

Others besides us were packing. Since the Jews had won the war in "Falastina," our Arab neighbors were avoiding us, behaving as if an Israeli foe was lurking in everybody's backyard. To spare the feelings of old Moslem acquaintances, also partly out of fear for the safety of our families staying behind, all those leaving said that they were going to start a new life in France. There was still another reason for this deception. The French government had an agreement with the Bey of Tunis affirming that none of the latter's subjects would be allowed to join the enemies of the Arabs. It was therefore necessary that we make our way to the newfounded State of Israel by detour. First we had to cross the Mediterranean to Marseilles. And even though everybody was aware of our true destination, no one could deny that we had boarded a boat for France.

"Juicy knuckles . . . thick, fat oxtails . . ." chanted the kosher butcher in Bab Salah Street to attract buyers, worried at the steadily diminishing number of clients. "Eat, children, eat, fill your bellies while you can. In Eretz Israel you will chew on stones. . . ."

In between sobs Fortuna had confided to me that she was with child. I had to try and act like a husband. From the proceeds of our furniture I bought her the two golden bracelets which still encircle her left arm—investing the rest of our money in provisions. They might tide us over the difficult start in the new country for, in spite of the Bible calling it the "land where milk and honey flows" more and more letters arriving from Israel spoke of food shortages. For this reason, only one corner of our two trunks was taken up with our handwoven blanket, a few sheets and our wedding clothes. Most of the remaining space was filled with cans of olive oil and bags with rice, beans, dried couscous, coffee, tea and sugar. To think that I had to sit on the lid in order to fit in ten pounds of salt makes me laugh. The shores of the Dead Sea are broiling with it far and wide, glittering icily in the heat of the Judean desert. The dried pepper and pepper pulp, on the other hand, were worth every inch of space they occupied. Without mixing them into the plentiful but pale and tasteless food we were to receive on the boat, in Marseilles and at the immigrants' camp in Israel I would have been unable to swallow one bite.

One day before our departure I lifted the cage with my quail (the only thing left in our room) from its hook on the wall. I could not take it with me, nor would I leave it behind. After one last visit to Rabbi Shushan the slaughterer, weeping Fortuna stuffed the bird with parsley, rice and a hard-boiled egg, making it into a farewell roast.

Slowly chewing as the domes and minarets of Tunis were dropping one by one behind the shoreline, we ate my bird the next after-

noon on the boat taking us and some forty other Jews to Marseilles.
When was I going to eat stuffed quail again? I felt homesick already,
remembering my mother's white wrapper steadily shrinking before
vanishing altogether, my sister, already taller than my mother, trying
to comfort her.

"Write and make sure to wear your fringed garment when you
step on the sacred soil. . . ." My father had kissed me through the
paling threads of his once so fiery mustache. "In a few years I will
send you your sister. Find her a good husband and . . ." His words
had been swallowed by the rattling of chains; the anchor was lifted.
Sensing that something extraordinary was going on, my brother Fraji
had run up and down the pier with wildly flapping arms.

Tunis was gone and so was my quail. Warily my glance shifted to
hysterical Fortuna whom I had been forced to tear out of her mother's
arms halfway up the gangplank. Seeing her composed and dry-faced,
wiping our plates, I could not believe my eyes. Having stopped crying for good, she would turn into the best wife anyone could wish
for—that is until her family caught up with us years later in Safed.

The last strip of our native land had vanished. Nothing more to
gaze at but the frothy trail of the boat and a couple of lonely sea gulls
shrieking overhead. I knew how they felt all alone between sky and
water. Pulling Fortuna down with me onto a heap of coiled-up rope,
we found that both of us were trying hard to cheer each other up with
endearments and smiles—the flighty groom and his bewildered bride
were becoming husband and wife. What a wife! Always cheerful,
rarely a complaint. So long as times were hard Fortuna stood by me
through thick and thin. Things only began to turn sour years later
when the ship of our marriage sailed into calmer waters and we both
became somewhat plump around the middle.

As for now, still feeling lonesome, we were descending into the
steerage where, having been assigned our quarters among a dozen
horses, we found plenty of company making the passage to Marseilles like us. In fact, the boat was so full of whinnying and scraping
four-legged travelers that we got little sleep during the three days and
nights it was fording its path across the seas to France. Whenever I
looked up from our blanket, serious brown eyes were peering at me
from above. Soft noses were pushing through the bars around us. I
did not mind the scrutiny as long as they kept quiet. However, either
because of the stink of manure, her pregnancy or the boat's stomping
progress through the rolling winter seas, Fortuna's stomach became
terribly upset. She was much better on the next boat, a big vessel
sailing under a brand-new Israeli flag that took us from Marseilles to
Haifa. Here we slept in real beds, conversed with two-legged voy-

agers, Jews from so many different countries that hearing the chatter in the dining room, I fancied myself in the Tower of Babel.

On the evening of the fifth day, having been told that we were nearing the coast of Israel, Fortuna and I lay down on our berths all dressed. It must have been around midnight when the sudden silence of the engines made me sit up. Then chains were rattling, orders shouted in a language which seemed to be the tongue of the Holy Scriptures. We had come to the end of our journey!

Hundreds of passengers were scrambling up on deck to view a big port full of ships, lights and a night sky blocked by an illuminated mountain. The town of Haifa, people said it was, and the mountain range was the Carmel. The Carmel . . . Elijah . . . the classroom at Talmud-Torah school came to my mind—my classmates and I kicking each other under the long table, listening with half an ear to Rabbi Parienti talking of the Prophets.

Palmidi was already in Eretz Israel. Dooha and Reuben would soon follow me. Who would have thought that we were going to set eyes on the very mountain from where the Prophet Elijah had driven his flaming horses up into the sky? With Fortuna close to me, I stood leaning on the railing staring into the night, at the clusters and rows of a thousand tiny golden pinheads stuck in the back of a crouching giant. Only windows, a young man from Morocco kept saying beside me, streetlights climbing up dark hills. I wondered what the embroidered giant might look like in the morning light. Every child knew that the earth of Eretz Israel was full of stones. Would a vast desert fortress rise from rocks in the morning mist? Would I see bearded Jews climb up and down its stairs and through its paved alleys?

Though nobody would be allowed to disembark before sunrise, I did not go back to sleep. For the rest of the night I stood bent over the railing, my eyes straining southeast toward Jerusalem—my thoughts gliding and trembling with the light on the water. This big port was but a threshold, the gate through which His people had to pass to go up to Jerusalem, the center of the world. From there, seated on His throne high up above the Temple mount, the Almighty ruled the universe. Was it for real, then? Was I, Fallu from Nabeul, face to face with Elijah's mountain, on my way to worship Him in David's city?

I would make good in the land of my fathers, I promised myself. I would work hard and raise my sons under His watchful eye. With heart and soul I yearned to help my brothers till the sacred soil, upright, God-fearing men whose lips never let escape a lie.

The lights went out. I climbed down to the quarterdeck to awaken Fortuna. As I had promised my father, I put on the fringed garment, got my prayer shawl and phylacteries and was sorry not to have grown forelocks and a beard in time. The harbor was slowly creeping out of the dusk as I joined a large crowd of immigrants from Libya, Morocco, Tunisia and Algiers. We stood as one waiting for the sun to rise, our faces turning toward Jerusalem. From lead the bay was melting into yellow silver. We could now begin to lay on our phylacteries.

By the time I was through with my morning prayers and could look to the west, a beautiful, big town had come aglow. Shell-colored, tree-shaded, gently sloped on green hills, it bore no resemblance whatever to the desert fortress of my night. Right in the center, in a cypress garden halfway up the Carmel, a temple with a golden dome was trying to outshine the rising sun. What better omen could there be?

Keeping our eyes on the lucky sign, Fortuna and I, eager to kiss the soil of Eretz Israel, let ourselves be shoved down the gangplank. How I had longed for this moment! The sacred ground on which we stepped ashore was concrete, the first obstacle I was to meet in the new land. Concrete to my left, concrete to my right! Pushing through the shouting, laughing, crying crowd, I found at last a patch of earth on which to kneel.

"Blessed be the Lord, King of the Universe, Who let me live to see this day," I thanked God from the bottom of my heart. Then I followed Fortuna to the customs' shed from which we emerged as Israeli citizens, proudly waving brand-new identity cards.

With only a handful of officials to fill out forms and hundreds of immigrants to be processed not everybody came out of the shed named and aged the same as when he had gone in. What happened was that Fortuna's and my birth dates were reversed. A year younger than myself when I had taken her for wife, it has been the opposite from the day we disembarked in Haifa!

"Rafael Uzan, son of Hamus and Meesha, born in Nabeul, Tunisia, in nineteen hundred twenty-three."

"Fortunée Uzan, daughter of Abraham and Camoona, born in Nabeul, Tunisia, in nineteen hundred twenty-two." There it is, black on white. Every time I open her identity card Fortuna flies into a rage. After thirty years, she still has not got used to the idea that she is now the older one.

Assembled into groups to be sent to different parts of the country, Fortuna and I climbed on a truck with a group of newcomers. Had my ears gone out of gear with the noise and confusion? Would an Israeli driver besmirch the tongue of the Holy Scriptures with Arab curses? Red lights, green lights! Cars were honking as we drove through a thoroughfare lined with trees and shops. Sidewalks were crawling with pedestrians seemingly obsessed to get some place in a hurry.

I could no longer ignore what I had not fully grasped in the first fluster of arrival, namely that very few of the port officials, stevedores or passersby were bearded or wore skullcaps. I was puzzled. No trace whatsoever of the hooded figures of my dreams: the long-robed rabbis keeping close to walls, afraid to brush against a woman.

In their stead, bareheaded youths and men were striding along as if the astonishing number of females walking in their midst was no concern of theirs. Nor did they appear in the least embarrassed by their short and tight dresses, some girls even wearing trousers! Who could explain the withered faces with painted mouths, gray hair unguarded by a scarf? I couldn't. Fortuna might have thought it was out of embarrassment that I would not answer her questions. But no. I simply did not know what to say to her. Everything seemed upside down. I felt like someone trying to think standing on his head. Where was I? Had the boat taken a wrong turn? How could these men and women be the Chosen People?

Once we left the town behind us, the sights—still a far cry from my stony fancies of the night—were becoming more reassuring. With the difference that here there were more trees, the occasional fields and orchards were greener, the sand dunes and familiar blue of the Mediterranean on our right resembled the shores of Cape Bon. On our left the Carmel was unrolling—a green, interminable ribbon, cut short at last at the entrance to a broad plain and the immigrants' camp of Binyamina.

Warbling sahrutas, all the camp's residents had come to the gate to receive the newcomers. There also was an orderly, waiting pump in hand to spray us with antiseptic foam.

"No lice, no lice," I begged in Arabic and French as he was concentrating on my wife's thick, dark locks.

"Microbes, microbes," the orderly insisted with a friendly smile, enveloping Fortuna and me in a thick white mist. A pair of ghosts, we went to join the lunch queue.

I shall never forget the taste of my first meal in Eretz Israel. It was awful! There may be countries where people like to eat overcooked noodles spliced with stale coconut. In Nabeul, however, we were not used to it. When I am hungry I must eat. Seasoning a heaped plateful with plenty of red pepper that I had been smart enough to take along, I closed my eyes to gulp down the stuff while poor pregnant Fortuna belched only to look at it. Having spent the last of our money in Marseilles and unable to supplement the camp food, I understood that if she was to bear a healthy son I must find work at once. Putting her to rest in the tent that now was our home, I went for a walk to the adjoining village.

"*Torah v'avoda,*" Torah and work—that was what I would find in Eretz Israel, I had been told. All right, I was going to try.

"*Avoda . . . avoda . . .*" I shouted in Hebrew, knocking on all the doors of Zichron Yaakov, one after another. But people either shook their heads or gave me explanations I could not understand. In the end I came to the house of an old woman who first pointed to the peeling walls of her home, then to a bucket with fresh lime. I nodded enthusiastically. Nothing was easier than whitewashing. A hundred times I had seen the Arabs do it. Grasping from her gestures that the woman wanted me to start work in the morning, I returned to the camp to bring Fortuna the good news and just in time for another plate of noodles. To be fair I must add that it was now accompanied by bread and some sort of fig compote.

Still determined to begin my new life on the right foot, I said grace after the meal as well as Shma Yisrael before bedding down for my first night of repose on a soil that had never been haunted by spirits. Lying on the narrow camp bed, confused and overtired, I stared up at the canvas roof so near my face.

"How goodly are thy tents, Jacob, thy dwellings, O Israel," I hummed in my heart, trying to lull myself to sleep with the comforting words of the morning prayer.

"Ooooh . . . hoooh . . . ooh . . . hooh . . . hooh . . . hooh . . ." The thin whine of an infant rent the night, swelled into heartbreaking crying. Soon a host of children were wailing from all sides. It was frightening. For hours Fortuna and I sat huddled on one bed, waiting for dawn to light the slit in the tent opening. How could Jewish parents be so indifferent to the suffering of their own flesh and blood? In Nabeul even Bedouins would take better care of their children. The last thing I had wanted was to start life in Eretz Israel with complaints. After such a grueling night, however, I had to speak my mind. The whole breakfast line broke out in laughter.

"Children wailing their hearts out . . ." The old-timers of the camp were holding their sides with laughter. "Jackals, they were a pack of jackals . . . having a good time in the vineyards!"

Standing in line morning, noon and evening got me wise to other things besides jackals. Starting out in the middle of the queue why was I always last to be served? Breathing the morning fragrance of the orange groves, I turned some questions over in my mind as I walked to my whitewashing appointment. Would I have to push and shout with the rest of them? My neighbors seemed to get what they wanted in this fashion. Tramping briskly along the dirt track I was beginning to see that in the land of my fathers straight paths would not necessarily take me far. Being a good Jew and relying on the Almighty was all right, but I would have to look out for myself besides.

No work would be too hard for me I vowed, plunging both my

hands into the lime to mix it. Soon enough they started itching, then burning like hell as I was scraping the old whitewash off the walls. By the time I had sealed all the cracks with plaster I could have screamed with pain. Too late I had remembered that nobody in his right mind, neither in Nabeul nor in Israel, would mix fresh lime without the help of a stick. As I had seen the Arabs do at home and holding onto the brush with fingers half of whose skin had been eaten away, I painted all the walls over twice; nothing mattered besides turning out an even white surface and getting paid.

It felt good walking back to Fortuna through the dusky groves, my aching hands calmed by a generous application of the old woman's olive oil. Money with Hebrew captions was tinkling in my pocket. That was but part of the story. I also had landed a job with the village cows, on top of which the kind people of Zichron Yaakov had filled the canvas bag of their new cowherd with bread, cheese and oranges.

At one of the farms I even was offered a room where Fortuna and I could have settled—but didn't. Perhaps I would have ended up as a farmer instead of a painter had it not been for the cows of Zichron Yaakov, the most fiercely independent, jaywalking beasts any cowherd has ever had to watch. Every half hour or so one or two of them would disappear, and every time I rediscovered them after a great deal of climbing, tranquilly grazing on the edge of a cliff or a steep ravine, my heart would miss a beat. No, these hills were not made for me, I decided. I must live by the sea. Regretfully handing in my resignation, I returned to the safe, flat camp of Binyamina.

As always, when I could not find Fortuna in our tent I knew where to look for her—at the soldier's kiosk by the roadside. Overcome by homesickness, the moment I left her she used to wander over there to sit on a stone for hours, searching in vain for a face from Nabeul among the tired recruits stopping for refreshments. She would probably be upset if I told her that I had given up the cowherd job. Never mind, my hands had healed. I figured that I would make a fine orange picker. Surveying the ripening fruit in the groves beyond the wooden barracks, my eyes strayed down the road to where a fair young woman was emerging from the dark foliage. Who was this woman steadily advancing toward me?

I knew her. Could I be dreaming? No, I told myself. I was in Eretz Israel, going to meet my wife at the kiosk of Binyamina. . . . Nevertheless it was my cousin Miriam who now threw her arms around me. Once too shy to let me carry her bucket in front of others, she was now kissing me in full view of the camp.

"Save me, Fallu, save me!" She held fast to me, wetting my face with her tears. My darling cousin, my gentle dove, did not seem to care whether she hugged me in front of the whole world. Why, mountains I would have moved had she shown me that much ardor six months earlier! Instead, dreams from way back were quickly turning into a nightmare.

Gaping at the blubbering young woman protesting her love in public, clinging to a dumb-struck golem as to her last hope on earth, a large crowd was forming around us. And what if Fortuna came along? The horrible thought gave new life to my arms. Limply they rose to try and disentangle my neck from Miriam's desperate clasp.

"You see," she sobbed into my ear, "just as Tootoo saw us in her water glass . . . together in Eretz Israel. You cannot send me away now, we belong to each other. . . ."

"Too late, Miriam, too late . . . too late," were the only words I was able to stutter, at last keeping her at arm's length and wiping her soggy face with the toilet paper cautious Fortuna had put into my pocket. My heart went out to my poor cousin, so miserable under the kerchief of a married woman. Her mouth puffed up, the warm gray of her eyes washed out by tears.

Whether out of frustration to see me wed to another or because her family had forced her into it, two weeks after I had taken Fortuna for my wife she had stood under the velvet canopy with a young man from out of town. I had not been too keen to hear the news, but my aunts, of course, had dwelled lengthily on her beautiful wedding and the handsome stranger who had led her under the huppa. Several times I had passed the little stand in the market where he sold and repaired eyeglasses. He was a good-looking fellow in a thin-lipped, closemouthed way, I could not help admitting. Nor could I help noticing the bottle of arrack always standing under the table laid out with steel and horn-rimmed spectacles.

No more any of my business, I had scolded myself, sweeping him and his bottle into the same corner of my mind where I had had such a hard time to shove Miriam earlier. Why did she have to slip out of there with such a bang? How on earth had she known where to find me?

She had heard about the letter I had sent my parents, my cousin managed to explain in between sobs. Aware of my plan to leave for Eretz Israel, she had accepted the stranger for the reason that he was going to take her there and once they arrived in Haifa, she tricked him into entering the camp of Binyamina.

"What else could I do, Fallu? I would have died so far away from you. . . ." Taking in her drained little face, the tendons moving so tightly under the skin of her thin throat, I could well believe it. Oh, God, what was I going to do? Myself close to tears I took her by the hand and led her behind the barrack, out of the sight of curious onlookers. A long, long time ago I had led her like this to the back of Nisria's house in Bab Salah Street, a chubby little girl with pale lashes.

"Miriam," I chided her gently. "We are both married now. . . ."

"Yes, don't I know it," she said bitterly. "Every waking moment I curse the star that shone over my huppa . . . a lying star." She frowned at the heavy ring circling her middle finger. "Around the neck of a bottle, that's where it belongs. That's what he is married to. Look what I got for having obeyed my parents." Fresh tears welling up, she showed me an ugly black mark at the base of her throat. No, I thought to myself, that is what you got for having had so little faith in me. What was the use of hurting her more with the truth or telling her that I loved my wife. Better to let her believe that fate was against her.

"Miriam, listen to me," I said aloud. "Listen carefully. When Tootoo told you your fortune she skipped something she saw swimming in her water glass because she wanted to make you happy and get a nice fat fee. Nobody can doubt that she saw you and me in Eretz Israel together—here we are—but she could not have overlooked the child growing in Fortuna's belly either. It shows already. Only yesterday she had to let out her skirt. So, please, try to understand and don't make trouble. I am married for good now."

Miriam had stopped crying and did not say a word. I only wish I could forget the look she gave me when I said good-bye to her. I never saw her again. Good souls told her husband what had happened by the barracks and there was a big commotion. Threatening to abandon his wife if he did not get a transfer, he whisked her off to another camp the next morning.

Fortuna, who always took things more calmly during pregnancies, made less of a fuss than I had expected. Telling her about the encounter before others had a chance to give her their version, she seemed to believe me. After all these years, however, she will still not allow me to visit my cousin or have her as a guest in our house. Here and there at funerals and weddings some relative will give me her regards, sighing dolefully when I ask how she is doing.

XXIX
Safed

In Binyamina, dust settles fast on anything, and I had had my fill of camp life. When Fortuna's cousin arrived to take us to Upper Galilee, I leaped at the opportunity to leave. From his account the town of Safed where he had settled was paradise on earth. Only later on did I understand the motive behind his glowing descriptions. A bachelor who had not tasted a hearty Nabeul dish for months, he was counting on Fortuna to cook for him.

Safed had the healthiest air in all of Israel, he said. Clear, cold water from mountain springs, friendly people, housing up for grabs, fruit trees and, most important, plenty of work for everybody.

"What do you mean, clear mountain springs?" I sat up on my camp bed with a jolt. "Haven't I told you over and over that I cannot live in a place where there is no seashore?"

"Calm down, cousin . . . as much seashore as anyone could wish for; Safed has got everything!"

Well, we hoisted our trunks and mattress, first on a train, then on top of the bus which was to take the three of us on an interminable trip up into Galilee. I remember how baffled I was at hills that from afar looked blue, turning green and brown the moment we came close. Their crowns were studded with small houses built of stone, their shrubby slopes with herds of sheep and goats. Drowsily watched by husbands napping among the wild flowers or chatting with each other under carob trees, groups of Arab women in long trousers and bright dresses were working in the fields. Decently covered heads close to the ground and broad behinds up in the air, they stood firmly planted amid lettuce and cabbages, gay yellow, orange, and lilac blobs on mounds of juicy green. Maybe I had found the Land of Milk and Honey after all!

One thing was sure. This was a thousand times better than the mad bustle on the asphalt and concrete of downtown Haifa where we had changed from train to bus. "The mountains skipped like rams, the

hills like young sheep . . ." I had always been wondering at hills dancing in the middle of a psalm. Yet now, seeing them rocking and gliding
by the bus's dirty windows these words were beginning to make
sense. It went without saying that the Almighty had to watch with a
stern eye over Jerusalem and what was left of His holy Temple. Upon
this northern corner of His land he seemed to look with a playful
twinkle. Against the peaceful background of Galilee, my fervently
toiling pioneers either sat on tractors or lay snoring in the grass.

All that was fine with me, though I felt somewhat stupid to have
carried two cans of oil from Tunisia to France and from there to Israel
when, as far as the eye reached, the countryside was covered with
olive trees. So old and gnarled were some of them they might well
have seen Rabbi Bar Yohai and his son Rabbi Meir light fires on the
heights, calling Jewish farmers to take up arms against the Roman
invaders. The road twisted steadily upward, the bus smoked and
belched. A last tortuous climb and we arrived at our destination—
Safed. The next stop could only be the sky, I thought, taking in steep
slopes, houses straddled on each other, juggling amid a maze of stairs
and terraced yards to get to the top of the hill.

"W-w-where is the sea?" I squeezed through chattering teeth,
asking myself whether mountain air had to be that chilly to be whole-
some.

"Patience, Fallu, patience . . . here you are." Smiling Fortuna's
cousin led me to an opening among the houses from where a ravine,
thick with pomegranate bushes and olive and almond trees opened
into a valley. Gently it slipped down toward a beautifully blue ex-
panse of water.

"Do you believe me now?" he grinned. "Prepare two lines with
bait and we will go fishing together. It's about ten minutes' walk
down there." I breathed more easily. This was all that mattered. The
cold and the climbing I would have to take in my stride, I decided,
still shivering with an inward sigh of resignation.

Had someone in Nabeul told me I was to spend the rest of my life
on a mountaintop I would have laughed in his face. Yet I had to admit
that in its crooked-looking and neglected way, the place was rather
pretty. It took me weeks to understand that Safed's clean air and
Fortuna's cousin had played a trick on me. That blue sheet of water,
looking so close and beckoning so invitingly, lay at a distance of six
miles from Safed as the crow flies. And at that it was no sea either,
only a big sweet water lake—something I had not even known existed. By the time it dawned on me that I had been cheated and that it
took a bus ride of about an hour to get down to the water's edge, it
was too late. I had set up house, children were arriving one after
another. Later I started to paint and was trapped on the hills forever.

As with the lake, most of the cousin's glowing stories proved to be only half true. Fruit trees there were many, but what use were they in the winter? As for friendly people, the Safed old-timers, stingy mountain-ghetto dwellers, were not much taken with penniless Jews from all over the world, suddenly fallen on their town like locusts. Little did the natives know of Hitler's death camps or of the persecution of their brothers in North Africa.

Lack of work was the big problem. For me, neither clear mountain springs nor bubbly air could outweigh unemployment. Besides, driving winter rains, occasional snow and a permanent hoarse throat from icy drinking water made them mixed blessings. One promise Fortuna's relative had made, though, stood the test: housing was up for grabs.

Many of Safed's little stone houses had been abandoned by their Arab owners. Gaping at the new immigrants with empty doors and windows, they stood waiting to be taken care of. Others, their walls cracked and blackened by fire, barely kept upright and seemed beyond repair. Curled around a central wooded peak, the town's main street was only now beginning to come out of its shell-shocked stupor. Most of the shops still remained closed behind their bullet-riddled shutters.

The war that had just ended had torn the hills of Safed into two opposing camps. Hanging from the northwestern slope, the small Jewish quarter had been cut off from the rest of the world for months, starved and vastly outnumbered in men and arms. Sometimes skimpiness has its good side. Used to living on next to nothing, trusting in God and being brave beside the old mountain, Jews had been able to hold out, fighting off their attackers until help came in the form of younger, well-trained brothers from the plains.

What these latter lacked in ammunition they had made up with noise, hurtling barrels filled with rocks and flaming kerosene from the steepest heights. The tiny, homemade cannon that they brought with them had given two or three roars before petering out. Since it was raining the Arabs had put two and two together, linking the drizzle with the noise. In the larger Moslem part of town one broken sentence had been racing up and down the stone-paved stairs and alleys:

"Atomic bomb, atomic rain . . . the Jews have an atomic bomb . . . run, run for your lives!" That same night the whole Arab population of Safed, men, women and children, had fled in panic, on foot, on horse and donkey back, to seek refuge in Lebanon and Syria, their next-door neighbors to the north. So there were plenty of houses for Fortuna and me to pick from.

"Wait till the Arabs come back and find you in their houses. They will kill you . . ." said the Safed old-timers, not without a note of smugness in their voices. (Neither the prayers and psalms I knew by heart nor the French knocked into me by Monsieur Mauricet's ruler could help me to understand them. Since the Jews of Safed spoke some sort of Arabic besides Hebrew, also a strange-sounding German called Yiddish, I muddled through with a mixture of my native Judeo-Arabic and the little German I had picked up from my former captors.) I had not left Tunisia and come to the land of my fathers to be afraid of Arabs, I said to them, hammering a mezuzah to the gate of a four-room house built around a courtyard with a cistern.

Silence greeted me as I first stepped over slippery leaves and rotting firewood. Bats took off through the paneless windows. A cat hurried in and out, carrying its litter to safety. The mustiness of years of charcoal smoke hung in the rooms. Mixed with the smell of mildew were mouse droppings and rancid cow fat. Hesitantly advancing amid rags, potsherds, rice and rusty pans scattered on the stone slabs, I almost stumbled when I saw the sandals. Neatly they stood side by side in all that mess, not even moldy yet, the brown leather sandals of a three- to four-year-old. The air in that house was hard to breathe. I turned to walk away.

An inner voice stopped me in my tracks. "Fool! You have a short memory. One pair of sandals and you give up? Have you forgotten how your Arab friends clapped and stamped. . . .How they cheered as the Germans dragged you half-naked through the market? The 'klabs' and 'son-of-dirty-Jew-bitches' they hissed after you were enough to build a bridge of curses from Nabeul to Jerusalem. . . ? This land belongs to you. Dig in if you want a better life for your children!"

I turned up my sleeves, went back into the smelly room and swept out everything—sandals first. To get rid of the mustiness, I gave a fresh coat of blue lime to all the rooms. Fortuna scrubbed the floor with green soap and chlorine and we moved in. Furnished with only our trunks and two narrow iron beds of the kind every new immigrant received from the authorities, our four rooms seemed immense. We would fill them with children, I thought, happily squatting on the ground as in the good old days before I had become refined.

To drive out the cold and dampness I fashioned a tripod from the clay found in abundance in the ground, gathered charcoal in the ruins, then caught a pigeon or two for Fortuna to roast on the fire. She was afraid of the newfangled kerosene cookers that sputtered like motorcycles. Besides, I had no money to buy her one.

Altogether it was a good start, especially if one took into account that customs had handed us our trunks almost untouched. Thank God we had had no expensive fabrics, carpets or candlesticks to pack, in contrast to many other families whom I had seen shrieking and tearing their hair over half or completely empty crates. My prayer books, the dried couscous, the olive oil and even my wedding suit had not been attractive enough to tempt thieves.

Notwithstanding that we had been lucky, our provisions were slowly dwindling. Time had come to get myself a job, join a synagogue and put away some money for a brit milah. For the old Safed shoemaker who finally took me on, I worked for only one day. Counting the eighty piasters he had shoved into my hand for nine hours of drudgery, I understood that this would never do. It was the first and last time I ever worked at my trade in Israel.

The next morning I did as all the other newcomers—I trudged to the labor exchange. It was still early, but the steep stairs leading up to that all-powerful institution were already crammed with Jews. Some were spicing their angry Hebrew with Arabic and Russian curses, others mouthed juicy Yiddish and Rumanian, bitterly spat-out Polish, Hungarian singsong, and elegant Ladino, all of them shouting as those on the upper steps kept banging on an iron door. After someone pounded it with a rock, it was opened from the inside, drawing everybody helter-skelter into a very high-ceilinged, very bare lobby where they pushed toward a tiny window in the middle of a concrete wall.

"Your name, comrade . . . age . . . how many children?" a voice repeated as a hand listed the lucky ones close to the opening.

I loved the way the Jews of Eretz Israel would address each other as comrades. Whatever our origins, we were all brothers come to build up our country with *Torah v'avoda.*

"Without elbows, comrade." A heavy Bulgarian in front of me rammed his knee into the buttock of a stevedore from Turkey who was very much out of place in the Safed mountains. Shouting in ever louder Spanish of the Middle Ages, the two started a fistfight. Others joined in and a shutter slammed over the window. It took several more days and a great deal of pushing before I was finally listed.

"Not that it matters one way or the other," one of my fellow Tunisians from the island of Jerba tried to comfort me. "First in line are electricians, blacksmiths, drivers and fathers having many mouths to feed. They get two, sometimes even three weeks of work a month. Next to grab a job are those who have someone from their hometown on the board or belong to a party. Then come the Moroccans knowing how to use their fists, also the Turks, hard workers and stronger than all the rest taken together." Since unborn children did not count, I was at the tail end of the list. With luck I could nevertheless count on five days of work a month.

Every afternoon I climbed the steps to the labor exchange where around four o'clock a husky fellow would jump on a table to call the names of the fortunate ones appointed to report for work at dawn of the next day. Three men for chores at the hospital, fifteen to the municipality for gardening and street cleaning, twenty to building sites, thirty-five to road construction, and forty to afforestation, the job that was the lowest paid.

Only Fortuna's growing belly gave me the patience to endure those rowdy afternoons at the labor exchange, pushing and shoving, hanging on the lips of the towering announcer. Sometimes, as I was still waiting for my name to be called, he would be kicked off the table. In the end, rewarded with a few days' tree planting, I had to go back to the unruly morning crowd to receive my salary and be placed on the list once more. When nobody volunteered to take the well-paid, seemingly simple job of tar stoker for road construction I grabbed it eagerly. On the first afternoon I returned home from work Fortuna drew away in panic, frightened out of her wits by the black man entering her lonely yard.

"I'd rather go hungry than see my poor husband turned into a Booshadia," she would sigh every evening, begging me to stay home as she washed me and my clothes in kerosene. I so disliked the labor exchange with its screams and scuffles and so resented having my biceps examined by the foreman that I did not need much persuasion. On top of these indignities, I was disturbed by the sight of people slipping into the mysterious depths beyond the concrete wall by use of some magic password. For a minute or two, as the hand kept steadily writing, the voice in the window would drop to a murmur after which the intruder would reemerge through a side door and disappear into the street with a forced air of unconcern.

Again it was the knowledgeable Jerban who came to my aid, explaining the riddle. Those fortunates admitted to the other side of the wall got their jobs out of turn with the help of a charm, he said, a powerful spell called "protectsia."

"It gets you through the thickest walls. If you want to get ahead in Eretz Israel you'd better learn how to use it." He slapped my back with a cackle.

The charm was a dirty trick. I felt very stupid. Now I understood why the other morning the truck that should have brought me to the tree-planting site had been filled with its contingent of laborers before I could get on. Fate, I had thought, hanging my head in the company of half a dozen others, each with a now-useless lunch bag slung over his shoulder. The Jew from Sousse, however, elderly head of a large family, would not resign himself so easily.

"In the name of God, take me with you. . . ." he had pleaded. "For weeks I did not get a single day of work. How can I show my face before my wife and children?"

For an answer the foreman had angrily banged on the driver's cab, ordering him to start the engine. The truck had barely advanced a few yards when it screeched to a halt again, trying to avoid the Jew from Sousse who had thrown himself in front of it. The driver had backed up to get around him. The man had darted to the rear, forcing the truck to stop altogether. Crawling under, he had lain there among the four wheels, shouting: "Work or death!" Hoisting him up in the end, they had squeezed him in with the laborers, trying to laugh the incident away with some lame jokes.

The ugly scene was once more passing through my mind as I sat on the stone slabs of my yard, Fortuna standing over me and dripping kerosene. Her belly gently pressed against my sticky head, she was busily scraping the tar off my face.

"Please, my dear husband," she begged for the hundredth time. "I promise, I will eat very little and the clothes for the child I can make myself . . . only don't go back to that dirty work. . . ."

"Not any dirtier than the whole labor exchange," I muttered as I put on clean clothes to go out for a stroll.

Inside burning with anger, outside hot and tingling from Fortuna's rub, I felt an urgent need to air my skin and thoughts. Maybe, because it is so close to Heaven, Safed has a lot of stars, more than any other place I know. That evening they were out by the thousands, lonely big stars and icy splinters blinking through the thin mountain air, dusty ribbons trailing from one end of the sky to the other. Most of them were much larger than they looked, Rabbi Yitzhak of Bab Salah Street had told me once. Some stars might easily be as big as a house, he had added thoughtfully, gazing up at the skylight of our synagogue. I wished someone would explain to me why the hand that had put all those stars in orbit did not put His people in their place down here. Reigning from His throne over Jerusalem, He could not help noticing what was going on right under His nose in His own land. With His little finger He could have made a clean sweep of all those wheeler-dealers of the labor exchange. Yet He did nothing of the sort and I, who this time had sincerely wanted to turn into a good Jew, could find little Torah and still less avoda in the land of my fathers.

The friendly star that had shone through the lattice shutter in my father's house was nowhere to be seen. It had been mine, watching over me. As long as I could remember my mother had told me so, but now I could not find it anymore. I was feeling terribly low. Fear crept into my heart that my star might have stayed behind in Nabeul. Of course it had not. In the summer, after the birth of my eldest son when I had found steady work at the municipality and moved to a house farther down the slope, it reappeared in our bedroom window. That night though, under the frosty February sky, I was so homesick that I yearned for Rabbi Haim's frown, Rabbi Ghez's stern advice, the twinkle in the eyes of old Rabbi Yitzhak Bishlino. I had nobody with whom to talk things over. Fortuna was a fine wife but she was a woman; my friend Palmidi was far away; and the rabbis I had met here were not of the saintly, hooded kind who give their counsel freely for a kiss on the wrist. What was I to think of a town where slaughterers haggled over the fee before they would consent to whet their knife? How could I trust rabbis who affixed a price to burials and circumcisions? From the day I had disembarked in Haifa, searching the concrete maze of the port for a patch of sacred ground to kneel on, all that I had been looking forward to in the Promised Land turned topsy-turvy. One by one, my hopes had toppled. My dreams burst like soap bubbles just as I seemed about to grab them. No longer could anyone play me for a fool. From now on I would go my own way. Kicking stones out of my path, I sent the whole labor exchange to hell.

I did not go to pray Maariv at the house of the Jerban that evening and from then on set foot in a synagogue only on the High Holidays. Landed right in the middle of newborn Israel's struggle for survival, I had come down so rudely that many years passed before I finally stopped sulking. It took nineteen years and two wars before I made the pilgrimage to Bethlehem and Jerusalem to face my dreams once more. The image of Rachel's tomb inside Baruch Tarbulsi's glass pen never left me however; the yearning was always with me.

XXX
The Birth of an Artist

Adrift on a sea of stars that February night, I threw more than dreams overboard. As we were preparing for bed, Fortuna was shocked to see me fold my fringed garment, putting it away in a corner of the trunk where it has remained undisturbed to this day. Instead of getting up with dawn to pray, hurry off to stir more tar or stand in line at the labor exchange, I took it easy the next morning. For several days in a row I went to roam through the ruins of Arab houses. Under a mound of rags and fallen plaster I came upon a carved, wooden pestle; inside a trough full of oats I found a badly dented copper pot and a huge flatiron still stuffed with charcoal.

Shops were reopening, displaying brand-new pots and pans at reasonable prices, household appliances fresh out of factories and shiny imitation jewelry. Yet there were people willing to buy my junk instead—artists, they were called. Whenever I knocked on the doors of the crooked alleys that still today wind round the bald spot of the western hill, they would bargain for anything I had brought in my bag. The more useless the stuff the better they seemed to like it.

From the time of my childhood, playing with the contents of my father's peddler pouch or the old coins my grandfather used to find in the myrtle valley, I had taken a liking to scraps of cast metal and carved wood. The soil of Safed, spiked with tokens left behind by those who had occupied our land over the centuries, became a source of delight to me. Greeks, Romans, Persians, Arabs, Crusaders, Mamelukes and Turks—by and by I learned to recognize their coinage but at that time I would sell for near to nothing the valuable antiques I dug up. For my part, I believed that I was cheating fellow Jews out of their money. Never mind, I thought, if those artists could live off colored smears and scrawls it served them right to pay twenty-five piasters for a coin with a she-wolf suckling two children. Much as I enjoyed this kind of trade, the income from it was so little that Fortuna and I soon hit rock bottom; our provisions gave out.

One day in early spring my wife and I were sitting on the floor to share our meager lunch when a shadow fell on the bowl of beans between us. Looking up I saw a woman standing in the door. A welfare worker visiting new immigrants, she introduced herself with a friendly smile. Taking in the bare room, the beans and Fortuna's belly, she now inquired where we came from, whether I had work or knew a trade. Then she pulled a five-pound note from her purse. She was just doing her duty, I suppose, but I was stung to the quick. How did she dare treat me as a beggar in my own house! Who had asked her to come here in the first place, dangling her umbrella before my nose? Pushing away the five-pound note, I almost knocked it out of her hand.

"You can keep your money, I don't want it," I said, getting to my feet. "I have come here to work. If I wanted to go on welfare I could have stayed in Nabeul with my folks." She knew, she understood perfectly well, the woman tried to calm me, perhaps I would accept the money as a loan, though, just to tide me over the start? Leaning against the wall, Fortuna stood pushing her belly in evidence, her eyes pleading with mine.

"All right," I finally broke the silence, "on one condition. You must give me your name and address so that I can pay you back." It took two years and very irregular installments, but eventually I returned every piaster of those five pounds.

In March, after the winter rains, the sun brought out millions of wild flowers the likes of which I had never seen before. Tired of searching the ruins, I would now venture farther out to explore valleys and ravines. The warmer weather, trees in bloom, the birds building new nests and most of all the Sea of Galilee gleaming beyond my reach made me sick with longing for Nabeul. Irresistibly drawn toward the lake, I had climbed down some steep rocks when I heard the sweet babbling of water. Hidden by big walnut trees, I found an abandoned water mill at the bottom of the ravine, its wheel immobile in a lively little brook. Restless as I, it must be running to the lake, I conjectured. I was about to follow the stream into the underbrush when I spotted a donkey. It was the scraggiest, oldest, filthiest donkey I had ever encountered. Lame in the bargain, I noticed, as it tried to slink behind the walnut trees. Yet to me the white ass of the anointed one led by Elijah could not have been a more welcome sight.

If I know how to talk to anybody it is to a donkey. From the years at Talmud-Torah school I had kept the habit of carrying bread in my pocket. Inside the mill I found a rope, and before long the beast let itself be helped uphill by me, back to town. Sometimes pushing, sometimes pulling, I dragged it up the rocky, breakneck slope, both of us completely exhausted when we finally got onto a path. This in turn led us to a road. By evening we made our entrance in the courtyard of my home. Fortuna, quick to realize the importance of my find, ran to buy candles as fast as her shape would allow. She then went to light them over the tomb of Shem and Ever, the only truly ancient graves of Jewish saints available in Safed. (Later, when I was restoring these tombs for the municipality, I saw that they were empty, as was the shrine said to contain a hair of the Prophet Mohammed which the Arabs had built on top.)

Our cistern was as good as the fountain of youth. One thorough wash and my foundling shed years. After I had taken care of its foot and fed it well, the animal seemed eager to work for me. Miracles do not happen twice over. To keep my donkey out of harm I made it a collar from blue beads unearthed near a Mameluke grave, for though the ground of Eretz Israel is not haunted by démons, the evil eye is rampant in the air. Now ready to establish myself in the transport business, I walked the streets of Safed behind loads of concrete blocks, floor tiles or cans with lime and sand, feeling like a man again. More important still, I would come home to Fortuna with money in my pocket.

With the warmer weather, vacationers were arriving to cool off in the hills. My donkey would carry their luggage from the bus station to the hotels, its bell proudly tinkling, announcing that a porter was for hire. Its bell tinkled with a little jerk because of its lame hind leg. Since the strenuous afternoon when I had given the animal a lift all the way from Wadi Limon to my yard in the alley of the Jerbans, my whole life had taken an upward swing.

My best clients were the artists. Forever pottering around their houses and their yards, they were in constant need of building materials. Still keeping up the trade in antiques as a sideline, I had become friendly with most of the painters and sculptors, feeling at ease in their company. They, too, seemed to like me. Whenever we came face-to face in one of the narrow alleys of the Artists' Quarter they would greet me in French.

"*Bonjour*, Rafael . . . *Vive l'amour!* . . . Bring me a sack of goat dung for my pistachio tree. . . ." They would wave their broad-rimmed hats at me as I set out to work early in the morning. They would pass me once more around noon, when, weighed down with paint boxes, folding easels and a cache of still-wet pictures, they would stagger back up to their alley. It was a wonder to see why they went to such pains to produce completely useless objects, pictures that made no sense from whatever side one looked at them. I kept asking myself whether there was not more to them than the eye could see. Otherwise, why would anybody pay good money for them? And some people did buy these things, as strange as it might seem.

Working on a flower border in the garden of a painter with a bored, long face and a bossy wife, I overheard him charge thirty Israeli pounds for one single painting, more than my donkey and I made in a month. I had actually seen the client give him three ten-pound notes, tuck the bargain under his arm and walk away with a happy smile. It was the one picture I had been fond of, mainly because the left half, scarlet with black zigzags, reminded me of the Bedouin weave in my parents' bed curtains. Sinners roasting in the flames of hell, the painter said it was. At the other end the souls of the righteous, fat pink and yellow blobs, were floating up into the blue. The sale had shaken the artist out of his usual morose mood.

"Call it a day, Rafael, we have worked hard enough . . . let's have a cup of coffee. . . ." The painter had been furiously hatching dots and darts into thick smears of yellow oil color. Without turning his head from the easel, he gestured me near him with his brush. Then he added two teats to the lower part of his painting, two purple mountain peaks swallowing the yellow heavens. Were not the hills brown and green? The sky meant to be blue? It was then, following the artist's stare through the open window, that I caught my first glimpse of what painting was about. The sun had just settled behind the double crest of Mount Meron, Safed's tall neighbor. Purplish and menacing, the twin hills blocked a sky that to my astonishment was actually yellow. Even the painter's furious dots and darts suddenly made sense—swarms of swallows taking a last fling before nightfall.

"You see that mountain?" sighed the artist, tying it to the yellow sky with one long stroke of red. "It is my only friend. . . ."

The conversation taking too lofty a turn, I felt the need to return to matters at hand. I disclosed to the artist that in the basement of his house I had just come upon a dead cat and three nests with young mice. The painter wiped his brushes and came down to earth.

"Well then, Rafael, poison the mice. What are you waiting for? Throw out all the garbage and clean the floor with Lysol," muttered my benefactor under his sadly drooping mustache.

Someone who that easily got thirty pounds for a single painting had invited me for coffee! Well, I was going to show him that Rafael Uzan deserved his confidence. Early the next morning I returned with a big bottle of Lysol and some of the newly discovered DDT and cleaned the painter's basement with a vengeance. Having buried the cat and snuffed out the mice, I then removed a large roll of canvases inhabited by centipedes and spiders and every last bit of dirty paper stacked up in a corner, veritable paradise for roaches. I did such a thorough job that the disgruntled garbageman had to cart off two donkey-loads of trash.

Not yet satisfied, I was secretly working on a surprise for my new patron. Much of Safed's soil was clay. While fashioning the tripod for Fortuna, I remembered how the potters in Nabeul used to make all kinds of animals from similar stuff. Now I tried to do the same, deciding that only a whole zoo would do for my painter's yard. A donkey I could have shaped blindfolded. Camels I had seen the Arabs do a hundred times. A turtle was child's play compared to the cat, the dog and the rooster. An elephant, on the other hand, which I had never seen in the flesh, was more difficult. In the end, it looked even more beautiful than the rest of my menagerie with its big trunk and ears like cabbage leaves, I thought, at last setting up all the animals among the terraced borders.

The painter seemed delighted.

"Come quick, Shoshana!" he called his wife. "Only look at that. . . . I tell you there is yet an artist to come out of that fellow!" She dismissed me and my animals with one glance.

"Leave the poor devil alone, Grishka," she frowned. "Why put notions into his head? By the way, Rafael, I have been meaning to ask you where you stored the paintings that were in the basement. My husband has an exhibition coming up."

Taken aback by her question I tried to recall every single thing cluttering that filthy storeroom of hers, slowly turning the trash over in my mind.

"What paintings?" I said. "I saw no paintings in the basement.

The broken wheelbarrow and runny hose I fixed. The tools I hung up on a board according to their size. Apart from that there was only a roll of smeary canvases covered with cobwebs and crawling with vermin. You cannot mean all those stacks of dirty paper with roach eggs in between the sheets? I had a hard time making the garbageman take the stuff without a tip. No, if there had been any paintings there I would have seen them. . . ."

"Oh, my God! He has given them to the garbageman!" Holding his head with both hands the painter had sunk down between the turtle and the elephant as his wife bombarded me with silly questions.

"What garbageman? What did he look like? Where did he go?"

"What all old Jews with a beard look like," I explained patiently. "And he went where all the donkeys take the garbage—below the ice plant where they make the goat cheese. . . ."

Off she went like a rocket, running after every garbageman and street cleaner in town, promising a reward to whoever came up with the canvas roll or the dirty papers she persistently called "watercolors." Convinced that she must be crazy, people beleaguered her door from morning till night, pocketing tips for faded wedding photographs, Turkish generals dangling in shreds from broken gold frames, calligraphed acknowledgments for donations to a yeshiva, and even a defunct, fly-bespattered king of England—none of which she was looking for.

Meanwhile the artist and I were spending our days at the municipal garbage dump, going through mountains of stinking, smoldering refuse. Nothing turned up, no paintings at all. Not even charred remains of them. At that time Jews, eager to help build up their country, were working hard and garbage people stoked their fires properly.

While I have throughout the years enjoyed friendly relations with the artists of Safed, my new patron never hired me again. I, on the other hand, lost all liking for clay animals for a long time.

Other serious matters were on my mind. My first Passover as the head of a family, however small, was close at hand, and soon afterward Fortuna would have to give birth. How forlorn we felt, huddled together on the singed carpet I had salvaged from a burned-out house. How different was my Seder from the one I had looked forward to a year earlier in Nabeul, chanting "Next year in Jerusalem!"

As the good Jewish wife she is, Fortuna had prepared a Seder plate with the five symbols and, tears of longing for her family choking her voice, kept bravely singing parts of the Haggadah after me. Not too sure of my own voice, I would try to comfort her in between hymns of praise and joy, promising that soon we would have a son, that there were many more Passovers to come with lamb instead of chicken, with all our folks around us and our children asking the four questions.

On that miserable Seder evening it took more than the obligatory cups of wine to make me believe in my own promises. Come midnight I had not even heart enough to go out into the yard so as to squeeze a wish past the Gates of Heaven. Nevertheless, everything later came to pass the way I had then painted it before Fortuna's tearful eyes. Not only did she bear one child after another, but eventually all our close relatives did join us in Safed so that we once more had big, joyous family reunions.

About a fornight after our first Passover in Israel I was opening a letter from my father when something fell out of the envelope. It was a threaded needle carrying a message from my mother. Unable to write, she used this little bearer of her love to let us know how much she had missed us at the Seder table. How that same needle had sewn up three portions of stuffed intestine—a large chunk for me, a smaller one for Fortuna and a tiny thimbleful for the child in her womb.

My father wanted to know about the prospects for peddling and baboosh making in Safed. He wrote that the fallahs had become too hostile for a Jew to risk entering the villages. How was I going to make him understand that in Eretz Israel shoes came out of factories and hawkers were planting trees or paving roads, if they were lucky?

The letter had slipped from my hand. Still clutching my mother's needle, I sat on an upturned kerosene can in my yard, staring at the clusters of budding grapes shooting from the vine. Other springtimes came to my mind—those of my childhood in the walled yard of our Italian ancestor, where my grandfather's vine had caught the sky in a net of tendrils and gnarled branches. A fallah now reaped its grapes and enjoyed the evening breeze seated inside the gate under the same inscription that had taught me my first Hebrew characters. "If I forget thee, Jerusalem, let my right hand be forgotten," read a row of glazed tiles immured in the wall built by my great-great-grandfather on the shores of Cape Bon.

So here I was, at last in the land of my father's dreams and prayers. "A man beneath his own fig tree and vine," as the Bible says, slowly striking new roots under the vine, planted by an Arab. The spin of the wheel was somewhat confusing, but be that as it may, next Passover we would have homemade wine to drink, no matter whether red or white.

Apparently cooking our dinner, Fortuna was keeping unusually quiet. Any day I would have to dash to the grocery and from there telephone the first-aid station. No midwife to run to in Safed; an ambulance with howling siren would take Fortuna to Tiberias to have our baby in a birth clinic, all expenses covered by the sick fund.

Thankful to belong to the latter, an offshoot of the all-powerful labor organization, I was reminded of old Rabbi Bishlino's saying that even a thorn in one's foot can have its uses.

According to my father's letter, things were going from bad to worse for the Jews of Nabeul. Desperate to leave, but finding it impossible to sell their property, some of them, such as Ramoo, the owner of the beach café, had nailed planks over their doors and windows before leaving rather than to sell out to the Arabs for a pittance.

Warming to my heart the touch of my mother's needle stirred my longing for her, for Nabeul and the carefree days of my youth. Until the Germans had felt compelled to introduce our town to their notion of order, all had been running smoothly, including relations between Arabs and Jews. There had still been answers to questions then, and a Jew did not have to rack his small brain to explain how the world worked. Everybody had had his place, his duties and to whom he was accountable: to his father, the Almighty, the rabbis and to the French authorities.

Here in Israel, strangely enough, people seemed largely answerable to themselves, forming their own opinions on each and everything by picking this and that from a dozen different newspapers.

I was tired of pondering the mysterious entanglement of Jews and Arabs, of the incomprehensible ways of the Almighty and the labor union. I felt as if I were stranded on a fence with one foot hesitantly hovering over the rugged, wobbly ground of my new home and the other one still lingering in good, old, worm-eaten North Africa.

Was it Fortuna's strange silence, my mother's threaded needle or perhaps the bewitching smell of fried fish and garlic coming from the kitchen? Seated on the kerosene can waiting for my dinner, I was drifting away on fumes of garlic and wings of fancy, softly landing in the sand of my native shores, right in front of Ramoo's restaurant. Having for months been wondering whether the palm saplings planted last spring would take to the poor soil of the beach, I was amazed to find a row of trees shading the promenade leading to the jetty. The restaurant was full of eating and drinking fishermen despite the indisputable news of its closing. Ramoo had sailed to Israel, my father had written, yet in my imagination I could plainly see the proud innkeeper standing in the door of his establishment. Fat and rosy as ever in his old black dinner jacket, he was shouting his head off, threatening to choke Shishi, the dwarf, with his towel as he bargained with him for a catch of mullets.

Down by the jetty things were just as lively. Trailed by a band of dolphins a sailboat was coming in, merchants from the island of Jerba beginning to unload their pottery on donkey carts. Italian fishermen were folding nets, children splashing and diving in the waves amid the fleeting light of sea-gulls' wings. Tony, who had taught me to catch cuttlefish when I was a boy, was giving old *Santa Lucia* a fresh coat of paint: orange, deep blue and black with white letters. The boat looked so beautiful I felt my fingers twitch with envy. Pulling myself out of my daydream I stood up: if Tony could paint so could I.

Before our relations had cooled, my former patron, the artist, had let me have a handful of dried-up watercolor tubes and one of his used brushes. Entering the house to get them out of the trunk I came upon Fortuna slumped on top. She held her hands pressed to her back.

"Your flounders will keep warm, Fallu. I left them on the ashes," she said in a thin voice. "Better get me to the clinic before you eat them."

That night, down by the banks of the Sea of Galilee, my eldest son was born. High up on the mountain in Safed I sat waiting for the dawn and for good news to break. Too restless to sleep I took the colors and the brush out of the trunk and, by the feeble light of a kerosene lamp, prepared to receive my firstborn. My son would have no need to weave his picture books from shadows lurking in the corners, as his father stretched out on a sheepskin, had done. Like those of my new friends, the artists, I would brighten up my house with paintings. While daydreaming under the vine that afternoon, I had vowed once and for all to clap my hands on those shifting, teasing memories.

Since the watercolors were too dry to be squeezed, I ripped open the hardened tubes, dissolving the pigment on a plate with the help of water. Then, on the back of a full-size, antiquated tax form, I outlined Ramoo's restaurant, the palm trees and the jetty, little Shishi, the Jerbans and the fishermen, putting everybody in a compartment of his own. I took great pains filling in the whole bunch of them with color. Even though painted on the back of an old tax form I wanted my first picture to be neat.

Toward morning a rich catch lay spread out before me, the gaily colored fancies of my afternoon safely shored up with a border of flowers of the fields, with pigeons and purple grapes, crimson pomegranates and pearly fishes. Patience. With time I would manage to lure back all my childhood, every happy moment of my youth. My son would be able to raise his chubby little fingers and point out the

Friday market, the Booshadia and the monkey men, my mother Mee-sha singing as she sat tatting silver lace and the whole family rejoicing around the Seder table made of orange crates.

"Elan," which means sapling in Hebrew, I was going to call my son. Proud and erect as a young tree he would grow up in his own country; no need to teach him to bend with the wind.

The deep black of the windowpanes was graying; dawn crept in, dimming my flickering lamp. I nailed my picture to the wall, where Fortuna had readied the laundry basket for a crib. Then I strode out into the crisp morning air to catch the first bus to Tiberias.

Glossary

Amalek. Ancient nomadic people who lived in the Sinai Peninsula and who carried out treacherous attacks on the Israelites. Since then the name *Amalek* has been used to describe any archenemy of the Jews.

Aslama. In Tunisia, Arabic greeting meaning *peace.*

Babooshes. Pointed leather slippers which were worn in place of shoes in Moslem countries.

Bastinado. In Asia, a form of corporal punishment that consisted of beating the soles of a culprit's feet with a stick.

Betar. Zionist youth movement of the followers of Ze'ev Jabotinsky.

Binti. Arabic for *my daughter.*

Booshadia. Goblin.

Bootalish. In Tunisian folklore, a sprite that appears in one's dreams.

Brit milah. Covenant of circumcision.

Dar'booka. Finger drum.

Durra. A variety of grain-producing sorghum.

Effendi. A title of respect in countries that once were dominated by the Turks.

Etrog. A citrus fruit among the Four Species used on Sukkoth.

Fallaka. Device for holding the legs of the delinquent during the bastinado.

Fisha. Arabic for *forward.*

Gauloises. French brand of cigarettes.

Gemara. Commentary on the Mishnah. The Mishnah and the Gemara together comprise the Talmud.

Golem. In Jewish legend, an artificially created robot-like man.

Gorni. A term used for the Jewish immigrants from Leghorn (Livorno), Italy, who settled in Tunisia from the seventeenth century on.

Hameen. A stew of meat, chick-peas and potatoes which is kept warm on hot ashes for the Sabbath meal.

Hametz. Leavened food unfit for Passover.

Haroset. Sweet fruit paste symbolizing the mortar which the Jews used for building the pyramids.

Hubeiza. A weed with a lentil-like fruit which is edible when cooked.

Huppa. Wedding canopy.

Hush-hash. A medicinal plant.

Imam. The leader of prayer in a mosque.

Jebba. In Tunisia, a long gown for men.

Kappara. Hebrew for *replacement.* The ancient custom of transferring one's transgressions to a rooster to be slaughtered for Yom Kippur.

Kashabia. In Tunisia, a long gown for men loosely thrown over other garments.

Klab. Arabic for *dog.*

Kommandantur. In German, a building with offices for military administration.

Le Maître. French for *the master,* often referring to a schoolteacher.

Maariv. Jewish evening prayer.

Massajoo. Judeo-Arabic for *this matzoh (which we eat).* Matzoh specially consecrated for the seder ritual.

Mevorah. Hebrew for *blessed.*

Mezuzah. A small piece of parchment inscribed with the Shma Yisrael which is rolled, placed in a case and attached to the doorpost of a Jewish home.

Minaret. Slender tower attached to a mosque.

Mincha. Jewish afternoon prayer.

Minyan. A quorum of at least ten Jewish males over thirteen years old which is needed for a prayer service.

Mishna. The first part of the Talmud.

Mohel. One authorized by rabbis to circumcise Jewish males.

Monsieur L'agent. French for *Mister Policeman.*

Mukhtar. The mayor of an Arab village.

Muezzin. In Moslem countries, a crier on a minaret who calls the people to prayer at the proper hours.

N'doralnik. Judeo-Arabic term of endearment.

Neo-Destour. The ruling socialist party of Tunisia which obtained independence from the French.

Otsbana. Stuffed derma.

Pitta. Flat, round Arab bread that can be opened to form a pocket and stuffed.

Qadi. A minor Moslem magistrate.

Qaid. One heading a qaidate in Tunisia.

Shaharit. Jewish morning prayer.

Shalom aleichem. Hebrew greeting meaning *peace be with you.*

Shamas. Sexton of a synagogue.

Sheikh. The chief of an Arab tribe.

Shekel. Israeli currency.

Slichot. Early morning prayers for forgiveness recited during the month preceding Yom Kippur.

Shma Yisrael. The opening words of a declaration of the basic principle of Jewish belief.

Sidi. Arabic term of address similar to *Sir.*

Sou. Small denomination of French currency.

Sukkah. Temporary structure with a roof of bows built to commemorate the tabernacles of the Exodus.

Sukkot. Festival of the harvest and of the tabernacles.

Tarboosh. Worn by men of Moslem countries, a brimless cap of felt shaped like a truncated cone.

Tu B'shvat. An early spring festival celebrating the rebirth of the trees.

Vercingétorix (72–46? B.C.). A Gallic chieftain defeated by Julius Caesar.

Vizier. In old times, a minister of government in Moslem countries.